# Social Assessment:

## Theory, Process and Techniques

### Third Edition

# Social Assessment:

## Theory, Process and Techniques

### Third Edition

C. Nicholas Taylor
C. Hobson Bryan
Colin G. Goodrich

Social Ecology Press
Middleton · Wisconsin

Taylor, C. Nicholas..
    Social assessment : theory, process and techniques /
C. Nicholas Taylor, C. Hobson Bryan, Colin G. Goodrich.
-- 3rd ed.
    p. cm.
    Includes bibliographical references and index.
    ISBN 0-941042-36-7
    ISBN 0-473-03245-7 (New Zealand)

    1. Social sciences--Methodology. 2. Evaluation
research (Social action programs). 3. Economic
development--Social aspects.   I. Bryan, Colgan Hobson,
1942- II. Goodrich, Colin G. III. Title.

H61.T365 2004              361.6'1'072
                           QBI04-200022

Social Ecology Press is publisher of the third edition in 2004.
Second Social Ecology Press printing 2008.
Previously published in 1995 by Taylor Baines & Associates of
Christchurch, New Zealand.

Social Ecology Press ™
PO Box 620863
Middleton, Wisconsin 53562-0863
USA

Telephone/Fax 1-608-831-1410
Toll free 1-888-364-3277
Printed in the United States of America

10 9 8 7 6 5 4 3 2

# Contents

**LIST OF FIGURES**

# PREFACE

International interest in the development of procedures and techniques for social assessment continues to expand. Areas around the world are grappling with increasing pressures on their natural resource base, issues of sustainable development, and the need to assess and manage the social outcomes of policies and projects.

This third edition of *Social Assessment* is in response to a need to extend expertise and capacity in this important and growing field. It builds on over two decades of teaching, practise, and networking with fellow assessors around the world. First published in 1990, new ideas were incorporated into the second edition in 1995, along with general editing and updating. This process was repeated for this 2004 edition.

The focus of the original text was towards the New Zealand context and experiences in social assessment, although the contents had much wider application. The theory, process and techniques have now developed into a cross-cultural and international base for practice and training, a base that covers New Zealand, North America, Australia, Africa, Asia and the Pacific Islands.

We have adopted the term **social assessment** in this book in preference to the term social impact assessment. The use of social assessment in this text reflects our desire to overcome the frequently negative connotation of the term impact. Too often, social **impact** assessment is seen as an activity that highlights undesirable social effects and therefore, by implication, hinders constructive change.

In many instances we use the more generic term **effect** instead of **impact** to underscore our position that the process of social assessment can involve subtle as well as not so subtle change. This use of the term effect also connotes that the process is much more widely applicable than a formalised environmental reporting and audit procedure. Social assessment can challenge and complement conventional areas of assessment for public policy and the management of change, especially economic and bio-physical assessments. It has the potential to boost anticipatory and participatory planning, and helps to manage change in the pursuit of the best outcomes for society in the long term.

The text begins with a critical examination of the historical background of social assessment, the common problems that have emerged, and new perspectives leading to possible solutions for these problems. This focus on both constraints and prospects for a new approach continues in Chapter 2 with a discussion of the orientations of practitioners to the field and typical work environments in which they tend to operate. Shifts in orientation are advocated, towards a new, issues-oriented approach detailed in the remaining chapters. In Chapter 3 a theoretical overview is provided along with base assumptions for the new approach, assumptions drawn from environmental sociology and other innovative areas of social theory. The process of social assessment, including the need for adequate institutional arrangements and capacity to support the process, is examined in Chapter 4. In Chapter 5 a flexible, analytical approach to the collection and analysis of data for social assessment is introduced. Then various techniques for collecting social data are discussed, including secondary data and surveys in Chapter 6, and information on economic impacts in Chapter 7. Finally, in Chapter 8, qualitative and consultative methods are discussed as fundamental to the issues-oriented approach. Short case studies are used throughout for illustration.

Our social assessment experience has covered a range of activities large and small. These include planning for major energy and infrastructure developments, rural and agricultural development projects, assessments of community needs, and evaluation of natural resource and economic policy. Graduate courses in social assessment began at the University of Canterbury in 1983 and at the University of Alabama in 1984 and continue to this day. They have been attended by students in resource management, sociology, geography, and many other disciplines. Teaching these courses has offered many opportunities to develop the material presented here.

The material has also benefited from the authors' involvement in leading in-service training courses in social assessment under the auspices of the University of Canterbury, Lincoln College (now Lincoln University), the International Association for Impact Assessment, the US Forest Service, the Australian Environmental Institute, The Social Impact Unit (Western Australia), Edith Cowan University (Perth) and the Development Bank of Southern Africa.

We take considerable pleasure in seeing students and past course participants working at, and extending, the practice of social assessment. Frequent promises to students, course participants and clients that we would combine our ideas into a text provided a strong incentive to complete this project in the face of other work commitments and the logistical constraints of international collaboration, and then to update it two times.

The collaboration of the authors would have been impossible without the financial support of the Fulbright grants to Dr Bryan in 1984 and Dr Taylor in 1986, and institutional support from the Centre for Resource Management at Lincoln University, the Sociology Department at the University of Canterbury, the Sociology and Geography Departments at the University of Alabama, and Taylor Baines and Associates. The staff of these organisations also helped in many ways.

The first edition was published by the Centre for Resource Management, Lincoln University. The original work received financial assistance from the New Zealand Ministry for the Environment, along with personal support from Dr. Tom Fookes. In the second edition, the new material on linking bio-physical and social variables was developed out of Bryan's experience in developing a national training programme for the US Forest Service. We are indebted to the Forest Service for this opportunity to refine these ideas. Material on soft systems methods was developed in collaboration with Julie Warren, with funding from the New Zealand Foundation for Research, Science and Technology.

Additional insight and encouragement came from members of the New Zealand Social Impact Assessment Working Group, and since 1990 from the New Zealand Association for Social Assessment, which became the New Zealand Association for Impact Assessment. We acknowledge in particular Julie Warren and Mary-Jane Rivers who commented on the first edition, and Jamie Newell, Di Buchan and many others over time. Similarly, our links with the International Association for Impact Assessment and its SIA Section have provided much intellectual support. We note in particular the leadership of Rabel Burdge, Frank Vanclay and James Baines. Dr. Burdge was instrumental in getting us started on this project and, along with Nan Field, seeing this third edition to press.

We thank Gerard Fitzgerald for his enthusiastic support and creative contributions, and along with Geoff Kerr and Ruth Houghton, willingness to include material as associate authors in Chapters 6, 7 and 8. We also acknowledge the invaluable assistance of Ms Tracy Williams of the Centre for Resource Management for her editorial work on the first edition, and her commitment and encouragement. Cilla Taylor helped with moral support and comments on this third edition. Erik Norder has given his support throughout, and provided graphics and other technical assistance. He was responsible for the preparation of the second and third editions for printing.

# CHAPTER ONE

## Social assessment: a critical appraisal

### INTRODUCTION

Social assessment provides a process for research, planning and management of change arising from policies and projects. Leading authors in the field agree that social assessment is a process for "analysing and managing the intended and unintended consequences" of change arising from policies and projects (Interorganizational Committee on Guidelines and Principles for Social Impact Assessment, 1998; Vanclay, 2002: 387).

The social assessment process uses social analysis, monitoring and methods of public involvement to document and manage social effects. It is focussed on individuals, groups, communities and sectors of society affected by change. The process is firmly established internationally as an important aspect of environmental assessment procedures and decisions, and the development and implementation of projects, programmes and policies (Burdge, 1985, 1998). It is used and practised by international development agencies, by government agencies, developers, non-government organisations (NGOs) and community groups. These very positive applications see social assessment contributing to more informed decisions and improved, more sustainable, social and environmental outcomes.

However, social assessment has not always led to socially responsible outcomes. This chapter therefore includes discussion of problems that appear to be endemic to the process. It also describes the considerable potential for practitioners to move beyond these difficulties. The potential for social assessment is expanded through the rest of the book, detailing a forward-looking approach that is now practiced widely.

The purpose of this chapter is to highlight turning points in the history of social assessment and to provide a critical overview of current problems and trends in the field. A cross-cultural and historical perspective is presented to enable the reader to understand better the various constraints that have arisen in establishing an effective presence for social assessment. The focus is international, with an emphasis on the United States and New Zealand.

### HISTORICAL BACKGROUND

#### Origins

The origins of a distinct field of social assessment are usually traced to the United States and the National Environmental Policy Act (NEPA) of 1969. A major stimulus for NEPA was the Santa Barbara oil spill. As some observers of the social period have noted, affluent Americans were faced with a direct affront to

**their** environment - black, gooey oil on their previously pristine beaches. Whether this was the determining factor or not, NEPA came into being soon after the spill. The Act requires Federal agencies to use a systematic and interdisciplinary approach, to ensure there is an integration of the natural and social sciences within environmental design and planning in decisions that may have an impact on the environment. The result, at least in numerical terms, was impressive. In the first 10 years after NEPA, almost 12,000 environmental impact assessments (EIAs) were completed. Around 1,200 lawsuits were filed contesting these assessments (Freudenburg and Keating, 1982: 72).

The social dimension, although specified in NEPA, was rarely included in much detail in these early assessments. It can hardly be claimed that specific projects were approved, rejected or changed radically on the basis of social assessment. However, many decisions were affected by the recognition of social factors in more subtle and indirect ways (Freudenburg, 1986).

Impetus for New Zealand's 1973 (revised in 1981) *Environmental Protection and Enhancement Procedures*, came from controversies such as the proposed raising of Lake Manapouri for electricity generation in the late 1960s. There are interesting parallels between the Manapouri proposal and the Santa Barbara oil spill in that they both struck a note of widespread public discord leading to formal environmental assessment requirements. These New Zealand procedures were derived from and had similarities to NEPA but lacked legislative backing.

In New Zealand, the Commission for the Environment was the agency for overseeing the procedures and reporting to the Government on the effectiveness with which they were being applied. Its primary role was to audit (review) Environmental Impact Reports. However, the Commission, without an established legal mandate, often served at the pleasure of the Government.

The first 10 years of environmental assessment, both in the United States and New Zealand, were characterised by a number of problems related to the inclusion of a social dimension within the overall assessment process. Sociologists and other social scientists were slow to define the social dimension (Freudenburg and Keating, 1982). When the social dimension was defined, this part of the analysis was still often left out, perhaps because the results sometimes called into question the results of economic analysis, went against political judgements, or simply failed to deliver a useable contribution to management.

Economic analysis often was substituted for social analysis and this problem continues. The substitution is understandable in that the study of economics is built around the structure of choices. Its quantitative nature also makes economics more immediately applicable to the needs of decision makers. When the economic analysis did move into the social area, the focus of the investigations was often on population change, and the quantifiable effects of developments and resource management decisions on jobs and demand for community services.

Public participation, although not an explicit requirement under NEPA, sometimes became confused with social assessment. The process of public participation was typically very limited and often simply provided the opportunity to make submissions or appear at formal hearings. These early efforts at public participation should therefore not be confused with a consultative process of social assessment as advocated in this book, even though some social impacts were identified by fledgling attempts to encourage public participation.

Rather than confining social assessment to the projection of social effects in terms of alternative plans, some planners and decision makers held the view that 'abstract' futures could not be predicted with any degree of accuracy. The strategy they employed was to involve affected populations in the design of their own futures. This strategy, not surprisingly, did not go over very well with managers of development projects who were faced with the concrete constraints of their development or programme options; nor did it necessarily fulfil legal requirements, although people sometimes became more involved in the decision process than ever before.

Paradoxically, while there were problems of little, if any, social analysis, there was also the problem of too much social analysis. This was more often the case when academics were given contracts to do the work. Keeping their traditional community research model in mind, there was a tendency for the study to become a lengthy social overview of the community or area in question, lacking any real focus on issues or projection of likely social effects. Such studies did, however, usually provide baseline data for subsequent, more focussed, assessments.

In New Zealand, an early piece of social assessment research that has gained international recognition was a large project monitoring impacts of the Huntly thermal power project (Fookes et al., 1981). The research received substantial government backing. However, the monitoring was regarded by many planners, developers, and others involved in the practical side of impact assessment and mitigation as largely an academic exercise. Some resulting scepticism about social assessment among development agencies hindered further funding and institutional support for social assessment monitoring work. Nevertheless, the substantial data base that was collected has not been used to full affect, although some of the findings have been useful for the planning of further projects. For example, it was found that rapid growth in the town of Huntly was limited because the workforce was prepared to commute considerable distances from larger population centres. This commuting factor has since been widely applied to project planning. Furthermore, out of this and other efforts at social monitoring a process developed for social assessment that merged appropriate data collection, identification of issues and mitigation of impacts at a community level. The Huntly research laid the ground for the phase of 'rapid growth' in social assessment that followed in New Zealand. This parallelled the influence community impact research had on the development of a strong base for Social Impact Assessment (SIA) in North America (Bowles, 1981).

SOCIAL ASSESSMENT

## Consolidation

From the late 1970s natural resource and planning agencies moved towards improved procedures for environmental impact assessment generally and, to a varying extent, social assessment specifically. In the United States all was not well with the NEPA process. The Council on Environmental Quality (CEQ, 1978) evaluated the implementation of NEPA over its first nine years and concluded that:

- environmental analyses had not been conducted in a uniform manner

- technical language in many of the reports precluded public understanding and response

- these environmental documents in some cases had become ends in themselves rather than a basis for better decision making

- there was a tendency for environmental documents to discuss virtually all environmental matters related to a proposed action, rather than to concentrate on significant issues

- there had been corresponding excesses in paperwork, delays, and duplication of effort.

As a result of this critique, there was a new emphasis on a preliminary inquiry, to focus attention on significant impacts, and on the production of documents that were shorter and more analytical rather than encyclopaedic (Hill, 1981). The focus, in other words, shifted to analysis.

An example of this shift in emphasis and strategy for social assessment within a government agency is provided by the United States Forest Service. The Forest Service had been labouring under the assumption that social assessment implied using long 'laundry lists' of variables in a how-to-do-it fashion. The agency was not unique in this sense; other natural resource-based organisations had employed similar approaches. The following principles were employed in the redirection of Forest Service policy (Bryan and Hendee, 1983):

- focus should be restricted to the social concerns revealed in the scoping process

- social effects should be sought in an analytic rather than encyclopaedic manner representative of four broad categories of variables: lifestyles; attitudes, beliefs, and values; social organisation; and population/land-use

- before collecting new data, all existing data bases should be utilised. The idea is not to gather as much data as possible, but to gather as little as necessary for the task at hand

- there should be explicit recognition that social effects may be positive or negative depending on the context in which they are viewed

- both direct and indirect social effects should be addressed

- no one method or approach for data gathering should be recommended. Rather it is recognised that the appropriate methods and approaches for social analysis will vary with the kinds of impacts anticipated

- the area for the assessment might vary with the proposed action and the effects being investigated

- the format for reporting of social effects will depend on what is found. If the social effects are deemed by the investigating team to be especially significant, then a separate social assessment might be warranted. Otherwise, it would be permissible to integrate the social dimensions into other sections of the report

- it should be recognised that individual social effects sometimes may be subtle and defy precise interpretation, but cumulatively these effects may be very large. Therefore, the assessment of cumulative effects is an important and necessary process.

Shifts in emphasis in the environmental assessment process were also evident in New Zealand. Expanded industrial development based on energy projects was promoted by the government in the late 1970s and opposed by active and vocal environmental groups. A 'fast track' piece of legislation, the National Development Act (NDA), was introduced in New Zealand in 1979 and amended in 1981. The aim of the Act was to thwart the delaying tactics of environmentalists and others who opposed proposed developments, particularly developments that were part of the 'think big' strategy (i.e. the National Government's policy of prioritising large-scale industrial development).

Although the NDA gave legislative backing to the consideration of social effects, inadequacies in the 'fast-track' process were quickly exposed. A conspicuous example was that issues for the indigenous, Maori people received inadequate attention in hearings for a large synthetic-fuels plant in Taranaki. Subsequently, local Maori groups exposed a number of problems concerning a proposed ocean outfall for effluent that would result in the pollution of their traditional seafood resources.

The Government attempted to dismiss the importance of social effects of the 'think big' projects. It gave primacy to technological feasibility and economic arguments - arguments that did not necessarily pass full and careful scrutiny. Given experience of the social effects of the 'think big' projects, combined with awareness of the growth of social assessment in North America, the social component of environmental impact reports subsequently grew in recognition and importance in New Zealand. The Commission for the Environment audits began to place greater emphasis on the social dimension of impact assessment, and the impact reports themselves treated social effects more seriously.

As the major energy projects unfolded under 'think big', their very real social impacts were an important focus for the establishment of a more advanced process of social assessment. There were numerous impacts in such areas as housing and social services, and these have been documented in monitoring research. In addition, comparisons between land projects and overseas energy projects allowed parallels to be drawn and further suggestions made for future planning (Taylor and McClintock, 1984). In preliminary planning work, the previously limited community profiling, with emphasis on potential negative attitudes towards a development, was expanded to a recognition of social assessment as a participatory process of planning. Social monitoring demonstrated the need to continue this work throughout the entire period of rapid change, with a commitment to public participation and community development as part of this process.

With the change to a Labour Government in July 1984, the role of agencies dealing with environmental matters was changed radically. In fact, the outgoing National Government's vulnerability can be traced in part to its perceived weaker stance on the protection of the environment in general and the role of the Commission in particular.

Through the efforts of a newly formed national SIA Working Group and network, further improvements were made to the assessment process at this time of organisational change in environmental administration. The Group comprised practitioners from different central government departments involved with social policy and social impact research, social planners from regional government, especially where major projects were being built, academics, and people involved in community development. Their work on refinement of principles for an effective process led to the publication and wide distribution of *Social Impact Assessment in New Zealand: a practical approach* in 1985. Secondary activity included networking and clearing of information. Other issues that concerned the group included plant closures with industrial restructuring, changes in rural communities due to new 'free-market' economic policies, and introduction of new computerised technology in work places.

In the late 1980s, the Labour Government set out to tackle the problems that had been identified by criticism of the existing system of environmental management, and considered propositions for re-organising central government agencies and legislation for resource management. During this time the SIA Working Group was in a good position to argue for a social emphasis, as a counter to the otherwise predictable emphasis on biological-physical and economic concerns. The Group argued for an integrated perspective, that recognised economic change is also social change, and that an assessment of the social effects of policies and projects must be carried out whenever social effects are likely to occur (SIA Working Group, 1988).

6

The SIA Working Group took an active interest in the resource management legislative reform, and the draft Resource Management Bill. The Group supported much of the Bill's content, including mandatory requirements for impact assessments, mandatory monitoring, and wider public participation. These concerns were largely met in the Resource Management Act (1991), discussed below.

Meanwhile, in Australia, social assessment grew rapidly as a field during the 1980s, taking leads from the United States and New Zealand, and also Canada. The Australians were also active in developing their own approaches, especially through work with indigenous peoples (Cowell et al., 2001). In Australia the institutional basis for social assessment developed through the mandate for environmental assessment, as outlined in Wildman and Barker (1985). There are special complexities due to the different requirements for each state and at the commonwealth level. As in New Zealand, the legal basis for social assessment was under review, with states such as South Australia attempting to update and clarify the assessment process, with legislative and administrative directives regarding the process and increased public participation (Government of South Australia, 1989). Wildman highlighted the need for improvements in process and approach to back up the improvements in legal mandate. For social assessment to make an effective contribution to policy, project planning and the management of change, there needs to be focus on social issues and improved techniques for community involvement. A handbook by Wildman and Barker, and papers in Hindmarsh (1988), provided the basis for these improvements. In-service training was initiated in several states. In addition, Western Australia took an important initiative in establishing their Social Impact Unit, one of the first stand-alone agencies for social assessment in the world (Duffecy and Pollard, 2001).

Marking the end of an era of consolidation for social assessment, the New Zealand Resource Management Act was passed in 1991 in association with major restructuring of local and regional government. These changes provided a turning point for social assessment practice. The Act included wide, mandatory requirements for impact assessments and "social" and "cultural" were clearly included in the definition of effects. There was mandatory public involvement and community consultation, and also monitoring of effects once change takes place. The new legislation emphasised greater flexibility, and placed an onus on regional and district councils, tribal authorities, interest and community groups to promote the need for social assessment on an ongoing basis (see Case study 1.1).

*Case study 1.1: The New Zealand Resource Management Act (1991)*

*The Act is an innovative piece of environmental legislation because it promotes sustainable management of natural and physical resources. In order to facilitate this approach it integrates management of land, air and water. Within the Act the environment is treated as a whole and when authorities are planning and making decisions, the focus of their decisions must take this perspective into account. The Act is the principal statute for the management of land, subdivision, water, soil resources, the coast, air, and pollution control, including noise control. It sets out the rights and responsibilities of individuals, territorial and regional authorities and central government. The Act sets up a system of policy and plan preparation and administration which allows the balancing of a wide range of interests and values.*

*The Act provides a response to the 1987 report of the World Commission on Environment and Development. It seeks to meet the needs of the present population while keeping environmental options open for future generations, and does this by recognising the connections between the natural and physical environment on the one hand and the social and economic environment on the other. This is done quite specifically in three key definitions within the Act; 'sustainable management', 'environment' and 'effect'.*

*Sustainable management is "...managing the use, development, and the protection of natural and physical resources in a way, or at a rate which enables people and communities to provide for their social, economic, and cultural wellbeing and for their health and safety while - (a) Sustaining the potential of natural and physical resources (excluding minerals) to meet the reasonably foreseeable needs of future generations; and (b) Safeguarding the life-supporting capacity of air, water, soil, and ecosystems; and (c) Avoiding, remedying, or mitigating any adverse effects of activities on the environment." (s.5.2)*

*Environment includes "(a) Ecosystems and their constituent parts, including people and communities; and (b) All natural and physical resources; and (c) Amenity values; and (d) The social, economic, aesthetic, and the cultural conditions which affect the matters stated in paragraphs (a) to (c) of this definition or which are affected by those matters". (s.2)*

*Effect is defined as "..the term 'effect' in relation to the use, development, or protection of natural and physical resources, or in relation to the environment, includes: (a) Any positive or adverse effect; and (b) Any temporary or permanent effect; and (c) Any past, present or future effect; and (d) Any cumulative effect which arises over time or in combination with other effects - regardless of the scale, intensity, duration, or frequency of the effect, and also includes - (e) Any potential effect of high probability; and (f) Any potential effect of low probability which has a high potential impact." (S.3)*

*Hence when considering what the effects on the environment are likely to be, the environment must be seen as a network of ecosystems, including people and communities. In this network, social, economic, aesthetic and cultural effects should be considered in the promotion of sustainable management of natural and physical resources.*

*A final point to note in relation to the Resource Management Act (1991) is that consultation is central to the whole process. In the Fourth Schedule to the Act, which addresses "Matters that should be included in an assessment of effects on the environment...", clause (h) recommends that there be "An identification of those persons interested in or affected by the proposal, the consultation undertaken, and any response to the views of those consulted (s.88)."*

## International practice

The 1990s saw wide international practice of social assessment become entrenched. The World Commission on Environment and Development (1987) report on *Our Common Future*, widely known as the Brundtland Report, highlighted the issues around sustainability of development and reinforced interest in EIA and SIA (Burdge, 1998). In the face of environmental disasters and recognition of poor project planning, decision makers moved further from narrow engineering and economic criteria for decision making (Burdge, 1991). International interest in environmental issues was refocussed by the "Rio" conference in 1992, with further recognition of, and some action on, issues of sustainability. A parallel move was the growing recognition given to indigenous people's issues, perhaps manifest most dramatically in the reforms in South Africa in the early 1990s.

Recent publication (Burdge, 2003 Guest Editor) of a double issue on Social Impact Assessment in the journal *Impact Assessment and Project Appraisal*, highlights the field's development. Indeed this publication is but one of a number of books and publications that provided substance to the field. In 1990, the first edition of this text was published as the first comprehensive New Zealand text on social assessment, and it was used widely within New Zealand and internationally, with a second edition in 1995. Burdge (1998) published his revised book on SIA, Dale et al. (2001) published a major book on institutionalising of SIA and Becker and Vanclay (2003) published a new *Handbook of Social Impact Assessment*. Lockie's (2001) review covered many publications in the field since Freudenburg's comprehensive effort in 1986.

This substantive literature on social assessment has assisted training and institution building, through university and in-service courses. A number of these courses were held in conjunction with the annual International Association for Impact Assessment conferences, and the range of international participants at these courses indicated the expanding nature of the field. Furthermore, social assessment is now taught as an integral part of many courses available on EIA around the world.

In the United States, themes of biodiversity and ecosystem management predominated as timber harvesting practices in the Pacific Northwest were held responsible for the possible demise of the northern spotted owl and Pacific salmon. The policy of the US Forest Service was refined and strengthened further, with a trend towards management and evaluation in terms of bio-physical, or 'natural' system boundaries, as opposed to political jurisdictions. There was also a more systematic attempt to translate the effects of environmental alterations to impacts on human systems. Guidelines for the conduct of social assessment were developed and standardised for agency personnel through a comprehensive programme of in-service training courses that worked towards the integration of bio-physical and social assessment. The CEQ directed the attention of other federal agencies to a greater focus on social assessment.

The most significant development in the United States was the publication of *Guidelines and Principles for Social Impact Assessment* by The Interorganizational Committee on Guidelines and Principles for Social Impact Assessment in 1994. These guidelines demonstrated a greatly increased consensus by the social science community and public agencies on the nature and process of social assessment. Their purpose was to provide guidelines and principles to assist agencies, private interests and affected people in understanding and using SIA, while fulfilling requirements under NEPA and agency procedures (Burdge and Vanclay, 1995; Interorganizational Committee on Principles and Guidelines for Social Impact Assessment, 2003).

A further significant development in international practice was the spread of social assessment into development planning in multilateral agencies such as the World Bank, Food and Agriculture Organisation (FAO) and Asian Development Bank. The World Bank Environment Department (1991),Asian Development Bank (1994 and updated), FAO (1992) and the Development Bank of Southern Africa all produced detailed procedures and manuals for social assessment. Aspects of social assessment are now incorporated into policy and project documents along with gender analysis and particpatory procedures (see www.worldbank.org, www.adb.org and www.iied.org) and these organisations employ significant numbers of social experts (Francis and Jacobs, 1999).

Social assessment also became established in many other counties, some supporting the development with institution and capacity building. These countries include South Africa, where a number of workshops and training courses took place from 1993 with involvement from this book's authors. In the European Union, environmental legislation or regulations of each member state are driven by the *Council Directive 85/337/EEC of 27 June 1985 on the Assessment of the Effects of Certain Public and Private Projects on the Environment*, amended in 1997 with SIA integrated somewhat slowly (Glasson, 1999). In Southeast Asia, there was progressive development of EIA procedures from the late 1970s, although progress has been varied (Leu et al., 1997), especially recognition of the social dimension of environment and the need for the assessment of social impacts. In Malaysia, for example, procedures for environmental assessment of land-use plans and major projects included a social dimension, although there was limited professional and institutional capacity to carry out the social assessments.

Development of impact assessment in Europe saw important, parallel, areas emerge and applied internationally. The first was work on strategic environmental assessment (SEA), that is assessment of the environmental effects of programmes, plans and policies compared to a focus at the project level. SEA practitioners advocate an integrated approach incorporating social analysis (Brown and Therivel, 2000; Eggenberger and Partidário, 2000). SEA can also incorporate gender analysis (Verloo and Roggeband, 1996). Health impact assessment (HIA) is another complementary field (Vanclay and Bronstein, 1995), also applied at the project, programme and policy levels.

Capacity building and institutionalising of social assessment are important aspects of developing practice. The New Zealand SIA Working Group moved to a formal constitution as the NZ Association for Social Assessment in 1990. The Association took an active role in promoting social assessment, including developments in concepts and methods, training and the maintenance of standards of practice, through a regular newsletter, regional groups and annual conferences. Interestingly, this association expanded its interests to include all fields of impact assessment to become the New Zealand Association for Impact Assessment in 1998. This Association is affiliated to the International Association for Impact Assessment (IAIA see www.iaia.org), the leading organisation internationally for social assessment practitioners. The IAIA has an SIA section, which has made a bibliography of SIA and list of key citations available on its website. The IAIA has also published international principles for SIA (see Case study 1.2, Vanclay 2003).

### Case study 1.2  International principles for SIA

*A working group of the IAIA, convened by Frank Vanclay, addressed international guidelines for SIA. The result was a slow process over several years that uncovered a number of difficulties in developing guidelines, including the need to address guidelines to a specific audience. The guidelines group identified a number of audiences, including practitioners, regulatory agencies, policy makers, affected peoples and NGOs, special interest and local action groups, developers (proponents) and development agencies.*

*The international group therefore developed a set of basic principles from which guidelines can be developed for specific contexts and applications of social assessment. Principles include (our wording):*
- *ensure SIA takes place from early in decision making by qualified practitioners with sufficient time and resources for thorough impact assessment, and transparent processes, methods, and decision making*
- *consider all social impacts within a broad definition of environment, including the distribution of these impacts across social groups, and considering cultural differences in the experience of impacts, including different orders of impacts*
- *focus analysis on key issues and employ the precautionary principle with social issues as well as technical issues, conducting further analysis when uncertainty exists*
- *ensure data integrity and validation by cross checking with stakeholders, including community groups and/or NGOs and/or local authorities, and respect local knowledge and intellectual property rights of local people*
- *promote active use of SIA for adaptive management and mitigation of social impacts, including systems of monitoring and compensation if required*
- *include a commitment to involving all interested and affected peoples in the planning, design and implementation of change, respecting local knowledge*

*and protocols, and being aware of local power relations, social structures and any groups usually disadvantaged in the process of participation*
- *consider the needs of vulnerable groups and minorities and provide mechanisms for capacity building and enhancement of their participation in processes of change.*

*The IAIA SIA principles document is on www.iaia.org.*

## PERSISTENT PROBLEMS AND TRENDS

Through the transition of social assessment towards a more effective approach, there has been an emerging consensus among practitioners about the basic requirements for process and methods. Yet a number of persistent and troublesome trends are evident (Burdge and Vanclay, 1995).

### Whose domain?

This problem revolves around who is best qualified to take the lead in social assessment. The early answer (and the one you might expect) is that the sociologist is best qualified. But there are a number of academic backgrounds that prepare people to undertake social assessment. Anthropology, with its focus on culture, community and qualitative methods, is probably one of the most useful backgrounds for social assessment practitioners. Other disciplines within the social sciences have their strengths as well.

Too often, however, there are instances of social assessments conducted by inadequately qualified personnel. Burdge and Vanclay (1995: 45), in their discussion of problems confronting the field, raise the issue of appropriate training and the possibility of registering "... suitably qualified and experienced SIA practitioners ...". There are increasing numbers of university courses and other training programmes available worldwide to fill this gap.

In another aspect of domain, academics have begun an earnest quest to open up jobs in the public sector for their students (and for themselves) in response to diminishing opportunities for traditional university employment. While social assessment is a vehicle for employment, public agencies in many countries have been hit with retrenchment problems arising from budget constraints. As a result, social science staffing often remains far below adequate levels to provide sufficient social assessment expertise in natural resource management and planning agencies.

A beneficial result of this trend is that people with such diverse backgrounds as forestry and engineering are being exposed to the social sciences, and the social dimension increasingly is finding its way into organisational perspectives and decisions. Of course, the 'costs' of using available but untrained personnel are that sufficient expertise is not always at hand to undertake the social analysis, and the untrained eye is sometimes blind to potential social effects.

These questions of domain are explored further in Chapter 2 in respect to principal orientations to social assessment and typical work environments that practitioners find themselves in.

## Integration v. segmentation

Social analysis is frequently segmented within the EIA process. The reasons have seemed logical enough. The subject matter of social assessment, after all, is different from that of bio-physical concerns, as is the expertise required to do the analysis. Furthermore, differentiation in disciplinary areas is typically made in the various legal mandates for impact assessment. The interdisciplinary nature of EIA may be recognised, as with mention of economics, social science and the "design arts" under NEPA, and the employment of interdisciplinary teams in the US Forest Service regulations. But in actual practice, the EIA 'team members' frequently do different parts of the analysis without much consultation with colleagues in other areas (perhaps especially so with the social sciences), and the reports are often in the form of a series of analyses under different topics with little, if any, integration.

As noted under the topic of domain above, the scope and focus of social assessment can be determined by the academic background of those undertaking the job. Often the personnel assigned to social assessment have backgrounds that reflect the power and influence of a particular discipline in the agency in question. In the US Forest Service (and this would be true for most other natural resource agencies) economists have traditionally been the main social scientists on hand. Yet economic changes are highly interrelated with less easily quantified social changes, and it is most desirable to have economists and other social scientists working together on an interdisciplinary basis.

Further problems arise with political or institutional analysis that assesses the feasibility of certain agency actions being accepted by the public in the guise of social analysis. There is a danger that this type of analysis, or worse, 'public relations', may be accepted by officials as a substitute for social assessment. The public certainly should not be favourably impressed by a sophisticated method employed by an agency in the guise of impact assessment in order to implement a pre-determined course of action.

## Focus

The issues of domain and integration relate to the problem of focus. There are two special concerns for the social assessment process: can it be done sufficiently quickly to meet the requirements of decision makers, and can the results be presented in a way that officials can use? The first concern, for speed, is related to the question of focus, since broad, encyclopaedic approaches have resulted in unduly long time lines and unwieldy results for projects and policy making. This is a major reason why consultants outside the academic domain have often been involved in social assessment for large-scale projects. They often restrict their focus to a number of standard (usually economic and population-related)

13

variables. Private consultants are also usually in a position to respond to requests for proposals presented in limited format and with restricted times for response. Unsurprisingly, this narrow focus limits conceptual or methodological improvements.

The second part to the issue of focus is the requirement that the product be useful to decision makers. Results need to be presented in terms of major issues. Most practitioners simply do not research and present issues that centre around the major environmental and social concerns in question. It is essential that the focus of social assessment be **issues oriented**. The issues should be determined as early as possible during the preliminary investigation phase including the initial stages of public involvement. This approach does not mean that all issues considered must be those that the public recognise and articulate. The use of expert opinion is another means of identifying likely issues. Also, issues may be revealed later in the investigation as new information becomes available. Fast and useful social assessments are those that are analytic rather than encyclopaedic, and issue driven rather than general. An issue-driven, analytical approach is described in Chapter 5.

**Problems of concept**

The need for an analytical approach points to the problem of conceptualisation, a problem that plagues the social sciences in general. Investigations for a social assessment should be tied to theoretical or conceptual frameworks, literally the mental maps that direct an inquiry. Without such direction practitioners can reveal little more than general insights about their topic. They find themselves in the analogous situation of someone finding bits of a glass chair thrown from the top of a tall building and trying to make sense of the pieces without knowing that the original object was a chair!

There are two areas in particular where conceptual frameworks can be improved. The first is the provision of guiding concepts for the selection of variables for analysis in a social assessment. When variables are being selected in relation to the major issues of social change, there should be some kind of mental construct of the social realm from which the key variables are being drawn. In other words, one needs a view of what this 'social universe' looks like. This conception enables the investigator to determine if critical areas of social significance are being left out. A framework of variables for social profiling is provided in Chapter 6.

The second area where the absence of conceptual and theoretical constructs is of particular concern is in the analysis of community structure and community change (Taylor et al., 2001). The practitioner should have some explicit notions grounded in social theory of community formation and change. Broad theories of community are explored in Chapter 3 and there is a framework in Chapter 8 for understanding communities and sets of interest within them.

**Does the issue 'count'?**

The problem of whether or not the issue being addressed is important can be divided into three considerations: the first has to do with techniques of projection, the second with the problem of quantification, and the third with question of data validity.

Methods of projecting the future lie at the heart of social assessment, and much of the mystery of the process of analysis is tied up in this endeavour. In spite of the long lists of methods available to practitioners of social assessment, most fall into the categories of trend projections, multipliers or scenarios. Sophisticated computer modelling has been used as part of these techniques (e.g. Leistritz et al., 1994-5).

With regard to quantification, it is apparent that those sciences, such as economics, that most easily lend themselves to numerical analysis have wider acceptance among decision makers than those that do not. Numbers can enable the investigator to measure variables and to subject the units and measures to mathematical analyses. Numbers can provide efficient and effective summaries of information, and it is often easy to use these 'known quantities' in other systems of analysis (e.g. economic input-output analysis as discussed in Chapter 7). In fact, a substantial part of the data of social analysis can be quantified - numbers of jobs, income, population. It makes good sense to use these data to the utmost. Unfortunately, numbers can also hide value judgements made in their gathering and presentation.

There is a real problem taking into 'count' (literally and figuratively) those things that cannot easily be counted. Significantly, it is often precisely those variables that are most valuable to us that practitioners have most trouble quantifying. Examples include the meaning of a pristine landscape as a focus of spiritual life for indigenous peoples, the attraction of free-flowing rivers and streams in wilderness settings for rafters, kayakers and anglers (though the amount of money they spend in pursuit of their sport can be calculated), the social and psychological costs of a change of lifestyles (e.g. selling the family farm for a coal mining development). There is no magic way that these changes can be transformed into neat units of measure for statistical analysis and tabular presentation.

Surveys are a common mechanism by which new, countable, social data are collected. While surveys have a part to play in social assessment, the social assessment practitioner often does not have the luxury of time and money to collect survey data, so the answer to many data needs lies in the judicious use of secondary data, i.e. data usually (but not always) collected for purposes other than the investigation at hand, and at a time prior to the onset of the social assessment process. Examples of secondary data (see Chapter 6 for more detail) include data on housing and employment, newspaper articles, research reports, data collected for the administration of the education system, historical records, or monographs, and books by local historians. A review of secondary data should precede collection of new data. When it is established that primary data are needed for the social assessment, then the use of both qualitative and quantitative data will increase the range of methodologies available.

The key to establishing the validity of conclusions derived from diverse sources of data, is a cross-checking procedure to ensure that the directions of evidence provided by each source point at least roughly in the same direction. Inconsistencies are checked out and accounted for. Such cross validation (some researchers call it 'triangulation') is a simple and powerful method of establishing the 'truth' of conclusions (Hill, 1984).

A very powerful approach called analytic induction is available for organising and focussing this analysis within a social assessment, as discussed in Chapter 5. In brief, the approach is to develop an explanatory framework about a social context and how it is likely to be affected by a project, plan or set of alternatives. The framework is constantly revised in light of new data. When the investigator can account for all the seemingly discrepant information with this revised model, a strong case can be made for the validity of the conclusions.

**Problems of process**

It is perhaps surprising that there are still differences of opinion as to what the process of social assessment entails. Usually the split has been between academics who view social assessment as a research process, and government officials who view it in terms of their agency's decision or planning framework. In addition, there are distinctions made by those who see social assessment as a top-down planning process and others who see it as a bottom-up process for community development and empowerment. The different orientations that form the basis of these perspectives of the social assessment process are considered in detail in Chapter 2.

We contend in this book that there is a basic and logical process implied by the term 'social assessment' that is definitely not the same as the academic research process, and does not always fall neatly within the various governmental or community conceptions either. The process follows much the same logic as for the other elements of environmental analysis and management. Full details of the process are discussed in Chapter 4.

The process involves, first, a scoping investigation to identify issues around which to assess effects on certain social variables, determine the study area and sub-areas, identify groups likely to be differentially affected by the proposals in question, and, in effect, to plan the methods and approach of the analysis all the way from data needs and sources to projection strategies. At this early stage in the process it is usually appropriate to establish a basis for wide public consultation. Second, there is social profiling, or the description of the baseline as a point of comparison with the status quo and the projections of the various alternatives for action. Then there is projection and estimation of effects, and comparison of positive and negative effects for each of the alternatives. This comparison is made in terms of agreed decision criteria, and any standards established as part of the social assessment for the levels of social costs and benefits that the proposed project or plan is expected to bring about. As part of this comparison of alternatives, the status quo (or take-no-action alternative) is included (Bryan and Hendee, 1983).

At this point, those with the power to decide, settle on the best alternative to pursue after balancing the findings of the social assessment with the other elements of the environmental and economic analysis. Then, if a project, programme or policy proceeds, a system is developed to monitor and manage ongoing consequences, including the mitigation of adverse effects, followed by evaluation.

It should be clear that social assessment does not involve a research process in the strict definition of the term. That is, formal hypotheses are not posed to see if they find support in the data. Instead, projections are made based on data and procedures that are seen to be sufficiently reasonable and convincing for others to agree on their plausibility. Even so, it must be noted that these are projections of futures about which one can never be sure. The 'future' will keep changing as people react to the project or plans in their attempts to enhance the outcomes and minimise the costs for themselves and others.

The purpose of social assessment is to enable proponents and decision makers to make more socially responsible decisions, and, in a very direct way, to involve people affected by these decisions. Although the generation of new knowledge about communities undergoing change and the social processes underlying these changes may occur, the immediate goal is the best decision and management of change, rather than the generation of new knowledge.

All this is not to say that academic research and theoretical perspectives guiding this research are omitted. Ideally, the theoretical perspectives and data derived from the social sciences should provide the basis and guidance for social assessment, so that each new assessment is not part of a 'new Columbus' (or 'Captain Cook') syndrome: having to discover new facts and perspectives that have already been established. But many of the problems found in the social assessment process arise because established theoretical perspectives, methodologies, and data are often not used effectively during social assessments. The reason may be that a qualified social scientist who has this knowledge is not used for the social assessment (Burdge and Vanclay, 1995) or that much of the social science literature has not been translated into terms that facilitate its use or ready application to the process. Ironically, there is an abundant literature on community, social structure and social change that has often remained untapped for these purposes.

**Flexibility v. standardisation**

An issue that has persisted since the inception of social assessment is flexibility of the assessment process versus its standardisation. Early litigation under the terms of NEPA for the environmental impact assessment process, for example, tended to concentrate on the fulfilment of the format of the process, rather than the substance. This trend is true to a large extent even today. As a consequence, an emphasis on the form and format of the reporting documents can create a certain bureaucratic uniformity, where agencies become intent on meeting formal requirements rather than on the central issues. This state of affairs has been especially injurious to social assessment, since it reinforced confusion about the nature of the social assessment process.

Early on, with no established body of literature and confusion concerning the methodological logic of the process, problems arose for social assessments aimed primarily at meeting the bureaucratic, organisational needs of an agency. This confusion was exemplified in the early 'laundry list' approach to variable selection. Assessors were typically divorced from the wider process of environmental assessment being undertaken by an agency. They were simply to report their findings to the 'responsible agency official', who then used (or did not use, as was often the case) the report to meet the formal requirement to provide a social assessment.

At the same time, academics in particular formulated broad-based community studies of every conceivable social variable. The resulting social overviews, while providing good baseline data for later studies, often did not actually project social effects, were not issues oriented, and were seldom considered by officials in the final stages of the decision process.

Agencies such as the US Forest Service responded to this state of affairs by formulating methodological guidelines for the conduct of social assessment. The aim of these guidelines was not to contradict bureaucratic procedures but to elaborate on each step of the agency guidelines as part of logical inquiry. The idea was to use this logic to transcend the various bureaucratic requirements of site and project-specific assessments, and to standardise the procedures without denying sufficient flexibility for state-of-the-art application.

Thus, the format of each social assessment followed the basic process described above and detailed in Chapter 4. Where possible, social data were gathered by members of an interdisciplinary team. Decisions were then to be made by officials according to standardised criteria, although as discussed below these criteria were often inconsistent. The heart of the social analysis, the way(s) in which social issues were identified and projected, was left to those carrying out the analysis. The idea was to make explicit the logic and sequence of the analysis without prescribing specific techniques for doing it - a balance between standardisation and flexibility.

Where this process did not go far enough in some people's opinion was in the establishment of qualification guidelines for those who conduct social assessments, and in the establishment of a means for judging the validity of their conclusions. With regard to the former, agencies have been reluctant to establish criteria for expertise because of cutbacks in personnel budgets and the need to proceed with people already employed. They have not been in a position to hire social scientists. There has also been doubt among many people involved in the process of planning for and managing social effects about the legitimacy of the social science enterprise. The job prospects for social scientists may well improve over the long term, but the problem of legitimacy will depend largely on the effectiveness of social scientists in contributing to decisions. In the meantime, agencies are often 'making do' with available expertise and training people on hand to undertake social analyses.

## Decision criteria

Decision criteria are the standards used to make judgements about whether environmental effects (including social of course) are positive or negative. There are several problems in this area that pose fundamental obstacles to social assessments being effectively integrated into the process of decision making. Criteria used by decision makers are often not specified explicitly. These criteria are frequently difficult to specify. When criteria are specified, they are often developed at inappropriate points in the process (and by people who are at inappropriate levels in consent agencies). Sometimes these criteria are inconsistent, for example promoting biodiversity while maximising timber harvest.

Since decision criteria reflect basic values as to what ought to be happening in society, it is a risky business to link an explicit statement of these values to specific project outcomes. Some decision makers naturally shun this problem when they can. They prefer to 'let the facts speak for themselves' (which, of course, they never do) and assume the outcome of their actions is for the 'social good' - jobs, income, economic prosperity, and the like. Social wellbeing, in other words, can be whatever people assume it to be. The prevailing assumption is that technological accomplishments and a loosely defined path of 'development' will bring about social good.

A closer analysis of social outcomes will usually inject greater accountability into the decision process. It is little consolation to the social assessment practitioner at this point that much human reasoning is an exercise in creative rationalisation to defend and promote things in which people have a vested interest. People at risk from accountability, such as politicians and other decision makers, naturally want as wide a latitude as possible when it comes to justifying or defending actions to which they are committed.

As decision criteria deal in the realm of human values, and there can be a range of values held by social groups involved in a single case of decision making, the criteria can be difficult to formulate and defend, especially the more explicit the values get. It is one thing to talk about economic prosperity, it is quite another matter to specify that more jobs in an area will barely compensate for the 'costs' of large infusions of newcomers and resulting community conflict and instability. What criteria should be chosen? More jobs? Greater diversification of the economy? Population stability, or perhaps a rate of population increase that does

19

not strain a community's capabilities of coping? Preservation of cultural values? Enhancement of minority interests? Economic growth? More community facilities? The problem of decision criteria is compounded in that the fulfilment of some of these goals may preclude the fulfilment of others. In the absence of a systematic way of setting priorities, or a definitive policy, decision makers are left to exercise their own judgement about effects, or worse, to assume uncritically that there will be some general social benefit.

There is also uncertainty over who should set the criteria. In fact, criteria are often set or governed by the assumptions of those furthest from the assessment process. The result is that their criteria are seldom given close scrutiny until litigation or formal hearings. Even then, social assumptions may take on secondary importance to considerations that seem to be physical or technical. Most people are uneasy when dealing with social values, but since decisions about resource use rest on sets of assumptions about values, it is better to state these precepts clearly and early in decision making. This move will not happen without a policy framework in place to guide the necessary thinking. These are policies that should derive from wide public involvement and invite debate in the political arena, before, rather than after, the fact.

Perhaps one of the most important aspects about the setting of decision criteria is that their early and explicit statement makes it difficult for those with hidden values (agenda) to avoid exposure of their self interest. In this instance, hidden costs are not usually passed on to the anticipated benefactors of a project. For example, the construction of a dam can be 'sold' to a community on the basis of job creation and increased economic vitality for the area. The obvious benefits to those whose business is engineering and construction are considered legitimate. But what is not legitimate or placed to the fore are the hidden costs to the community of the 'boom and bust cycle' associated with the arrival and departure of a large, outside workforce. The community is left to pay taxes for expansion of community services (schools, recreation facilities, fire and police protection), while being told that a new tourism industry can be based on lake recreation, when, in fact, the original river had more tourism potential. Some community members do benefit but at the expense of others. Real estate speculators make money, but young citizens looking for new homes in the community may find themselves priced out of the market.

It may be that in the generalised example cited above, the overall national benefit of hydroelectric power outweighs the costs experienced locally and by specific social groups, but the early setting of decision criteria about social and environmental change forces a more careful accounting of costs and benefits before commitment to the project is made. We must make the assumption that full and early disclosure of who gains, who loses, and by how much, provides more comprehensive cost-benefit analysis and supports public involvement and creative public debate.

## The roles of prediction and participation

The problems in this area have probably accounted for more of the obstacles to effective social assessment than any others. They include the issue of predicting the future, the role of public participation in shaping futures, and the problems of diverse philosophies within the field. Public participation is not synonymous with social assessment. Nonetheless, social assessment should involve people affected by change in shaping their future.

It is rightly argued that the primary goal of social assessment is to anticipate a course of events following an environmental change and to manage them accordingly. It could also be argued that for all practical purposes 'social futures' cannot be forecast with any degree of accuracy, that people take action on the basis of any available information, and that the 'future' keeps changing as people react. Social assessment must therefore involve a strategy that both anticipates and reacts to change.

Theoretically, at least, projection of futures is possible. Though predictions are often tenuous (other scientists have similar problems), there are methodologies that offer plausible scenarios of the social consequences of future actions. The public at large and officials who represent the public can work with these scenarios, and the projections made serve as a basis for common discourse about the problems and prospects of the proposals. There may be disagreement about the projections, and the projections may indicate the need for mitigation measures, but the social forecasts are the essential ingredients of the social assessment process. The quality of these projections, the plausibility of the assumptions, methods, and conclusions, and how well they are presented, will have a lot to do with the success and acceptance of the overall process.

Another issue related to public participation as part of the social assessment process is whether it is indeed a participatory process, or just public manipulation. The answer to this question depends on how early the public is involved, whether the project is destined to be pushed, regardless of opposition or social consequences, and the view the developers or planners have of the social assessment process. In the long run, unless public participation is included in good faith early on, as an integral part of the process, issues can become polarised to the extent that opposition or support for particular proposals will not be based on sound information but on political exigencies and power. A well worked methodology for public involvement will aim to inform and involve the public in the decision process without the stalemates over issues that often occur. Nevertheless, decisions of any social consequence will usually involve some degree of social conflict. A broad view of social assessment in general, and public participation in particular, encompasses conflict identification and conflict resolution or negotiation as part of the decision process.

It has been difficult to obtain consensus among social scientists and other participants over philosophies and approaches to social assessment. The social sciences are 'low consensus disciplines' with a wide variety of theory and philosophy.  Social assessment inherits this legacy from its social science practitioners.  One definition of scientific knowledge is that experts agree that the information is 'true', for the time being at least.  The scientific method allows the experts a basis for such agreement by replicating results to determine if they are consistent.  The problem in social science is that fundamentally different philosophies guide its practitioners.  Some assume that the basis of society is consensus, others assume that conflict is the natural state.  Some assume that people and societies can be studied just as any other object of scientific investigation; others say that humans are 'special' and the principles of causality and determinism do not apply.  Some assume that planning is most effective as a technical process under central management, others argue strongly that it must be truly participatory with all social groups empowered to take part and have their concerns met.  Chapter 2 provides an analytic framework for guiding practitioners through these problems and their implications for social assessment practice.

## CONCLUSIONS

There is no easy way out of the dilemmas and contradictions surrounding social assessment.  We argue in this book that social assessment has to be an eclectic endeavour, using a variety of methods and perspectives.  Both centralised planning and community action have their place in influencing futures.

Our review of the field of social assessment demonstrates its considerable potential to strengthen social planning and place social criteria alongside economic and environmental criteria in decision making.  Social assessment is a process in which decisions with social implications are analysed from a social viewpoint before and after they are taken.

It is clear that social assessment has been hindered by a number of problems with approach and methods that have seemed almost endemic.  The practitioner is usually beset with time and money limitations, necessitating reliance on secondary data.  Often it is only possible to analyse crucial social variables with qualitative data as they do not lend themselves to quantitative techniques of projection.  Furthermore, such data are considered by some decision makers to be less 'scientific', less reliable, and less valid than 'hard data'.  These problems with data are often exacerbated by an unwieldy, 'laundry list approach' to collecting data.  Then there are investigators who attempt to research almost every facet of community life to be affected by a plan or project.  Social assessment requires an issues-oriented approach using both qualitative and quantitative data.

It has to be made clear to decision makers that careful social analysis and an effective social assessment process often reveal hidden costs (as well as benefits) of projects and plans that the developers and others pass on to the affected communities.  This informing and, therefore effectively empowering of social groups, is part of the problem of gaining acceptance for the social component.  Social assessment is often an exercise in disclosure of information that can be threatening to certain vested interests. Many proponents and officials therefore distrust social assessment.

The process has a way of making values more explicit and injecting a degree of accountability in the decision process. It can be said that every political decision is in fact an experiment in human behaviour, but the outcomes and implications of such 'experiments' are seldom clearly explored. The process of social assessment leads to this very type of examination, so it is no wonder that some politicians do not support what they see as an exposure of their prerogatives.

Finally, we suggest that social science has been more of a reactive than proactive enterprise. By this we mean that social scientists have tended to look at things after they have already happened and offered interpretations for these events, rather than anticipating change, and perhaps prescribing or influencing change before or during the fact. We believe that there is now a gradual move in a more proactive direction. While elements of the proactive mode have always existed in our work, we are arguing that we should hasten this trend and concentrate more energies in this new direction.

## SUMMARY

Social assessment provides a process for managing social change arising from projects, policies and programmes. Chapter 1 provides a brief overview of the development of social assessment as a field. An historical and cross-cultural perspective is taken to highlight turning points and many positive developments, as well as to identify persistent difficulties and constraints.

The background to the field can be traced to the NEPA legislation in the United States in 1969, and the institutional development that followed for environmental assessment and, subsequently social assessment, in that country and elsewhere. Social assessment has established an important role in many countries and multilateral organisations, primarily in environmental management.

There are diverse disciplinary backgrounds to the practice of social assessment, and these have led to conflicts of approach, but also to the development of an important, interdisciplinary perspective.

Problems of philosophy, process, focus, concept and method beset the field during its development phases. The problem of philosophy relates to technocratic versus participatory approaches. It also raises the question of decision criteria, and the accountability of proponents, public agency officials and political representatives.

Questions of process relate to the focus of social assessments towards either research or action. There is in fact a logical process that emphasises the focus of assessments on key issues for either projecting or managing change. This process of social assessment needs to be tied to conceptual frameworks for understanding social change and for substantiating and validating social issues. The information used in social assessment will usually encompass both quantitative and qualitative data sources. It is often the issues that are most difficult to count that are the most important to assess. Good assessments are usually analytic and issue-driven.

Social assessment poses a special challenge to the social sciences and involves a shift in emphasis from reactive to proactive approaches. It also poses a challenge to other disciplines to take part in an integrated approach.

# CHAPTER TWO

## Orientations to the practice of social assessment

## INTRODUCTION

Chapter 1 provided a critical appraisal of developments in the field of social assessment. Both problems and prospects were noted. In this chapter we provide an analysis of the field in terms of major orientations to social assessment practice, and then enlarge on the prospects available in a more proactive, integrated and issues-oriented approach.

Our review of social assessment literature and practice indicates that practitioners come from a variety of backgrounds. These backgrounds include social and environmental sciences in universities and research institutes, professional planning and engineering, community development, and special interest research or action groups. It is apparent that each background carries with it a characteristic orientation to social science, social policy and social development. We discuss these orientations in respect to characteristic work environments and from this discussion present some conclusions about possibilities that exist for working around inflexible and dogmatic positions.

## ORIENTATIONS IN THE FIELD OF SOCIAL ASSESSMENT

Social assessment can be seen in terms of two major dimensions. Each dimension reflects dominant and opposing perspectives and these are shown in the titles of the rows and columns in Figure 2.1. One dimension has to do with whether the primary perspective adopted in a social assessment is 'technocratic' (product oriented) or 'participatory' (process oriented). The second dimension relates to a primary perspective towards the use of information, as a basis for social action, or research and the generation of new knowledge for knowledge's sake. Hence, this dimension is shown as either 'action' oriented or 'research' oriented.

The technocratic-participatory dimension reflects the problem of values in social assessment, a problem that is important because social assessment is close to decision making. Put simply, social assessors are likely to have more success in influencing a group of decision makers if their products are couched in a framework of values that is align with those of the decision makers (e.g. values leading to being for or against a development or policy). A close correlation of values can lead to a mutually reinforcing system of social assessment and decision making. Practitioners are familiar with the results, where assessments do little if anything to enlighten or change the course of a particular policy, plan or development. Where assessments are governed by institutional funding, political, and other constraints, they can serve to facilitate, or even 'rubber stamp', development. They occur within a dominant set of values that legitimates a particular path of development. On the other hand, communities and citizen groups affected by planned change often have different sets of values that place them at odds with decisions 'from above'. One can often find groups fundamentally opposed to planned change, to preserve their way of life and bring about changes to proposed paths of development. Thus, a social assessment from their perspective can either support the process of change and development, or oppose and modify it.

The distinction between technocratic and participatory social assessment is not new to those involved in natural resource planning and management. Early in the development of social assessment, Tester and Mykes (1981) distinguished between participatory and technocratic approaches in North America, and Taylor and Sharp (1983) did the same in New Zealand. These authors noted that technocratic approaches, whether academic or applied in orientation, tend to be positivistic. That is, they aim to facilitate development by prediction, control, and management of impacts. In comparison, participatory social assessment emphasises an involvement in community action, either by action directly in opposition to a new project or by negotiation over the distribution of impacts. More recently, Roberts (2003: 260) distinguishes between "consultative"and "participatory" approaches at two ends of the "public involvement spectrum".

The research-action dimension reflects a difference between the study of change in and of itself and action to effect change, with or without data and analysis resulting from research. Social scientists have always been challenged in this way by change, as Berger and Berger (1976: 330) suggest: "social change is an intellectual problem in that it is a challenge to understanding; social change is also a political problem in that it demands practical actions". Once again, the distinction between applied and basic social research is not new to many social scientists involved in natural resource management. There is a common distinction made between applied and basic research for natural resource management by examining the social context of the research. It is possible to observe differences in work style, multidisciplinary orientation, research methods, and the application of research results to client needs, policy and action.

**Four orientations**

We use the differences found in the practice of social assessment by intersecting the two main dimensions and then distinguishing four orientations (Figure 2.1). For each orientation it is possible to discuss its characteristics in relation to the process of social assessment. These orientations are influenced by their different work environments that relate to their different approaches to social assessment. Within each orientation its characteristics constitute, in sociological terms, 'ideal types'. These constructs are used to draw out and illustrate principles and trends. The framework is particularly useful in assisting practitioners in social assessment to think critically about their own work and resulting approaches that they might take. In particular, the framework shapes thinking towards an issues-orientated approach.

**Figure 2.1    Orientation to social assessment**

| | ACTION ORIENTATION | RESEARCH ORIENTATION |
|---|---|---|
| **TECHNOCRATIC APPROACHES** (product oriented) | Action based on centralised social planning and management (government agencies, consultants) | Academic research (universities, private and public "think tanks") |
| **PARTICIPATORY APPROACHES** (process oriented) | Action based on social development at a community level (local community organisations, groups and community workers, organisers) | Advocacy research (foundation supported and independent research on behalf of special minority interests) |

At the centre: **ISSUES-ORIENTED APPROACH** (with arrows pointing inward from all four quadrants)

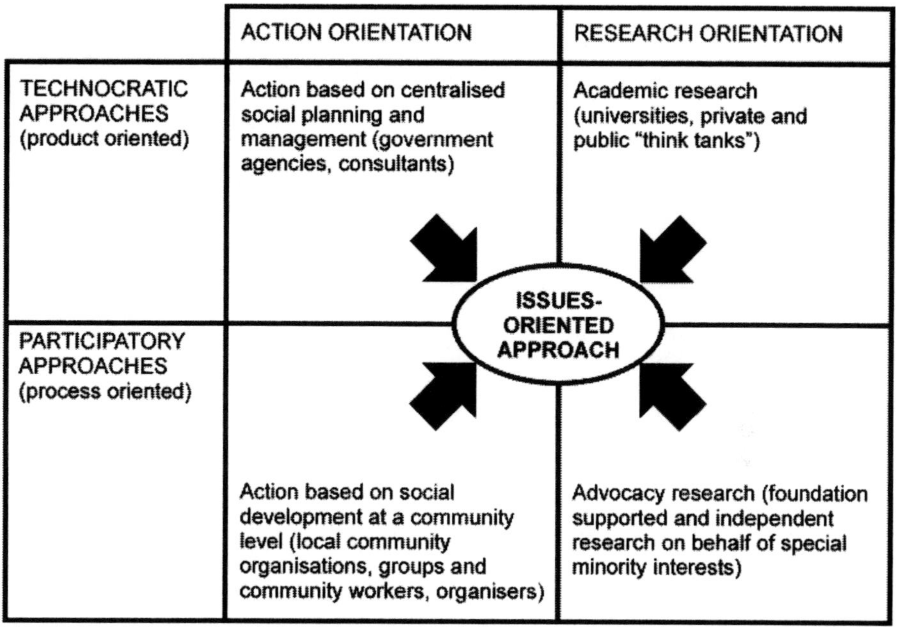

*Technocratic-action*

The technocratic-action orientation to social assessment is typical in government agencies charged with conducting or overseeing environmental impact assessment, and other public agencies charged with fulfilling legal requirements associated with the field of environmental impact assessment and natural resource planning and management. This orientation is also typical of private sector developers and of consulting firms that usually work to meet the needs of either the developers or the agencies. Resource development is usually organised within this work environment through a bureaucratic union of private sector capital and central government. The likely focus of people operating in these work environments is a centralised one aimed at 'informed' social planning and the management of impacts. The principal impetus in this approach to social assessment is to make 'top-down' decisions based on 'expert knowledge' within a formal and structured bureaucracy. Status and modes of career advancement inherent within this structure restrict individual opportunities for creative responses to social assessment and soundly-based natural resource and social policy.

*Technocratic-research*

The typical setting for technocratic-research work is the university, as well as some public or private 'think tanks' charged with evaluating policy issues.

Although social action may emerge from the results of academic research, the product of the research is generally assumed to be knowledge for its own sake. A variety of philosophical or ideological positions may be found in this type of work style, ranging from conflict (radical) to structural-functional (conservative) analysis, and in methods, from qualitative to quantitative.

Bureaucratic organisation in this setting is similar to that of the technocratic-action orientation. Career opportunities and research funding are based on limited criteria, usually performance in publication. Therefore opportunity for creativity in research methods, conceptual development, or advocacy research may be restricted by practices that are strongly established and reinforced by the normative conventions of the researchers.

*Participatory-action*

This orientation is in the same action dimension as centralised social planning and management, but the work environment shifts from national, regional, or centralised planning agencies to action at the local level. At this level is a 'bottom-up' attempt to organise for social change. Often this action is in response to policies originating primarily from 'above'. The work organisation will usually be semi-formal. It may be an existing community group that is in opposition to a development, or a group organised for the sole purpose of challenging a particular part of a development plan or policy. It may also be a group organised in response to needs defined locally. In some cases the organisation may have been established already as an arm of local government (e.g. community development programmes) and may come into direct conflict with wider agency objectives. Often status and authority in these work environments are consciously organised in ways that directly challenge those found in technocratic work environments, for example, an emphasis on group consensus, collective work, or the active participation and leadership of women members or minority groups.

*Participatory-research*

This orientation shares the fact-finding orientation of academic researchers but it is usually research done by or in collaboration with an interest group. Thus the research might be on behalf of indigenous people, feminists, social reform workers, environmental groups, labour unions, etc. The focus in this orientation tends to be research to validate the particular plight and need for changed conditions of the interest groups represented. Work status and opportunity in this orientation usually depend on the particular social and cultural needs of the group of which the researcher is a member, not the structured reward system of a large research organisation. Thus, the work environment is usually either informal or limited by special cultural needs, such as those found in a traditional tribal setting. New types of peer pressure might encourage or even force the researcher into new methods and concepts. In a traditional setting this innovation might mean the use of narrative research, for example. In an alternative employment group, radical theories of economic development might be appropriate, and for an environmental group, an ecological approach might be essential.

**Orientation conflicts**

Confusion and debate as to what constitute 'legitimate approaches' to social assessment have resulted from conflicts among particular practitioners or work organisations who are trying to legitimate their own approaches and ideologies. The most common conflict identified is between action in a technocratic, 'top-down' approach and action in a participatory, 'bottom-up' approach. To put it simply, community development activities that result in opposition are not in the interest of government or industry set on a particular development or policy. Top-down oriented management finds it difficult to take a positive view of community development processes that may end up significantly altering its plans and challenging vested interests. Nor is it easy for people operating from a strong community development perspective to take a positive view of opportunities that might exist for them to participate in programmes that originate from above.

The conflicts between so-called 'academic' and 'applied' approaches to research are also well known. In the academic setting the emphasis is usually on the publication of research results for the sake of theoretical and academic development, as well as professional enhancement. Generally this work takes place within the intellectual confines of a particular academic school of thought or paradigm. Well-established methods are used to test current concepts and deduce refinements to existing 'knowledge'. In contrast, most research in the applied policy sphere is a means of collecting and using data for an immediate objective. At one extreme this research takes place outside the rigours of any academic discipline. The results of such work are frequently unpublishable and viewed as 'illegitimate' in established academic settings. Such work is typically not seen as worthy in consideration of tenure and promotion.

On the other hand, academic work is often seen as irrelevant to solving applied problems by those involved in social action. Those doing applied research are sometimes viewed by community and special interest groups as 'selling out' to their clients. At the same time they can be viewed by their academic colleagues as doing irrelevant or unimportant work. Further conflict arises if the research setting and funding for applied work place any restrictions on academic freedom.

Conflicts are also found between the academic and advocacy research orientations. Applied and special interest research can both be seen by academics as unworthy of merit for promotion and consideration of tenure in their work environment. But there is a further problem, for when social science opens avenues for contributions to policy and planning, it is often the academic approach that is seen as most legitimate. Academic research lies firmly in the technocratic dimension. Participatory research has often evoked uncomfortable challenges to established academic thought, regarding both theory and methods. Examples have included research by indigenous people, women, and environmental groups. These groups have moved towards issue-identification using innovative concepts and methods that have sometimes been at odds with traditional, discipline-based approaches to research.

Inherent conflicts exist between action and research in the participatory dimension. Community action, for example, will create pressure to collect data that support a particular stance by advocacy researchers. The data may not necessarily support this stance, however, and conflict can result from pressure on the advocacy researchers to compromise the integrity of their research process. It may be necessary for groups in advocacy positions to compromise some of their ideas about appropriate concepts and methods for research, in order to make a well-argued contribution to social policy when enabling practice has made available an opportunity for their input.

Coalitions are also formed. They may, for instance, be formed between people in the participatory-research orientation and those involved in participatory-action. However, coalitions may also be slow to form in spite of similar agendas, due to the 'baggage' or unique characteristics of each group. For example, a community action group may be hesitant to link with participatory researchers who have taken a different stance in another context.

## TRANSCENDING THE ORIENTATIONS

Implicit in our description of the four orientations to practice of social assessment and the common conflicts between them, is that those working from a particular orientation will find it productive to take views from those with other orientations into account. For example, those with technocratic-action orientations are finding that citizens likely to be affected by a policy or project want to be involved in decision making. Those with academic research orientations are being pushed to investigate the more immediate and practical problems of the 'real world'. Some academics have moved to central planning agencies, and others in some instances have taken on advocacy research. Community-level social development workers and advocacy researchers are finding that formal and informal channels are opening up enabling them to participate in environmental impact assessments, planning, and other decisions affecting their own lives or those for whom they are advocates. Some special interest advocates and researchers are spending time in academic settings by becoming involved in special interest departments of teaching and research institutions.

### The middle ground

The best prospects for developing new approaches to social assessment are found in the increasing number of individual practitioners who have made moves away from a strong adherence to orientations embodied in their familiar work environments. Most importantly, we note the prospects that arise from practitioners who move towards the middle ground (Figure 2.1). The middle ground, which we see as providing the dynamic and creative setting for a proactive, issues-oriented approach, requires a two-dimensional shift in stance.

Previously, social planners have noted the importance of a single dimension move from technocratic to more participatory approaches. Rothman (1974: 6-7), for example, suggests that both technical social planning and social action can have the potential to meet new and more desirable social goals. In fact, he maintains that 'social progress' will be met best by a merging of technical (expert) and lay knowledge. This merging of information is the basis of 'enabling' planning practice, as suggested by Forester (1980) and discussed in more detail in Chapter 3. He considers the political implications of communication in planning and describes how much top-down communication in technocratic planning approaches is 'disabling'. Improved strategies of communication can produce a more democratic process of planning. Communication from the top down and an openness to communication from the bottom up will encourage participatory planning. In Forester's suggestions for such communication strategies there are an implicit understanding of the need to break down many current, elitist practices, or, in Roberts' (2003: 276) words, "relinquish some control".

These moves across the technocratic-participatory dimension are important. But, to achieve the middle ground, shifts in the action-research dimension must, if possible, occur at the same time.

**Implications of the middle ground**

Social assessment in the middle ground should be a productive activity. First, research in this area involves grass-roots sociology. The academic is challenged not just to make a better contribution to technocratic policy formation but to work closely in areas where there are social changes involving community and special interest groups. Technical planners are challenged to become more familiar with the constraints and potential of social science research. They are encouraged to take a more humanistic perspective towards planning and investigating different paths of development, and to ensuring better communication and more participatory approaches. Advocacy researchers are challenged to broaden their innovative analysis into critiques of existing social theory and methods, and to find avenues in which to make effective contributions to social policy while still validating and advocating for special issues. Community development facilitators and special interest groups are challenged to use social science research to build their cases. They also need to continue to critique existing research and policy, often through coalitions with other groups, broadening their efforts beyond the needs of single interests.

A second productive area results from the effort that has to be made when practitioners attempt to operate in different work environments. Social researchers have to take on new positions in terms of social concepts and social theory. Practitioners involved in social action are likely to give direction to social change at both the level of community organisation and the level of bureaucratic organisation. Thus, there is a great potential for the formation of creative and responsive social and natural resource programmes and policy.

## CONCLUSIONS

Characterising social assessment in terms of four major orientations to practice helps to identify the potential of the middle ground. Practitioners can make a more positive and proactive contribution to the decision process by working in the middle ground using an issues-oriented approach. The approach can contain the following elements:

- recognition of social assessment as a process

- better conceptualisation and analysis of the human environment

- identification and focus on key issues

- the use of participatory methods

- conflict identification, resolution or negotiation.

A participatory, proactive process for social assessment emphasises early consultation and resolution of potential conflicts in planning and decision making. The process helps to mobilise communities and interest groups to participate in change, usually through techniques of information exchange and issues-oriented research methods. An emphasis on early consultation is usually very cost effective, bringing all participants in a decision-making process together to identify effects and deal with the distribution and management of their costs and benefits. In this participatory approach the social assessment process itself becomes part of any change being analysed. For instance, the process could be instrumental in setting up forums for discussion of social impacts, thereby encouraging community groups to take a definitive role in managing the direction of social change.

Through the issues-oriented approach described in this book, there should also be close integration of social and environmental impact assessment. All environmental issues are ultimately social issues, and the process of assessment is conceptually the same. Our approach implies the use of integrated, anticipatory and participatory methods and processes. In Chapter 3 we examine the conceptual basis behind such an approach.

## SUMMARY

In Chapter 2, orientations to the field of social assessment are discussed to identify major philosophical and institutional constraints to an issues-oriented, consultative and proactive approach. Social assessment is dominated by the strong orientations, philosophies and work environments of particular practitioners. By identifying these orientations it is possible to consider prospects for new directions in our practice.

There are two dominant and opposing perspectives to social assessment: technocratic and participatory. Intersecting the technocratic-participatory dimension, the research-action dimension reflects the difference between research conducted for its own sake and the application of information to a set of actions. Four main orientations can be described from the 'boxes' produced by the intersection of these two dimensions. Debate within social assessment about approach often reflects the conflicts inherent in these dimensions.

Innovative theory and method within social assessment have tended to originate from practitioners who have transcended the limitations of their orientation, often in conjunction with shifts between work environments. The middle ground, reflecting a two-dimensional shift in stance, is of particular importance. It involves 'grass roots' sociology and more humanistic and participatory perspectives on planning and decision-making. Advocacy researchers and people working from a community or special interest group are also challenged to broaden their perspectives and take advantage of opportunities to participate. As a result of these creative efforts a more participatory and proactive process has emerged. It emphasises better conceptualisation and analysis, a focus on issues and consultation, and provides for informed negotiation and the mediation of conflict.

# CHAPTER THREE

## Theoretical considerations for social assessment

### INTRODUCTION

This chapter presents the underlying assumptions used in our teaching and practice of social assessment. As explained in Chapter 2, social assessment practitioners can be distinguished by their different orientations and work environments, each of which reflects different values and ideologies. As a process to anticipate and manage social change arising from projects, programmes and policies, social assessment usually involves practitioners from government agencies at central, regional and local levels. It also involves the private sector, social researchers and participants from various special interest and local groups.

These distinctions between orientations include an important general distinction between technocratic and participatory approaches to social assessment. But this distinction is not made primarily in terms of theoretical perspective. Rather, work environments and orientations towards planning and research are the usual basis upon which we categorise different practice. For instance, we regard 'radical' social theorists as technocratic in approach if their work is not grounded in social action and 'enabling' practice. In other words, the fact that they are 'radical' in their thinking does not necessarily imply that the radicalism moves from intellectual debate to overt action. The practice of social assessment benefits from a critical view of society and, therefore, a critical view of sociology. Thus we advocate in this chapter a new set of basic assumptions for the practice of social assessment, assumptions that lie in environmental sociology and critical theory.

Social scientists have often reified the role of theory without necessarily using it effectively to direct and interpret their analytical work. Part of this problem arises out of the position that theory holds in the social sciences. Rather than providing a set of suppositions about the nature of the world from which testable propositions (hypotheses) are derived, theory often becomes the focus of the analysis itself. Hence, we see theory studied in its own right (meta theory) rather than as a tool used to interrogate social reality.

There have, however, been efforts to write theory specific to social assessment and the most notable of these include Dietz (1987), Rickson et al. (1994), Slootweg et al. (2001) and Becker (2003). The sum of these contributions is exciting in the sense that social assessment is perhaps more grounded in theoretical and conceptual models than acknowledged by practitioners. Dietz proposes a framework using Habermas' pragmatic approach to policy, while Rickson et al. stress the need for theoretical guidance, and elaborate key (and guiding) concepts that are located within the fields of community and organisational theory. Slootweg et al. propose a conceptual framework to assist with integration of social and environmental analysis. These authors provide important contributions but, as this chapter indicates, there is no single theory underlying the practice of social assessment. What is most important in the development of the field is an appreciation of the guiding and informing role of theory. As Rickson et al. (1994: 89) state, "It is only through the use of relevant social theory that professionals assessing development know what to ask (what data to collect) and what data mean when they have it". Becker (2003: 130) points out that a practical conceptual framework for analysing a specific case can be derived from a number of comparative studies.

This chapter explains and examines some basic assumptions for social assessment, first by briefly discussing classical theoretical perspectives in sociology, and then by adding the assumptions of environmental sociology. The central theme is of a pervasive social-environmental interaction that provides a conceptual basis for sustainable development and enabling practice.

## COMMON SOCIAL PERSPECTIVES

Established areas of social theory are grounded in the work of the three main classical theorists of sociology: Durkheim, Weber and Marx, described by Humphrey et al. (2002) as conservative, liberal, and radical perspectives respectively. In the terms of Catton and Dunlap (1978), who proposed a new environmental paradigm for sociology, work in these traditions is all part of one human-exemptionalism paradigm. This traditional paradigm has an anthropocentric view of humans as somehow separate from and superior to natural processes.

Some authors, such as Kilmartin et al. (1985: 6), have noted the obvious base of this new environmental paradigm in the human ecological approach described below. While the human ecologists were one important source of ideas for the new environmental paradigm, we note, in line with the argument of Humphrey et al. (2002), that the liberal and radical theorists have also made major contributions to environmental sociology. We diverge from Humphrey et al., however, in our acceptance that there is a new environmental paradigm, even if it is only incompletely formed as yet. This new environmental paradigm is already making an important original contribution to social theory. For us, it provides the most useful current theoretical advances in sociology, and particularly for the sociology of natural resource management and base assumptions in social assessment (see Figure 3.1).

Before examining the paradigm of environmental sociology in more detail, the theoretical contributions of each of the classical human-exemptionalism perspectives are examined.

**Figure 3.1    Theoretical perspectives for social assessment**

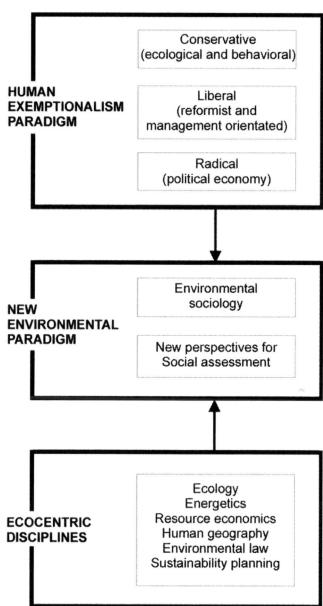

## The conservative, ecological-behavioural perspective

The threads of human ecology theory can be traced back to the 1800s and the work of Comte, 1798-1857, and Spencer, 1820-1903, who were also important figures in the founding of the conservative school of thought within sociology. Comte elaborated upon ideas about the essential unifying factor of collective life, a theme that was later to dominate the conservative perspective in sociology. In Comte's case this essential unifying factor was 'consensus', by which he meant common habits, beliefs and traditions. These ideas were further developed by Herbert Spencer, who, working within an organic model of society, was to place considerable emphasis on the notion of a society consisting of specialised functioning parts, each of which was considered to be essential to the survival of the whole.

It was left to Durkheim, 1858-1917, to bring together these two conceptions of group integration through 'consensus', and 'differentiation and interdependence', into a single theory. Durkheim developed a theory of an evolutionary sequence experienced by societies, involving change from social unity based upon consensus (mechanical solidarity) to unity based upon differentiation and interdependence (organic solidarity). Increases in social density necessitated this change, leading to large, mobile populations that were distinguished by a division and specialization of labour, and hence by interdependence.

This refinement of Durkheim made it easy to draw upon the organic model earlier provided by Spencer and to add the biological and evolutionary concepts of Darwin. Parallels were later drawn between the ecology of plants and animals and the ecology of human societies (Hawley, 1950).

Further important work in the human-ecological tradition was carried out in the United States by the Chicago school of the 1920s and 1930s. For Park (1936), the dominant figure of the Chicago school, human ecology was an attempt to apply to human beings a type of analysis previously applied to the interrelations of plants and animals. Park developed an understanding of the city as a source of social disorganisation, a physical organisation that breaks down the strong and intimate relationships of rural life. The city was seen by Park as a domain in which individuals compete for basic resources, resulting in predictable patterns in the use of urban land in particular.

Based on Park's work, two further schools of thought developed. The first was the idea of spatial analysis, or mapping, of the city. Here, the work of Burgess is renowned. He provided a theory of the city in the form of a series of concentric rings radiating out from the central business district. The second school of thought is dominated by the work of Wirth, who examined patterns of behaviour, or ways of life, in different localities of the city. This work led to a great deal of subsequent research on 'suburbia' in particular. Kilmartin et al. (1985: 8) trace the thrust of modern planning and community development to this tradition. Based on this research much effort has gone into the creation of community, where it has been assumed that urban life works against personal relationships, support networks, etc. Public and voluntary agencies have also been driven by these models in their 'social welfare' approaches.

Most importantly, the human ecological perspective introduces the notion of social systems and provides insights into society-environment relationships and community dynamics. These ideas are picked up in the new environmental paradigm below.

## The liberal or reformist perspective

Critics of human ecological and behavioural theory point to its conservative emphasis on ecological determinism and failure to see beyond the concept and benefits of competition to an understanding of social conflict and the dominance of powerful groups. The earlier work of Weber (1818-1883) provided the basis for new analysis of these social problems in the wake of urban conflict in the 1960s. Weber advanced an understanding of bureaucracy, the instruments of power and domination, and the acceptance of these through the development of legitimating ideologies.

The growth of a hierarchical, impersonal bureaucracy is seen here as the primary element of organisational changes in modern industrial society. Studies therefore have focussed on the growth of institutional structures, i.e. structures controlled by a managerial elite. Much work has focussed on means for reforming these structures to provide changes in the distribution of resources. Most particularly, the 'freemarket' philosophy of the human ecologists was rejected in favour of planned state intervention in the economy and social life.

Links can be made between this institutional analysis and the understanding of historically-based patterns of dominance in society. Elite groups reinforce their dominance through inheritance of authority, power and status. Here, Weber's notion of life chances is most important. Weber is able to show how power, when stabilised by a legitimating culture, can lead to a stratification of differences among groups in society. These ideas encourage an analysis that identifies the failure of the social system to allocate equitably natural resources and also infrastructure and services such as housing, education and health.

Improved resource management and planning, including techniques such as triple-bottom-line accounting, are therefore a basis for reform within this perspective. They also include emphasis on greater public access to the policies and decisions of governments, public management and private corporations.

## The radical or political economy perspective

By the mid 1970s a broad critique of sociology had developed. The critique provided a holistic view of society in which its components were analysed as parts of the advanced capitalist economic and political system. Such changes as new technology, the movement of people into cities and development of suburbs, or industrial projects and restructuring are therefore seen as intermediate, not underlying, causes of patterns found in social life. Planning, therefore, is seen as an instrument of capitalist organisation. The only real source of social change in this paradigm is radical social change.

The political economy perspective views society in terms of five principal spheres that form the interlinked cycles of the capitalist system: production, exchange, circulation, consumption and legitimation. While crises do occur in the system, the private sector, the state and the labour sector generally work together to avoid major conflict (i.e. maintain consensus) and ensure political and economic stability (cultural hegemony).

Production of commodities from resources is the first sphere. In the modern world economic system, natural resources are highly immobile, labour generally immobile and capital is highly mobile. Therefore, production tends to shift to cheaper labour markets or to cheaper or more abundant resources, where there is rapid growth in urban infrastructure. Production also moves as close as practicable to markets for the commodities that are sold.

Exchange, circulation and consumption are the three spheres for moving, marketing and consuming primary products. Time and costs become critical in these spheres, with their form having major implications for the value of a product from a producer to its consumer. Here the city is important, as the urban form and infrastructure affects movement of labour, products and consumers. There is encouragement for individual consumption (e.g. low density housing, private cars, owner occupation). Services suitable for private capital are supplied in a collective form by the state (e.g. education, drainage, public transport). Credit is vital to modern systems of circulation and consumption. Credit institutions, which are expanding rapidly with the use of computer technology, fund increased consumption.

Legitimation is the sphere in which the system is controlled. Legitimation includes the process whereby institutions such as the law (courts, police, etc.) repress any radical change, and reinforce the workings of the system. Processes of legitimation ensure that the future of the system is seldom questioned and environmental and social costs are unevenly distributed. Ideologically, the benefits of private property and individualism are promoted, especially through home ownership.

A major advantage of this radical perspective is that it alerts sociologists to the importance of power relations and guides questions relating to who wins and who loses in developments. The major problem with this perspective is that it is highly structural. It emphasises economic determinism and tends to neglect long-term resource constraints. It also relegates key actors, social groups and social movements to minor roles in the process of social change.

# THE NEW ENVIRONMENTAL PARADIGM

The new environmental paradigm comprises environmental sociology perspectives and also draws on a number of ecocentric disciplines (Figure 3.1).

## Environmental sociology

Catton and Dunlap (1978) provide the seminal discussion of the new environmental paradigm in the context of sociological theory. They argue that the three classical perspectives discussed above have in common 'anthropocentrism' as part of their world view. Therefore these perspectives represent different parts of a human-exemptionalism paradigm. Catton and Dunlap argue that much more attention needs to be paid to the dependence of human society on ecosystems, and the laws of thermodynamics.

The core notion of environmental sociology relates to the insistence that social systems have significant interactions with physical and biotic systems and vice versa. Thus, environmental sociology works from the assumption that there is an interactive relationship between social and natural environments (Duncan, 1961; Schnaiberg, 1975; Catton and Dunlap, 1978; Humphrey and Buttel, 1982; Humphrey et al., 2002). The human ecosystem is viewed as sets of dynamic interactions between physical, biological and social systems. This perspective is not new to many cultural anthropologists, geographers and environmental sociologists. It has been applied in some outdoor recreation research and other applications of sociology to natural resource planning and management.

Given these interrelationships, environmental sociologists can and do include in their analysis socially significant facts as well as the more orthodox 'social facts'. Their interest is in the ways by which society and the environment interrelate, the cultural values and beliefs that cause people to use the environment in particular ways, and the implications of this use for social consensus and conflict (Humphrey et al., 2002). Furthermore, environmental sociologists are interested in the dynamics of the society-environment relationship. A basic tenet is that alterations to bio-physical systems (E) over time will inevitably have social (S) consequences, and vice versa.

$$\frac{\Delta S}{t} \Leftrightarrow \frac{\Delta E}{t}$$

Social change processes can therefore be both direct or indirect, resulting from changes in the bio-physical environment as well as from social processes, as noted by Slootweg et al. (2001).

This integrated perspective encourages environmental sociologists to challenge notions of social and economic 'progress', especially progress whereby industrialised society is viewed as 'freed' from the restrictions of its biological/physical environment. In contrast is Schnaiberg's (1975) social-environmental dialectic, which contains a basic proposition that ecological disruption is linked to social disruption, and vice versa. Schnaiberg proposes that there will always be a conflict between the economic expansionist goal of societies and the physical/biotic base that provides the raw materials for this expansion. Quite simply, it is a zero-sum game where the more you take or use, the less there remains, as detailed by the second law of thermodynamics. Many subsequent commentators on society and environment relationships have worked from this basic premise.

## Carrying capacity

Before considering the implications of Schnaiberg's dialectic for sustainable development, it is useful to consider some other key concepts drawn from ecocentic disciplines and often overlooked in the human-exemptionalism paradigm. The idea of carrying capacity is a key concept. The term carrying capacity has its origins in the physical-biological literature. As early as 1929, however, the concept began to be applied to human-environmental relationships, for example, in relation to the effects of high visitor use on vegetation in national parks (Verberg, 1975). Catton (1983) has emphasised the concept of carrying capacity, and an understanding of the physical limits of social life, as fundamental to the new environmental paradigm. Catton defines carrying capacity as the amount of use (of a given kind) a particular environment can endure year after year without degradation of its suitability for that use. It is important to note that Catton (1980), in his book *Overshoot*, provides other concepts that extend this definition.

### Ghost acreage and limiting factors

Ghost acreage (or 'phantom' carrying capacity) was a concept introduced by Borgstrom in the 1960s. He divided ghost acreage into 'trade acreage' and 'fish acreage', meaning that societies could increase their carrying capacity by means of trade of either abundant or scarce resources, and fishing from global oceans. Thus, it can be seen that densely populated nations in particular can harvest oceans and trade products including food. Catton (1980) adds to Borgstrom's two notions the idea of 'fossil acreage', or 'importing from the past' (or, we could suggest, the **future**, where the use of resources now imposes constraints on their use by future generations!).

Catton also notes the importance of Liebig's concept of limiting factors: "whatever necessity is least abundantly available (relative to per capita requirements) sets an environment's carrying capacity" (1980, 158). Thus, linked to the notion of ghost acreage, it can be seen that a human population can increase its carrying capacity beyond that set by a limiting factor. But, as Catton says: "Trade does not repeal Liebig's Law". Only by knowing Liebig's Law, however, can we see clearly what trade does do, in both ecological and social terms.

*Social carrying capacity*

It is important to add an obvious social component to these definitions. The principle of 'social carrying capacity' introduces this component. Here it is assumed that carrying capacity should be linked to user satisfaction in relation to the activity of different social groups (Bryan, 1983). This principle points to dual concerns. First, the amount and type of use of the environment should not impair continuing use if sustainability is to be maintained. But whereas physical-biological limits set carrying capacity of sustainable use, social carrying capacity sets limits for human satisfaction. Furthermore, these are separate but related concepts. So physical-biological carrying capacity may exceed social carrying capacity, and vice versa (Bryan and Taylor, 1987).

Our understanding of social carrying capacity can be extended with the concept of cultural niche. This concept relates to the idea that the environment can have different attributes for different uses and user groups. Conversely, society is made up of many groups with different values, cultural characteristics and resource needs. Social groups occupy different cultural niches depending on their cultural characteristics: the blend of social organisation, technology, cosmology, etc. that is sustained in a relationship with the bio-physical environment. Whereas anthropologists and cultural geographers have been able to describe the cultural niches of some pre-industrial societies in detail, especially for island societies, this is obviously a very different task for a post-industrial society within a world social-ecological system.

Various groups may define different niches within the same ecosystem to satisfy their needs. But these niches can overlap, causing competition and social conflict. The use of one resource may preclude the use of another, either synchronically or diachronically. For example, the opencast mining of coal on rich farmland will preclude current agricultural land uses, and also future uses of the stock resource. Damming a river will end all possible use of that ecosystem based on its free-flowing characteristics or fertile flood plains. But a new ecosystem and new resources, or potential cultural niches, will be created, such as reservoir-based fishing, recreation or transport.

An understanding of these social conflicts within any particular ecosystem can be increased by use of the concept of specialisation. The specialisation concept was first developed in its modern guise in the social sciences to apply to outdoor recreation management (Bryan, 1977, 1979) but has ready application in a wider setting (Bryan and Taylor, 1987). The principle is that people's orientations to, and behaviour in, resource settings in the practice of their sport will vary with their level of specialisation and where they are in their 'leisure careers'. The independent variables underlying this process are the degree of involvement in and commitment to their activity, variables that are affected by such factors as access to sporting opportunities and physical prowess.

On the resource side of the equation, a key principle is that an ecosystem has the potential to satisfy a range of uses from the general to the very specific. As use becomes more specialised, the cultural niche becomes more narrowly defined and linked to particular resource properties. Multiple satisfactions can be derived, and social carrying capacity increased, where an ecosystem can sustain a number of specialised uses, or a range of uses from general to specific.

The most intense social conflicts over use are likely to result when two highly specialised or exclusive uses are incompatible. Avoidable conflicts might arise when the supply of resources to satisfy less specialised uses can be substituted from a number of different ecosystems, providing a basis for trade offs. Specialisation will vary with the types of limiting factors in an ecosystem. For example, uses dependent on water, such as human settlement, irrigated farming or a thermal power station will be highly specialised in an arid area, where space may be abundant. They will be just as specialised on a small, freshwater island, with no limit on water but where space is at a premium.

# SUSTAINABLE DEVELOPMENT

### The social-environmental dialectic

The limits to use of the environment by humans, and degree of social conflict that arises, are set by both physical and social factors. Schnaiberg (1980) adds to the definition of limiting factors by identifying major biospheric threats to the biological survival of humans. These can include, for instance:

- the production of carcinogens and environmental toxins

- disorganisation and depletion of currently productive food systems

- disruption of future food systems

- damage to hydrological systems

- climatic changes harmful to human habitats.

It can be seen that these are socially-induced limiting factors, or mal-adaptations. These, in turn, can be linked to threats to production and the economy, such as:

- unemployment

- income reduction and poverty

- decreased profitability and capital formation

- decreased availability and increased costs of public services.

The logic of these interrelationships is inherent in Schnaiberg's social-environmental dialectic. It is also important in setting principles for sustainable management and planning, and ensuring that social, economic and environmental policy are always linked.

Schnaiberg's dialectic provides the following set of assumptions:

- economic expansion necessarily requires increased environmental 'extraction'

- increased environmental extraction inevitably leads to ecological problems

- these ecological problems pose potential restrictions on further economic expansion.

Past and current planning for development are still largely ignorant of this dialectic.

### Application of the social-environmental dialectic

Catton and Dunlap (1978: 46) summarise three syntheses of Schnaiberg's dialectic that can be related to different development strategies:

- 'an economic synthesis' that ignores ecological disruption and attempts to maximise growth

- 'a managed scarcity synthesis' in which controls are placed over the more obvious and disruptive ecological consequences of resource use and abuse

- 'an ecological synthesis' in which ecological disruption is minimised by controls over both production and consumption of goods, and resources are managed for sustained yields.

Many approaches to economic and social development inevitably fall within the first two syntheses. We argue that future practice of social assessment must reflect the third. Implicit within the concepts of environmental sociology is the notion that resource-based economic growth will create unexpected and often unwelcome environmental consequences and outcomes. Our framework suggests that these could include social consequences and outcomes. Often economic growth is an expression of the dominance of one set of interests over another. This dominance is not just a reflection of disputes between 'greenies' and 'growthists', it will also involve factions of 'growthists' themselves as they compete for scarce resources. In New Zealand, for example, the Resource Management Act (1991) is on the face of it a device for managing scarcity, and in some ways embodies an ecological synthesis in its definition of sustainability (see Case study 1.1). However, in practice the legislation has largely provided a process for managing conflict between adversarial parties in resource planning and consents for resource use.

In examining the social rationale for economic growth based on technological change, it is important to note that new technology needs new markets that can be encouraged by decreased costs of production and relative prices. There is an important problem here, though, when a decreasing workforce in extractive and manufacturing industries brought about by technological change reduces consumer demand. The essential problems for longer-term planning in both the private and public sectors is increasing employment in the service sector, increasing welfare payments to people who are unable to participate in the workforce, and at the same time a need to maintain a suitable level of income and patterns of socialisation that encourage high per capita consumption.

It is necessary, therefore, to examine the options for maintaining a society where technological change is focussed on an expanding service sector and its associated infrastructure (e.g. energy, transport and communications). It is reasonable to assume that producers act to promote a consumer society, but are also subject to both market and political forces. If the assumption is accepted that there are limits to further ecosystem withdrawals and additions, then further expansion of production needs to be limited.

These limitations could be achieved by at least two options for 'management'. The first is management from 'below' where environmental, consumer and labour groups challenge the consumer society through changes in the organisation of production and consumption. There may be, for example, an increasing interest in cooperatives, work trusts, and other alternative social systems, based around a new 'counter-culture' of job creation. Second, there is management from above, where the state might become involved in such activities as community development programmes based on increased use of labour, sustainable agriculture, the promotion of 'soft energy' options, or recycling programmes.

In considering these models we agree with Kilmartin et al. (1985) who, discussing the advanced capitalist city, maintain that the tension between planning and consumer sovereignty is a recurrent theme. 'Free-market' economic policies have frequently been tempered by the need for a social contract between capital and labour, to create the conditions for growth and full employment. These policies have also been tempered at times by the rule of social democratic parties. However, wide consensus about the direction of economic and technological change is now very difficult to achieve.

**Questions of development and underdevelopment**

Sustainable development models need to consider the unequal distribution of development within and between societies. In its simplest terms, development theory concerns the rise of underdevelopment through the systematic exploitation of peripheral regions by central, or 'core' economies. The simplest examples of this relationship are provided by an analysis of relationships between central economies and their colonial territories.

An analysis of core-periphery relationships specifies the winners and the losers as long as the relationship exists. It also specifies which sets of values and goals will dominate in any conflict of interests. Normally this model of the development of underdevelopment is applied across political boundaries to illustrate the relationships among different states. However, refinement of core/periphery analysis also provides an understanding of the different rates of development usually found within political boundaries. We are particularly interested here in resource-based activities in which many of the unwanted externalities or social costs of development are located at the periphery from where the raw materials for production are obtained.

The experience of cycles of booms and busts of economic development in such places as New Zealand's West Coast (Case study 3.1) provide examples where raw materials such as coal have been developed for the benefit of limited interests elsewhere in New Zealand and overseas. Within this exploitative relationship the value of the periphery continues only so long as the raw materials are economically extractable and transferable. The successive depletion of coal, gold, timber and fisheries in countries such as New Zealand, Australia, Canada and the United States has led to many external costs of production and, eventually, costs of depletion, being borne by the peripheries.

Major energy projects of the 'think big' era in New Zealand demonstrated the inter-regional differences caused by the selected injections of capital and labour for energy developments (Taylor and McClintock, 1984). The energy-rich regions obtained 'benefits' in terms of population increase and investment. It is also very evident, in hindsight, that these projects can be related to a pattern of 'winners and losers' in the regions affected. Assessments of the social effects of major energy projects documented the social problems that arose, identified the groups primarily affected, and elaborated upon strategies for coping (Conland, 1985). We can note, however, that this early social assessment work was essentially conducted after the fact, a trend emphasised by subsequent and reactive focus on social impacts of the wind down stage of construction of these projects.

## The social assessment process and cycles in resource communities

The sorts of social changes that took place around these energy projects are a common focus for social assessments. These changes take place in 'resource' communities that are at the interface of our society and its interaction with the bio-physical environment. Some comprehensive sociological data exist for resource communities experiencing rapid population change (e.g. Weber and Howell, 1982; Bowles, 1982; Taylor and McClintock, 1984; Freudenburg, 1986; Taylor and Fitzgerald, 1988; Taylor et al., 2001). In general, the cycles experienced in resource communities involve the establishment of a new industry and plant, and large increases in labour and capital in a locality. Then when capital and labour are reduced and the operation phase begins an important period of wind down occurs. Lastly, after a period of stability there is a period of plant closure, when a natural resource is exhausted, technology changes, or markets change. In between these main foci of change, on which social assessments usually or should usually be conducted, are periods of relative social stability.

Chapter 1 noted that social assessment evolved, in some significant part, around the construction of new projects, a process often characterised by rapid population growth, transient workforces, and inadequate social services. This phase is then followed by recruitment of the operational workforce, increased demographic stability and improved community services until a stable community develops (Lucas, 1971). This model can be extended to include a stage of community decline or wind down (Bradbury and St. Martin, 1983) when a resource is exhausted. It can also be extended to technology and market changes when workforces are substantially affected. Practitioners of social assessment have therefore given increased recognition to the stage of a resource development where an operating plant is closed down, or a social, economic or natural resource policy is radically changed. Those conditions create a special set of social impacts that frequently occur within boom and bust cycles, and there is now a substantial literature on the process of plant retrenchment and closure, and the topic of community decline (Ekstrom and Leistritz, 1988). Social impact practitioners have evolved approaches to mitigating the direct effects of changes on individuals and communities at this stage of the resource cycle. They have also recognised the need for a counter process of community revitalisation and local economic development initiatives.

Taylor and Fitzgerald (1988) refine this model of cycles of change in resource communities by suggesting that many localities experience a series of cycles and associated social changes. It should be noted that in any particular locality, different sets of historical processes may be operating at the same time in several different industries. While the local impacts of these changes may be assessed separately, the combined regional effects also need to be assessed. The origins of these changes can be traced to the same macro forces; hence, it is vital for those undertaking social assessments to understand and account for these forces and establish a social assessment process that deals with cumulative changes, with a strong predictive capacity. Events at each part of the cycle have different implications for the people in resource communities. Practitioners of social assessment must be sensitive to these cycles of change as they can invoke different requirements of the social assessment process, as shown in Figure 3.2. Some cyclical activity is illustrated in the case of the coal mining town of Runanga (Case study 3.1).

Given an understanding of the common cyclical change experienced by the people in these communities, there is potential to ensure that social assessment takes place in a proactive manner. Informed by changes in resource cycles, the practitioner can assist people affected by change to be forewarned and more creative in managing change. Taylor and Fitzgerald (1988) suggest that much social assessment that at present can be categorised as basically reactive, can be made useful given a wider approach that elaborates theoretical and empirical issues. Without such a proactive effort to analyse social change and contribute to natural resource policy over time, social assessment will at best be palliative, and at worse counterproductive, reinforcing existing patterns of change.

**Figure 3.2     Social assessment and the resource community cycle**

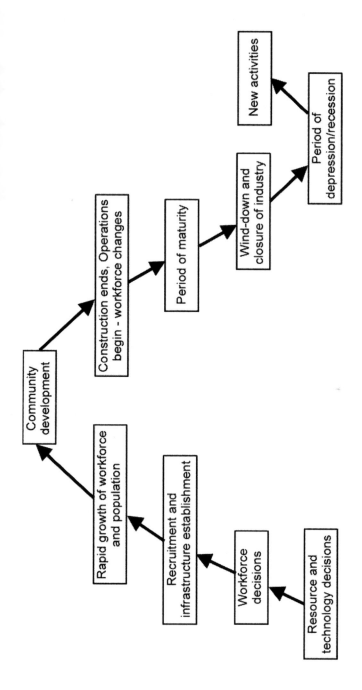

*Case study 3.1   The coal mining town of Runanga, New Zealand*

*From the turn of the century until the 1960s coal was the principal source of energy for transport, industrial uses, and domestic heating and cooking in New Zealand. Coal mining communities opened up around the main coal fields such as Greymouth on the West Coast of the South Island. Then a decline in coal use, and the decreasing cost effectiveness of the older state mines, especially on the West Coast, led to a succession of major mine closures. This decline culminated in the restructuring of the Government coal agency into Coalcorp in the mid 1980s, with subsequent mine closures and workforce reductions. The most specific impacts were on the small, traditional mining communities such as Runanga/Dunollie near Greymouth where, prior to corporatisation, 46% of the 174 wage labourers at the Strongman mine were living. The mine had been reduced to 22 workers by late 1988.*

*The process of restructuring in the coal mining industry is most dramatic when 25 years of slow attrition followed by rapid close downs in the 1980s are compared with the possible impacts of proposed new coal-mining ventures. These are ventures associated with new markets, corporate structures and modern mining technology. In most cases these new developments are taking place in localities with past connections to the use of coal resources but with much smaller workforces. The proposal first mooted in the late 1980s to mine two million tons per annum for export from a field near Runanga is one example. Here the new Coalcorp entered into a joint venture with Japanese companies for the proposed mine, which had a projected workforce of around 400 and a projected life of 20 years. It involves new technology for the West Coast mining industry, making it difficult for employees from the old coal mines to take part without substantial retraining. This proposal was further affected by government plans to sell Coalcorp to private interests, technical mining difficulties, and sensitivity to overseas markets. As a result there was considerable uncertainty about the future of the new mine in subsequent years, with it opening, closing and then reopening*

## Policy framework for sustainable development

Social assessment that is participatory, proactive and oriented towards social and environmental development requires a policy framework oriented to sustainable development. An integrated theoretical perspective as discussed in this chapter will encourage an integrated institutional approach (Dale et al., 2001).

An integrated approach to natural resource policy includes environmental, economic and social policy. The approach addresses themes pertinent to urban and rural areas, sectoral development and regional variations in levels of development. Some issues an integrated, sustainable policy would address are:

- dependency/autonomy, including the degree of reliance by communities and households on a narrow or unsustainable resource base, levels of economic diversification, nature and control of technology and technological change, outside control of decisions

- local and regional resource planning, including zoning, economic instruments and assessments and management of the cumulative effects of development

- regional development and the social desirability of regional assistance, improved national economic efficiency through stimulation of regional growth, improved targeting of assistance, dis-economies of concentrated national growth and urbanisation

- employment and livelihoods, and the stability and segregation of the rural economy and labour market, effects of instability on particular groups such as farm workers, women or indigenous peoples, equity issues, patterns of work and social organisation

- small business development, research and development assistance for entrepreneurs, and access of rural businesses to centralised infrastructure, resources and technology including information and telecommunications

- housing and residential infrastructure such as roads, quality water and sewerage systems, security, open space and recreation access

- community viability, including leadership development, maintenance of social services, costs of infrastructure and services, links between community viability and economic activity, community participation and the need for processes of social development that are locally based.

All these areas lead into the issues of social vitality, social well being and social development. Here, it is important to consider the extent to which local groups can participate in formulating policy. Wilkinson (1985: 348-349) reminds us, for example, that rural communities might once have been described as 'close knit' and 'self-sufficient'. While this may never have been entirely accurate for countries like the United States, Australia, Canada or New Zealand, we could certainly consider social relations in many places as loose-knit and dependent. Diverse and fragmented communities experiencing regional cycles of boom and bust, especially prolonged periods of poverty, pose challenges for 'bottom-up' formation of natural resource policy and processes of social assessment.

## ENABLING PRACTICE FOR SOCIAL ASSESSMENT

There are important implications for the practice of social assessment in the theoretical assumptions and issues of sustainable development outlined above. It is especially important for practitioners to review critically the institutional and political context for each social assessment, with a view to both the constraints and opportunities that might exist for their work. In this review an understanding of the role of information will be most important.

Tester (1985) provides specific instances in New Zealand, for example, where the private sector and the state work together to distort information and manipulate decision making according to narrow sets of social issues. These instances were particularly evident in the era of 'think big' development from the late 1970s to 1984, and the specific use of the National Development Act (1979) as an instrument to control decisions about social and environmental interests. Ironically, of course, this era saw the rise of social assessment in New Zealand that was much more participatory and inclined towards the establishment of a process, rather than a product. This change in emphasis occurred through the efforts of individual practitioners and community groups, despite the essentially reactive response to social impacts that prevailed.

Tester makes an important contention that planners need to examine critically their underlying assumptions about the liberal welfare state. Responses to the fiscal crisis of the state, and the concurrent restructuring of the private sector, will usually represent a strictly limited response. The 'rational' thinking inherent in this response is strictly bounded in the absence of a socially informed process of decision making and management. It becomes irrational, in the sense that, within the liberal-democratic model of the state, one assumes that the activities of the government are somehow geared to 'serve' the wider interests of the whole of society rather than narrow sets of interests. What is 'good' for a multi-national company, for example, is not necessarily good for a particular country or its environment.

Hence, a view of the government as protector of the public interest, mediating and negotiating on its citizens' behalf, may have limited application in the context of widespread and rapid social change experienced in many countries. A diverse number of institutions and organisations may appropriately be involved in the management of social change in these countries, including initiating and supporting social assessment. In this context the 'enabling' practice of social assessment becomes an essential part of a more complete societal response to social change.

Enabling practice is suggested by Forester (1980), who examines the implications of 'critical theory' for the practical actions of planning. He argues (1980: 283) that "planning actions are not only technical, they are also communicative...". Communication is, of course, a political activity, so Forester argues that Habermas' theory of communication in society is most useful in discussing planning practice. Furthermore, he explains that the theory is not simply useful in an 'empirical, interpretive, and normative' sense, but also in distinguishing types of practice in planning, and developing new approaches. Forester considers that Habermas' theory explains how the political-economic structures of society need to be understood as structures of communication. In these structures information can become distorted during planning and decision making according to the power or influence of different groups.

The 'spiral element' of Habermas' theory lies in the "contradiction between the disabling communicative power of bureaucratic or capitalistic, undemocratic institutions on the one hand, and the collective enabling power of democratic political criticism, mutual understanding, and self-determined consensus on the other" (Forester, 1980: 276). Forester argues that while many distortions of information within the structure of a political economy are inevitable, others are not. Many of the distorted sets of information and ideology surrounding social inequalities, consumer and market oriented decision making, and the organisation of resource development and use, can be unravelled by highlighting the actual processes of communication.

Forester provides basic ways by which it is possible to clarify communication and establish 'enabling' practice of social assessment. If this is not done the information, procedures, or reports of social assessment become part of continued disabling practice. Examples of practical strategies for disabling and enabling communication are provided in Tables 3.1 and 3.2 respectively. In the practice of social assessment, it is essential to promote a greater awareness of these ploys that are still as relevant today, and the role of information in driving participatory approaches. This is a key theme here that is continued throughout this book, as we discuss aspects of the social assessment process, the approaches that can be taken to the collection and dissemination of information in social assessment work, and the strategies affected people can adopt.

## Table 3.1    Twelve basic anti-participation ploys (after Howard, 1976)

**Act now, argue later**
The simplest and best of the lot, if you can get away with it. It involves building over the footpath, or felling the preserved trees, or allowing the listed building to fall to pieces, without telling anyone. With luck, the environmentalists won't find out until it's too late to do anything about it.

**Divide and rule**
Another old favourite, dating back to Roman times. Its most recent manifestation is the 'Choose-a-route' trick, designed to split up motorway objectors into three or four little camps, all at one another's throats.

**The bogus choice**
Allied to the above. You take all the possible options, eliminate the ones you don't want people to think about, add a few dummy ones to make up the number, and then offer them to the public.

**Markmanship**
So-called from Mark, ch.4. v12: 'That seeing they may see and not perceive, and hearing they may hear and not understand.' Most, if not all, official notices are written on this principle.

**Stone wallmanship**
Another golden oldie - the only equipment needed is a waste-paper basket.

**Passing the buckmanship**
There are two sub-ploys here - Crude Buckmanship (That's the responsibility of ... department) and Refined Buckmanship, practised between officers and the members of a council. The officer says "There's a good deal in what you say, but it's the councillors who decide policy and our job is to implement it". The councillors say, "There's a good deal in what you say, but we employ experts to advise us and it would be rather silly not to take their advice".

**Jam tomorrow and jam yesterday - but never jam today**
The would-be participator is told either that the scheme is already committed and they should have made their observations earlier, or that it's only a gleam in somebody's eye and it's much too soon for comments. The magic moment for participation is always in the past or the future.

**Confusionism**
Long, detailed answers to points that are almost (but not quite) the ones the community has raised.

**Nice chapmanship**
You write the worried or indignant householder a soothing letter, assuring them their views will receive the fullest consideration, that the by-pass is unlikely to be built for many years - in fact, assuring them anything that will make them shut up and go back to sleep and let you do the same.

**The cotton-wool wall**
For use if nice chapmanship doesn't work. You treat the objector with the utmost courtesy and consideration, supply them with all the information asked for, listen carefully to everything said, and then go ahead just as if nothing had happened.

**'Go away, you rude little boy'**
"We always listen to responsible comments, but we are less likely to do so when they are accompanied by insinuations of the kind contained in your letter." Practically an admission of defeat. (Of course, no experienced environmentalist would dream of writing a letter that really *was* rude - on the contrary, the more bitter the argument, the more polite the language in which it is conducted.)

**'I'm only trying to help you'**
You invite the objector to an interview, or seek them out during the adjournment of an inquiry, and tell them that in their own interests they really should withdraw - otherwise they'll lose credibility, become a laughing-stock, etc. Not recommended except against a most inexperienced objector - anyone else will assume (rightly) that your case is crumbling.

**Table 3.2**     **Communicative strategies, some pro-participation ploys (from Forester, 1980)**

| | |
|---|---|
| **Cultivate community networks**<br>Make wide use of liaisons and contacts, rather than depending on the power of documents, both to provide and disseminate information. | **Encourage...**<br>Community-based groups to press for open, full information about proposed projects and design possibilities. |
| **Listen carefully**<br>Gauge the concerns and interests of all participants in the planning process to anticipate likely political obstacles, struggles, and opportunities. | **Develop skills**<br>You need skills to work with groups in conflict situations, rather than expecting progress to stem mainly from isolated technical work. |
| **Notify people early**<br>Let less-organised interests know early in any planning process of issues affecting them (the more organised groups whose business it is to have such information won't need the same attention). | **Use informal channels**<br>Emphasise to community interests the importance of effective participation in informal processes of project review, and take steps to make such design-change negotiation meetings equitable to professionally unsophisticated groups. |
| **Educate**<br>Educate citizens and community organisations about the planning process and the 'rules of the game'. | **Be independent**<br>Encourage independent, community-based project reviews and investigations. |
| **Supply information**<br>Get technical and political information to citizens to enable them to be informed and participate effectively. | **Be politically sensitive**<br>Anticipate external political-economic pressures shaping design decisions and compensate for them soliciting 'pressure we can use' (e.g. countering vested anti-public interests) rather than minimising external pressure altogether. |
| **See...**<br>That community neighbourhood, and non-professional organisations have ready access to public planning information, local codes, plans, and notices of relevant meetings, and consultations with agency contacts, 'specialists' supplementing their own 'in-house' expertise. | |

# CONCLUSIONS

We have brought together theoretical approaches and assumptions from the social sciences. These are primarily the classical groups of social theory, assumptions of environmental sociology with their underlying notion of a pervasive interaction between society and environment, and other eco-centric perspectives. Theories of economic development and underdevelopment, and an understanding of cyclical change in communities based on natural resources, help to identify elements of a framework for sustainable development that social assessment can contribute to in a proactive way. Enabling practice of social assessment is based on an understanding of the importance of communication in sustainable development and environmental management.

We do not suggest that the mere knowledge of these theoretical approaches will change existing strategies of unsustainable development. We do suggest that ignorance of these approaches could reinforce existing, unsustainable strategies through social assessment that is reactive and limited in scope. As it evolves, a coherent new set of assumptions will provide a conceptual basis for future approaches to social assessment, and help partitioners contribute to policies for sustainable development and future environmental management. This set of assumptions should also, in turn, be productive in stimulating new theoretical development within sociology as a whole, with a better understanding of relationships between society and environment.

## SUMMARY

This Chapter has outlined basic assumptions to draw upon in developing a broad theoretical base for social assessment.

There are a group of common, anthropocentric and dominant theories within sociology that see human life as largely separate from and superior to nature. They can all be categorised as one human-exemptionalism paradigm that includes the theories based on the work of Durkheim (conservative), Weber (liberal) and Marx (radical).

A new environmental paradigm has emerged from these three groups of theory as well as additional perspectives on the environment and ecological processes. This paradigm acknowledges the dependence of social systems on the bio-physical environment and the interactions that take place in ecosystems, of which humans are a part. The new environmental paradigm provides concepts, such as social carrying capacity and sustainability, that recognise the social, economic and ecological context of human activity.

Schnaiberg's social-environmental dialectic links ecological and social change and helps to explain the limits to sustainable economic development. Syntheses drawn from this theoretical perspective provide a range of different strategies for development, from economic, through managed scarcity, to ecological. Theories of development and underdevelopment and resource communities are introduced as frameworks for analysing the differential effects of impacts, both negative and positive, between regions, across sectors of society and over time. Sustainable development policy requires critical analysis of society-environment relationships.

The important link between theory and practice can be established by examining critical theory and perspectives on information, power and the role of communication in planning practice.

# CHAPTER FOUR

## The social assessment process

### INTRODUCTION

This chapter considers the nature of the social assessment process. The process responses to our understanding of orientations to social assessment in Chapter 2, and the basic assumptions in Chapter 3 that lie behind enabling, forward-looking and integrated approaches to environmental assessment. The practice of social assessment struggled with poor definition of terms as the field developed, although there is now considerable consensus among practitioners about the main elements of the social assessment process. We draw attention to some of the inconsistencies in the literature, yet our central point is that there is a simple and logical process typically applied in practice. While there are refinements in presentation, the framework has not changed since the first edition of this book in 1990.

The process must truly be interdisciplinary, with all components explicitly integrated. We contend that all environmental alterations have social implications. This is not to mean that the focus of every analysis will be social, but that all environmental outcomes should be looked at, in the final analysis, as being social or potentially having social consequences. For example, a primary issue in evaluating impacts of a large-scale timber operation might be its impacts on a watershed and fisheries, and the economic and other social ramifications of their alteration. The focus of the analysis (and the environmental mitigation) might be on the location and design of logging roads and extractive techniques to reduce soil erosion and siltation into streams. But it is concern about the ultimate human or social implications of poor logging practices that should drive the analysis. So concern with endangered species may be a matter of ethical or moral consideration, or a commitment to the intrinsic well-being of the species in question. However, the ultimate and strongest basis of concern is with the implications of declining biodiversity for human ecosystems, where the endangered species provide the 'canary in the coal mine'.

This anthropocentric emphasis should not be mistaken as contradictory to the tenets of the new environmental paradigm, with its focus on the co-dependency of all living species. The fact is that impact assessment, by its very nature, is in the service of human beings to make wise decisions about environmental change affecting human futures. Furthermore, separation of the effects of our endeavours as impact assessors into 'environmental' and 'social' is to the confusion and ultimate detriment of the process. In the United States, the classic illustration of confusion about this issue can be found in the controversy over suspending timbering operations in the Pacific Northwest for environmental reasons, symbolised by protection of the northern spotted owl. Those whose jobs were threatened by the suspension or reduction of logging attacked the other side's arguments by posing the seriousness of the policy's impacts on their economic well-being and lifestyles against the protection of 'a few ugly birds'. Those on the other side, talked of the importance of protecting an entire ecosystem for future human options ranging from fisheries to tourism, centred around the qualities and size of old-growth trees. This benefit was measured against what they saw as the short-term loss of jobs in an industry that was on the decline anyway. Noteworthy here, is the observation that the simplest and easiest way to trivialise the other side's argument is to stop with the 'environmental' (i.e. bio-physical) or economic effects, without translating them into their social implications. A properly conceived impact assessment would evaluate human outcomes against human outcomes for all alternatives. In short, to have relevance for policy and decision making environmental effects must be translated to social implications through the social assessment process. This translation requires a high level of integration for environmental and social assessment.

**Objectives of the process**

This chapter draws in particular on the New Zealand experience during the 1980s because the basic principles developed there apply widely, through to the present time. The first attempt to set out a coherent and practical process for social assessment in New Zealand was published as *Social Impact Assessment in New Zealand - a Practical Approach*. This publication was prepared by a group of practitioners, who comprised the New Zealand SIA Working Group mentioned in Chapter 1. The publication was produced largely in response to impacts that emerged in the 'think big' era. It describes social assessment as a process "in which intended projects and policies are examined for their possible effects on individuals, groups and communities" (Conland, 1985: 3).

While as in many other publications this definition talks clearly of 'intended' actions, the process set out in it goes well beyond this limited definition to demonstrate how projects go through a typical series of stages in their development, and that social assessment should apply at each stage. These stages are:

- early investigation to identify the resource that may be used in the development

- decision making on how the resource will be used

- identification of the site where a plant will be built to abstract or use the resource

- construction of the plant

- wind down of construction

- operation of the plant

- closure of the plant.

It is suggested that "all these stages affect the quality of life of the people who live close to the site and in the region where the project is based" and, "a number of steps can be taken to protect communities from undesirable and possibly irreversible social effects arising from major projects, without affecting the positive impacts" (Conland, 1985: 2). These steps include:

- early planning and identification of issues

- a sound information base

- coordination between central, local and regional government and the developer

- involvement of local people in decision making and identification of issues

- monitoring to assess the social effects of the development over time.

A social assessment process that encompasses these steps usually needs to have the intention and capacity to manage social change at each of the stages of a project from planning and design through to operation. Furthermore, practice since the early focus on project planning shows social assessment is also applied successfully to programmes and policies.

As stated in Chapter 1, social assessment is a process of research, planning and management to deal with social change arising from intended and current policies and projects. It is focussed on individuals, groups, communities and sectors of society affected by change, although its focus is often local and regional. It is a process that uses social analysis, monitoring, and methods of public involvement.

One goal is to anticipate any social effects of change so that they are managed as early as possible. Another goal is to involve all social groups affected by change so that differential distributions of costs and benefits of change are managed, in a positive process of social development, a process that need not be lengthy or expensive.

The objectives of the process are to promote and maximise cooperation, coordination and communication among participants who represent all levels of the affected people, including the developer or proponent of change. The process is designed to form an early and continuing flow of information among all participants in the development, which will:

- ensure that information on social effects is collected and available to interested parties

- provide channels of communication about social effects

- alert all stakeholders to the social implications of change, so that strategies for planning and management are adopted by all participants to maximise social benefits and minimise costs

- clarify objectives of all interested and affected parties in relation to the project, programme or policy, and inform criteria for decisions and evaluation

- encourage public participation and involvement through existing channels such as community and non-government organisations and interest groups, and if necessary help build capacity and suitable forums.

Affected people need the capacity to obtain and use information on the full range of environmental effects, including social effects, participate in decision making and planning of change, and act as necessary in the process of planning and management of change.

Very simply, the social assessment should anticipate and describe social effects so they are managed as early as possible, and involve all groups in a process of social development that manages the benefits and costs of change. The process will usually involve local communities and interest groups, regional organisations and government, central government agencies, private sector groups and the developer or proponent of change, whether public or private sector in origin. The assessment may be organised in response to specific planning or consent procedures. It can also be initiated by affected groups, or by third parties interested in socially informed development and management.

**Strategic application of the social assessment process**

Much of the earlier practice and writing about social assessment applied the process to project planning and implementation. The process is also useful in strategic applications, in the same way that environmental assessment is applied strategically to the design of programmes, plans and policies as strategic environmental assessment (SEA). There is an expanding literature on SEA (Brown and Therivel, 2000); Eggenberger and Partidário (2000). Published cases are also emerging to demonstrate strategic social assessment (Baines et al., 2003a).

# COMPONENTS OF THE SOCIAL ASSESSMENT PROCESS

**Basic terminology**

Early recognition of a process of social assessment and a number of key terms defining that process came from Charlie Wolf, a well-known personality amongst practitioners and academics in the field (Wolf, 1983). Wolf's basic process contained 10 principal steps that became the core of many subsequent publications and manuals on how to do social assessment.

Krawetz (1981) published an initial critique of terms used in early social assessment work. She noted particular confusion over different components of the social assessment process, especially the activities of social impacts 'prediction', social impacts 'evaluation' and social impacts 'monitoring'. Krawetz advocated Wolf's model as a more consistent approach. Nonetheless, confusion remained amongst practitioners, not the least being a continuing focus on design and planning stages of social assessment, despite the articulation of activities such as monitoring, mitigation, management and evaluation in Wolf's model (if not in the order we advocate here).

Confusion arising from Wolf's model came as much from the use of terminology as the logic of what people were doing. For instance, the term 'assessment' is used in Step 6 by Wolf to describe the specific activity of estimating effects, when it is also used very commonly both to describe the general field and process of social assessment itself, and to refer to the specific activity of preparing a social assessment report. 'Monitoring' (Step 9) is distinguished from the activity of assessment although it makes much more sense to see social impacts monitoring as one important and integral part of the social assessment process. It also makes sense to see monitoring, mitigation and management as closely linked activities. Effective mitigation and management require the essential information on impacts derived from a monitoring programme. Finally, 'evaluation' (Wolf's Step 7) has developed a specific meaning in social policy research and policy planning, where it refers to the formal, retrospective evaluation of a programme or activity.

*Elements of the process*

Further definition and tightening of basic terminology reinforce the simple logic of the social assessment process. The publication by the New Zealand SIA Working Group (Conland, 1985) provided some initial resolution to this evident confusion in terminology. The approach we advanced in the first edition of this book and have used widely since then is summarised in Table 4.1. In this table the process is divided between the design phase and the implementation phase of a project, plan or policy. Although this is not simply a linear process, as we discuss later, activities associated with each element of the process generally build on each other as one moves down the table. Also, it is important to note that the dominant mode of analysis changes with each set of activities.

Impact assessment was initially dominated by the model of a standard research enterprise: identify the problem, collect the data, make the projections, and compare the results of different alternatives. The process as summarised in Table 4.1 is a more 'organic' approach, one that emphasises an on-going process of issue identification and analysis of effects, not just for the implementation of a project, programme or policy but for the implementation of these as well.

**Table 4.1        The social assessment process**

| Element of the process | Activities in the process | Dominant mode of analysis |
|---|---|---|
| **DESIGN PHASE** | | |
| Scoping | Identification of issues, variables to be described/measured and links between bio-physical and social variables, likely areas of impact and assessment boundaries | Projection of expected change - links to profiling |
| Profiling | Overview and analysis of current social context and historical trends | Collation and analysis of data about actual change, and social responses up to the current point in time |
| Formulation of alternatives | Examination and comparison of options for change based on the projection and estimation of effects | Analysis of issues and options - links to projection and estimation of effects |
| Projection and estimation of effects | Detailed examination of the potential impacts of one or more options against decision criteria | Projection of change including scenarios under different alternatives |
| **IMPLEMENTATION PHASE** | | |
| Monitoring, mitigation and management | Collection of information about actual effects, and the application of this information by the different participants in the process to avoid or mitigate negative effects, enhance positive effects and manage change in general | Collation and analysis of data about actual change, and social responses to mitigation and management strategies - may involve further projection of effects |
| Evaluation | Systematic, retrospective review of the social effects of the change being assessed including the social assessment process that was employed | Review of monitoring data and additional analysis of actual change and social responses over the whole period of change |

The assessment process is not done at one point in time to fulfil a legal or operational requirement for impact assessment, but is an on-going, iterative process of planning for and managing social change, reacting to issues and reformulating goals and strategies to increase social well being.  To use an analogy, the assessment can be viewed as a 'navigation process' into the future. Based on monitoring a course, continual mid-course corrections (i.e. mitigations) must be made to correct for unforeseen changes in the 'winds and currents'. The further from port the ship goes without such corrections, the further off course the vessel will be, with the real possibility that the planned (projected) destination is never reached.

*Clarifying the terms impact and effect*

While the terms impact and effect tend to be used interchangeably, and in some legal definitions they might mean the same thing, we talk here about impacts as specific, identifiable changes and effects as consequences. These terms follow common usage of the words, impacts being short and sudden and effects being longer term and consequential. In legislation and procedures one term might be used, when it implies both - as in the New Zealand Resource Management Act (1991) where effects are described as short and long term, temporary or permanent, positive or adverse, happening in the past, present or future and cumulative (see Case study 1.1).

One often hears the expression 'actual' impacts or effects. The adjective 'actual' is added to impact or effect to imply these are happening (measurable or describable) rather than projected or perceived. This use of the word actual is misleading. It is an accepted premise in sociology that where something is perceived it can be real in its consequences. For instance, people might respond socially to a perceived alteration to the environment, one that might be unproven in scientific' terms. They might stop recreating in a 'polluted' river, sell their home and drive down property prices due to 'electromagnetic radiation', or refuse to send their children to a school on a 'contaminated' site.

Another misuse of the term 'actual' - one often adopted by decision makers - is to use it for measurable, quantifiable impacts or effects (projected or otherwise) versus ones that are described (qualitative). As we explain in Chapter 5, this use of the word actual leads to prejudiced and incorrect use of social data. However, it is important to identify the likelihood of projected impacts or effects happening, and on identifying the magnitude and significance of impacts or effects in relation to other sources of social change.

**Scoping**

Scoping is usually the first step in a social assessment. It depends for its effectiveness on the techniques described in the following chapters. A preliminary investigation is made to identify issues and focus the social assessment, select the key variables for social analysis, and make an initial description of likely areas of impact and boundaries for studies to be conducted. Scoping usually involves the initiation of a consultative process, involving open and honest communication with public groups to:

- identify important issues relating to a proposed action

- determine the timing, depth and extent of the analysis needed, and plan the detail of the analysis

- link bio-physical effects with social outcomes.

If the social effects of the proposed action are potentially significant, then preliminary decisions can be made about the selection of critical variables to be included in the analysis, the extent of profiling required, data availability and collection needs, delineation of the assessment area, resources needed to conduct the analysis, and other information pertinent to the investigation.

Scoping is normally based on the initial collation and interpretation of available secondary data, as well as some collection of primary data through initial consultation work. If critical gaps in information are identified during scoping, the assessors may have to plan the use of social surveys and other research instruments to obtain additional data, usually as part of the activity of profiling. These data are then interpreted in terms of the major social variables under consideration.

Where the social assessment is part of an environmental assessment, the scoping needs to be undertaken from the basic proposition that all actions affecting the environment have social effects to varying degrees. Thus, the development of a procedure for establishing these linkages in the assessment process is a key step. Analysis to establish these linkages is an enterprise requiring cooperative and interdisciplinary effort. It is not valid to assume that somehow environmental effects and social effects are unrelated, or that the respective analyses should be done separately without reference to each other.

*Webbing and chaining*

For assessments involving analyses by individuals in a team, and especially a team with different disciplinary backgrounds, we recommend a specific process to link bio-physical and social variables in a 'web' of cause-and-effect relationships. The process is called webbing and chaining. This process is much more analytical than compilation of a matrix of project variables set against impact variables sometimes used by assessment teams, with the team ticking off, or even ranking, the intersecting boxes to identify possible issue areas. Although, as with a matrix exercise, it can be an initial 'brain-storming' process for members of an interdisciplinary assessment team.

To use a game management example, suppose a fire expert recommends selective burning of a forest to reduce future fire risk. The proposed action is discussed at a meeting attended by a wildlife biologist, social scientist and others. The wildlife biologist notes that one likely result of the selective burn is an increase in the browse base for the deer, with the likely result being an increase in the deer population, while the social scientist starts making initial estimates of the increase in number of hunters likely to be drawn to the forest and the associated economic impacts. Another team member then expresses concerns about crowding and hunter safety. Each of the issues (i.e. anticipated effects) in this initial scoping meeting is visually depicted and connected with lines and arrows of assumed cause-and-effect relationships among variables. This can become a working document for the team and then other interested and affected parties - whether lay-people or scientists - as they are contacted to identify their concerns.

Members of the team can offer the working cause-and-effects document to different stakeholders for their responses and contributions. A coding system is useful to delineate the major areas of concern for more detailed analysis where necessary.

In practice, this webbing of effects can become very complex, as Figure 4.1 indicates. In fact for complex cases it's useful to detail webs and chains in a series of linked diagrams, using colour to assist quick identification of the components drawn. Space on the page simply precludes this illustration being taken much further here.

The problem facing the scoping exercise is the need to be analytical rather than descriptive. Remember, it is an 'issues-driven process'. The use of this approach makes the effort truly interdisciplinary, as people in different specialities begin to think in terms of the linkages among variables. The initial exercises by the team become a reference point for any discussion of issues (anticipated effects) and serve to organise the analysis. Finally, if participants in the development of the web are always instructed to push the different connecting links to the social realm, then a truly integrated analysis bridging the gap between bio-physical and social concerns is assured.

The heart of the analysis is to examine further these early projections of effects, and the linkages, between them. Chapter 5 is devoted to examining the analytical approach in more detail.

## Figure 4.1 Webbing and chaining

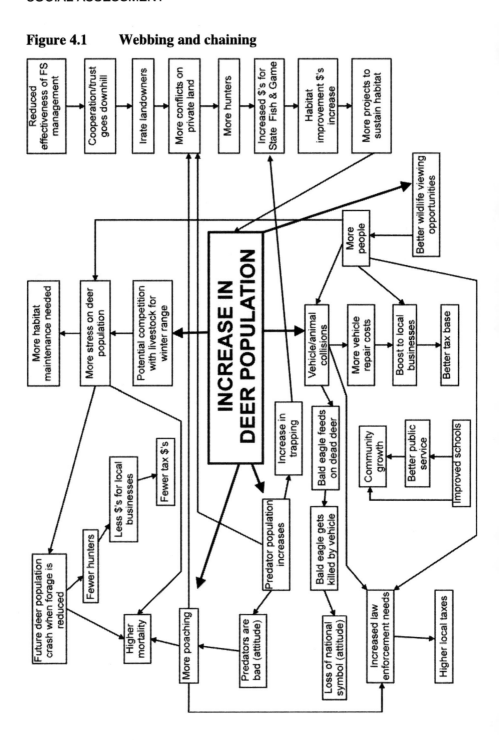

*The stakeholder analysis*

Social effects are not meaningful unless they are depicted in terms of the positions of the different stakeholders. Thus, in this interdisciplinary mapping of issues in a web of cause-and-effect relationships, all issues are driven to the social realm and who gains and who loses is depicted as well. It is not enough, for example, to calculate that a ski resort or mine development will bring in X amount of new dollars into an area economy, or generate Y amount of total economic impacts when these dollars are re-circulated through the economy from the multiplier effect. The analysis should include a breakdown of the community into different stakeholders to determine how they might be differentially affected by these impacts. Business people directly connected with the new activity might very well profit from a substantial increase in spending by mine workers. But young adults in the town employed in other areas of the economy might find that a shortage of affordable housing far outweighs whatever other gains they might experience indirectly from the business boom.

Note different alternatives for a proposed action should result in different outcomes for different stakeholders, so ideally alternatives should still be considered during scoping (this assumes social assessment takes place early in the planning process). The object, of course, is to maximize the positive effects and minimize the negatives, but this is difficult or impossible if all issues are not pursued in terms of their social implications for the different stakeholders. Thus a consultative approach to the assessment, to involve all interested and affected parties from the start, is necessary as mentioned previously and as discussed in Chapter 8.

**Profiling**

This activity is sometimes described as undertaking a baseline study, which tends to imply a less focussed approach than is necessary. The work involved in profiling should follow from the activity of scoping and can to some extent be initiated in conjunction with the scoping exercise. In this case the two activities, and any report produced from them, might conveniently be referred to as a preliminary assessment. A preliminary assessment report may be a useful milestone, providing an opportunity to consider formally what is needed in the way of more detailed assessment work.

Profiling involves some analysis and overview of the current social context, and of historical trends. The social characteristics and history of the area being assessed should be described as a point of departure for estimating effects of change. A social overview should be developed from the findings of the preliminary investigation for decisions having potentially important social effects. The overview contains an interpretation of data on social issues and trends, and will serve as a source of information for the process of decision making prior to the estimation and comparison of effects.

# SOCIAL ASSESSMENT

The social profile should include (Conland, 1985):

- a description of social trends and current conditions

- an analysis of significant social and cultural values existing in the assessment area and the relationship of these values to the proposed change

- a description of the local and regional economy and potential economic links between the proposed development and the assessment area

- maps depicting areas of influence of public agencies such as local authorities and their land use zones, tribal boundaries, and a narrative description

- a plan for the assessment of social effects, including social factors to be used, and definitions or interpretations of key variables and their sources

- documentation of data sources and a discussion of assumptions underlying their analysis and projection

- discussion of the reliability of data, inconsistencies, or gaps in the data that might affect the analysis.

Appropriate data sources of the following types should be used in the profile:

- available statistical data: census reports and other data compiled by government agencies, as well as by private organisations

- written social data: letters to editors, newspaper articles, written testimonies, histories, graduate theses, annual reports, and research studies pertaining to the local area

- observation and respondent contact data: talking and participating with people in the area, in their work, leisure, and other social settings; and systematically observing variables selected on the basis of the preliminary investigation and other important variables that may emerge

- survey data: where structured interviews are carried out or mailed questionnaires are administered. Preliminary investigation must precede the survey to validate the selection of questions and the variables the questions represent (see Chapter 6)

- public participation data: information gathered during the public consultation process (see Chapter 8)

- agency or project personnel: agency or project personnel are a source of descriptive data for communities within which they live and work.

Methods for analysing the current situation and preparing a social profile are discussed in more detail in Chapter 6.

## The formulation of alternatives

Alternative courses of action that emerge from the available details of the planned project or policy, and information gained during the scoping and profiling, are considered. This activity ideally occurs at a time when there is intensive interaction and communication between the social assessment practitioners and the proponents of the development and their design/planning team. Different sets of options, including 'no-go', are considered. Formulation of alternatives is therefore closely related to the projection and estimation of the effects of different alternatives.

The formulation of alternatives should take place wherever possible in the context of regional or national natural resource and social policies. The formulation should also take place in collaboration with staff of the public agencies involved in the strategic tasks of formulating and managing these policies and overseeing any consent procedures. In New Zealand, for instance, this sort of policy work is now undertaken at a local and regional level, under local government and resource management legislation. It then becomes important for developers to work with the local or regional governments responsible. In this way the project is more likely to fit ultimately with community objectives for development.

One of the concerns most frequently expressed by social assessment practitioners is that they have inadequate contribution to the consideration of alternatives. While, ideally they should have an input at the stage of policy formulation and resource planning, there are other levels at which social assessment contributions are very important, even if they were not tapped earlier. Levels include:

• social and natural resource policy, such as, decisions on the use of a wild river for scenic values, tourism, city supply or power generation

• the type of activity, for example, the type of power generation - run of the river versus reservoir

• location, for example, where a reservoir might be constructed - what farm land or settlements will be affected?

• operation, for example, the size and type of dam to be constructed - use of local or outside workers

• construction, for example the method of construction - location of the construction workforce.

Another factor that provides alternatives at all levels of decision making is timing. If, for instance, a dam is to be built quickly, there may be no time to train local construction workers in the techniques required, necessitating the use of incoming workers. Many negative effects can be mitigated given time alone. A further obvious factor is financial. Is a developer prepared to build the mitigation and management of social effects into the project costs from the start?

## Projection and estimation of effects

The projection and estimation of effects should include those of the 'no-action' alternative. They should also include the identification of likely needs for the mitigation and management of impacts. Alternatives for different resource uses or policies are examined and compared using relevant criteria, such as community stability and viability, quality of life factors, the creation of new jobs, economic growth, etc. In setting decision criteria it is important to note all the different views, both 'positive' as well as 'negative', of issues and potential effects. Different social groups, public agencies and private sector interests will most likely have different perspectives.

Specific tasks in this phase of work are to:

* determine the scale, intensity or significance, duration and probability of effects

* decide if risk analysis is needed

* compare effects and implied social, economic, and resource trade-offs

* display information in environmental documents as is appropriate and required by consent procedures.

Much social science literature over the years has focussed on development and refinement of techniques for the projection of social change, often with a particular emphasis on one or two types of techniques. In fact, whether in the bio-physical or social realm, accurate projections are difficult to make. The use of several projections techniques is a far sounder strategy than dependence on only one or two techniques. To revisit the navigation analogy, if the navigator only has one compass on board or must rely solely on the sightings taken of stars and planets, and the compass is not accurate or the weather is cloudy, projections of time and date of arrival (not to mention the current position) become problematic. Use as many different projection techniques as is reasonable, so as to be able to 'triangulate' to check the proposal is on track to its expected outcomes.

Social assessment practitioners have a number of projection techniques available to them. Some of the techniques are considered 'economic projection' methods, but these are included here, as we consider these to be part of our generic treatment of social effects. In other words, economic projections are simply one other way to calculate 'social' impacts. (A more detailed treatment of economic impacts is presented in Chapter 7.) In summary, basic approaches are as follows.

*Trend extensions*

This technique is simply the projection of a current trend into the future. Examples are projecting a trend in tramping (hiking) activities based on trail use figures for the last five years, or projecting a trend in timber industry job decline based on previous industry declines.

*Population multiplier approaches*

In this approach, current population size is multiplied by a coefficient to account for the amount of change in another variable. Examples are projecting an increase in demand for community infrastructure services (schools, medical facilities) based on projected population increases for the area.

*Computer modelling*

This approach involves the mathematical formulation of premises and a process of quantitative weighting of variables, effectively combining the above two approaches. The technique is increasingly available with specially written computer programmes. The greatest limitation is likely to be the availability of suitable base-line data for the analysis. An example is provided by Leistritz, et al. (1994-5) and their computer model designed to assess the social-economic effects of development projects on factors such as economic activity, employment, population and social services at a regional, county and district level.

*Consulting experts*

This is an obvious technique to take advantage of other people's knowledge. Such experts may include university researchers, professional consultants, local authorities, or knowledgeable citizens. In fact, in the early scoping stage of an assessment local officials and citizens are routinely asked about issues or anticipated effects. An especially useful tactic is to ask people in other places who have already undergone a similar kind of development what their experiences were (see comparison communities below). Note knowledgeable locals are experts on their local situation. Frequently the failure to tap and account for local knowledge, with sole reliance on technical knowledge, is a source of friction in environmental assessment.

*Comparison communities*

This technique is employed by comparing communities to be affected by an alternative with communities that have already undergone a similar action. An example is projecting the effects of a particular type of industrial development by determining what happened to communities adjacent to other such developments. Care must be taken to ensure that the communities in question are at least roughly similar in terms of basic characteristics (e.g. size, socioeconomic profiles) to ensure comparability.

# SOCIAL ASSESSMENT

## Institutional analysis

This is an analysis of the social structure of a community - usually in terms of the number, nature, and diversity of ways for the delivery of human services vital to the survival and prosperity of the community. An example would be projecting community response to a proposed, off-highway, motorised vehicle trail by determining the number of lawyers or other professionals in town, the presence and activity of off-trail motorised and non-motorised rental firms, etc. This type of analysis can be done out of the 'yellow pages' of a phone book by counting and listing the variety and types of services offered in a community (e.g. legal aid societies, planning authorities, medical specialists, accountants, financial planners). The analysis enables an assessment of the nature and strength of the community's infrastructure and the expertise underlying it. Generally, the more institutionally complex a community, the more likely it will be able to maximise its gains and minimise its losses in the face of proposed alterations. Note: in another context, institutional analysis is a tool to determine the 'political feasibility' of a proposed action - whether the community can and will mobilise, and how effectively to oppose or modify change out of its own interests.

## Economic base models

These projections are used when local areas derive economic vitality (e.g. employment) from exporting goods and services to other areas. A ratio is calculated to reflect the value of these 'exports' (called 'basic activity') as they generate other economic activity in the service of the export sector (called 'non-basic activity'). For example, if a mining operation is proposed for a particular area and is expected to employ 200 people, and the historic ratio of basic export of non-basic (service) employment is 0.5, then we can predict an additional 100 jobs will be created ($0.5 \times 200 = 100$). Thus, the total change in employment caused by opening the mine is 300.

## Input-output models

These focus on the relationship between what must go into producing a particular good or service ('inputs') and the level of production that results ('outputs'). Different producing sectors of an economy are compared in terms of the dollar value of input required per dollar of output. Adding all the changes in demand caused by the initial change produces the 'multiplier effect'. For example, for industry A, a one dollar change in demand for its output creates a total change in the economy of $1.34, a slightly higher multiplier than was found for industry B. If industry A is timber production and industry B is tourism, the overall value of timber production to the economy would be higher than tourism.

## Benefit-cost analysis

This technique is distinguished by its greater scope than the traditional models of economic impact analysis summarised above. All the benefits and all the costs of a proposed project or plan are weighed and balanced against each other, not just quantifiable effects measured by market prices.

*Willingness to pay*

This approach derives an indirect measure of the value of the externality (i.e. non-market impacts) to the individual. For example, in projecting the value of a lake resource, or a social welfare service, a survey technique might ask hypothetical questions of potential users about how much money they would be willing to pay to allow them particular levels of use. There is a large literature on this area of work, known as contingent valuation.

*Econometric models*

These involve a system of mathematical equations designed to capture the complex structure and interrelationships of a particular economy. For example, the practitioner might want to analyse and model industry-specific impacts in terms of different development scenarios. Although building such models is a time-consuming process and limited to variables for which data are available, many major universities maintain econometric models of their region that can be used to project and assess economic impacts.

*A note on scenario construction*

Scenario construction is sometimes listed as a separate and single projection technique. In fact, scenarios are comprised from the results of a variety of projection techniques and data sources, using the analytical approach discussed in more detail in Chapter 5. An example could include a number of specific projection techniques: a comparison community approach to see what happened in similar communities under similar conditions, population multiplier approaches to determine population and employment effects, and consultation with experts who are aware of likely impacts on different segments of the community (interested and affected parties), economy and the community infrastructure. The results of these different analyses would usually be combined into an overall model or scenario of likely impacts. This same process occurs when single experts or groups of knowledgeable people are called upon to 'construct scenarios' and develop sets of options. Most would use, at least intuitively, a number of techniques to develop images of the future, even if these are based simply on their and others' experiences or familiarity with the subject matter. Images of the future might also include an assessment of 'futures foregone', those options that would be given up irrevocably as a result of a plan or project, for example, river recreation, settlement and agricultural land use options after the building of a dam.

*Monitoring, mitigation and management*

Monitoring has direct application in the mitigation and management of social impacts that arise from a project, programme or policy. The main purpose of social impact monitoring is to identify any important discrepancies between expected and actual impacts or effects of an action. Adjustments may be necessary in the change being implemented to help reduce unanticipated and unwanted effects or to enhance benefits. It also provides a vital contribution to project evaluation, and forms a basis for comparison cases for the projection and estimation of effects at another time or place.

Monitoring should continue throughout the period of change so that the effectiveness of mitigation can be assessed. Feedback is provided on trends, impacts and current issues to help modify the programme of impact management when necessary.

Social impact monitoring was considered to be a basic requirement for advancing social assessment in Canada and other countries. Yet, as Krawetz et al. (1987: 15) found in their review of social impact monitoring in Canada, New Zealand and elsewhere, the reality of most social monitoring is that it is "a seemingly convoluted, chaotic and messy process". They advocate a systematic approach to managing this activity.

Social impact monitoring experience internationally highlights several points. The first is that impact monitoring should be initiated as early as possible in the social assessment process. Ideally, the monitoring process is closely linked to the scoping of a social assessment. Then social profiling provides baseline information for future monitoring. At this early stage in the assessment process a working relationship can be built among the potential participants in a later monitoring exercise: the developer, community and public agencies.

Although there have been extensive and very useful efforts at monitoring social impacts in New Zealand projects, at Huntly, Marsden Point, Taranaki and the Clutha River, for example, none of these efforts linked into a complete social assessment process. In the cases of the Huntly and Clutha projects, considerable effort was put into monitoring, but without clear links to mitigation activities. In some cases of plant closures and state sector redundancies, considerable effort went into activities to mitigate the effects of change and assist redundant workers, but without adequate monitoring. Another frequent problem regarding social impact monitoring is the difficulty of obtaining full developer cooperation, which appears to be vital if monitoring is to contribute effectively to mitigation and management.

Description and measurement of social change, and assessment of its significance, are major methodological problems in monitoring (Krawetz et al., 1987). It is notoriously difficult to differentiate among the various origins of specific social changes. Monitoring requires that some criteria are established to focus the effort around key variables (e.g. immigration, available jobs, housing or use of social services), and to concentrate on the key issues. Some typical topics of information collection for social impact monitoring are shown in Table 4.2. These examples are based on the authors' experience, and comparisons of monitoring projects in Canada, The United States and New Zealand (Krawetz et al., 1987; Fookes et al., 1980, McPherson, 1985 and Houghton et al., 1986a.).

**Table 4.2        Examples of social impact monitoring variables**

| Category of variable | Examples of variable |
|---|---|
| Project workforce characteristics | size<br>skills<br>age, gender, ethnicity<br>marital status<br>number and age of children<br>previous work history and residence<br>project expenditure and wages |
| Demographic | population by locality<br>age-sex structure<br>ethnicity<br>family size and household composition |
| Economic | labour market<br>unemployment<br>household income and expenditure<br>industry and occupational structure<br>training programmes<br>retail sales<br>business activity and outlook<br>local government finances |
| Infrastructure | housing and housing lots availability/prices<br>rental and temporary accommodation<br>health care<br>education services<br>transport<br>social welfare services<br>utilities |
| Community | community groupings and lifestyles<br>voluntary organisations<br>indigenous peoples groups<br>recreation<br>social problems |

Systems for the collection, storage and analysis of data are important in the monitoring system that is established. They should build on those used in the scoping and profiling work, including any files and data bases that are established at that time. The need to plan for monitoring in this way is a further reason for establishing the monitoring as early as possible in the social assessment process.

Monitoring should also be integrated with project management from as early in the process as is feasible. The most common possibility is to link the monitoring to any public liaison mechanism established as part of the process of change. Pubic liaison helps to focus the monitoring by identifying pertinent issues and is informed in turn by the monitoring data and any issues and trends that emerge. The consultative process involved is discussed in more detail in Chapter 8.

Participatory orientation (see Chapter 2) of the social monitoring is important as well. For instance, the involvement of affected groups and local organisations in the social assessment process will assist timely and relevant monitoring, and the application of monitoring information to the mitigation and management of impacts.

**Evaluation**

Evaluation is the final component of the social assessment process. It is an activity that is separate from, but complementary to, monitoring and the management of social impacts. Evaluation is usually initiated as part of the process established to manage a project, programme or policy change. However, external monitoring is also undertaken. Sometimes this external evaluation is on behalf of other parties, including affected people. It is also done as part of formal requirements, often by an outside agency, when it is usually referred to as an audit.

Casley and Kumar (1987) identify three typical times at which an evaluation should be conducted in relation to the stages of a development project. They are:

• in the middle of the implementation of a project, after its full social impacts have started to emerge

• at the end of a project's implementation

• and well after, ex post facto, a project, when the longer term effects can be identified.

Evaluation has been most clearly defined in the management of rural development projects, especially in projects undertaken as part of international assistance. Casley and Kumar (1987) treat evaluation and monitoring as distinct, but important parts of the management process for development projects. Compared with the ongoing activity of monitoring as an integral part of the management process, "Evaluation is a periodic assessment of the relevance, performance, efficiency, and impact of the project in the context of its stated objectives" (1987: 2). While evaluation should obviously draw on any data bases established as part of the monitoring activity, it may require additional data. Evaluation may also involve comparisons with other similar or related projects, or with geographical areas or social sectors or groups that have not experienced the set of social changes in question.

One aspect of evaluation often neglected is the evaluation of the social assessment process itself as an integral part of the management of change. Regular evaluation of the assessment process will improve the management of individual projects and will also contribute to the advancement of concepts and methods for the social assessment process in new applications, providing in particular the basis for future comparative cases (Taylor et al., 2003).

## The process and project/programme cycles

The application of the social assessment process described above can take place at different phases of the project/programme cycle, as illustrated in Figure 4.2. At the identification stage, social issues should be screened as projects are identified within the context of an integrated policy or strategy for development. As a tool in the design phase of a project, programme or policy, social assessment is more effective the earlier it begins. Then scoping studies will be carried out as the design proceeds and adds detail. Profiling of affected people and communities will usually be required at this time. In the more detailed design phase, social assessment should be applied in the examination of alternatives and assessment of likely social effects, both positive and negative. Procedures for incorporating social issues into the project implementation will also need to be established, including the process for ongoing monitoring and evaluation. There may be a need for institution building at this point. Ongoing monitoring (for adaptive project management) and periodic evaluation (for example, annual, mid term and end of term reviews) will be required during the implementation phase. It is also necessary to include social assessment in project/programme reviews and post audits.

# AN INSTITUTIONAL BASIS FOR THE PROCESS

Experience with social assessment has shown there are a number of institutional requirements. Capacity to utilise the process fully may need development and ongoing support. At the national level, for instance, there has to be coordination among agencies, an effort to define coherent social and natural resource policies, and the establishment of a national social research strategy and data bases for social assessment. Past efforts to carry out these activities have largely come from individual social assessment practitioners and their networks. These people, scattered among agencies, universities and local professional groups, have identified the need for a better institutional bases for social assessment. They have lobbied governments to obtain greater funding and legislative backing, and argued for a more proactive role for social assessment in defining management options and advising decision makers.

The institutional basis for social assessment is necessary at three main levels, central government, regional government and local (community). These are discussed in turn, followed by capacity needs that cut across all three levels: a research base for social assessment, training and professional development, gender analysis and guidelines for practitioners.

**Figure 4.2    SIA and the project/programme cycle**

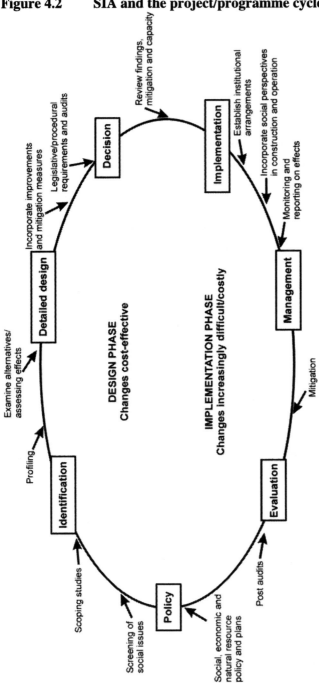

Source: Adapted from World Bank Technical Paper No.139; Taylor Baines (1993).

## Central government

Difficulties establishing an institutional base for social assessment are illustrated by experiences in New Zealand, Australia and other countries such as South Africa, as well as in multilateral agencies such as the World Bank and Asian Development Bank (Dale et al., 2001). Key successes institutionalising SIA at the central government level internationally include the:

- creation of stand-alone agencies, or dedicated sections within agencies, in various countries, usually at the central government level and sometimes at the state or regional levels

- recruitment of social scientists into government agencies and the allocation of resources to social assessment and social development

- increasing acknowledgment of the social dimension of 'environment' in resource management legislation in a number of countries, as well as formal requirements for social assessment and public involvement

- the wide range of research undertaken related to social assessment (Taylor and Dale, 2001).

These successes show that coordination of central government agencies, policy formation and research strategies need to take place within an integrated framework of social, economic and natural resource (environmental) policy. However, it is uncommon to find an integrated approach amongst the numerous agencies with responsibilities for these related areas of public management. At best, efforts at policy, research and coordination for social assessment at central government level are fragmented and largely limited to economic matters, along with some land-use and natural resource policies, and provision of social services and welfare. Applied research on social change is infrequent, often has little relevance to the management of change, and takes place without national data bases on social change and natural resource management.

In New Zealand, for example, there was an ongoing call for a central government agency for social development (Renouf and Taylor, 1985; Cronin, 1987; The New Zealand SIA Working Group, 1988). Such an agency was envisaged as an institutional base for social policy formation, social assessment and social development. Its work would include coordination of agency activity, advice to government, the administration of procedures for social assessment, and auditing of projects and policies with social effects. It would work closely with agencies involved in environmental and economic policy and management. Conland (1985) argued that development and effective implementation of social assessment requires:

- an adequate institutional base at the central government level

- a sufficient funding base, and support for skilled personnel

- legislative backing, a trigger mechanism, and quality control (auditing)

- mechanisms for allocating costs between the government, private sector and community.

In Australia, The Social Impact Unit of the Western Australia Government was a small unit established in 1989 but wound up in 1993 following a change in government. The Unit undertook to encourage both developers and communities to anticipate, understand and address social issues in decision making and project management. It also advised government through the Environmental Protection Authority on the social acceptability of project proposals. The Unit provided a basis for networking, training and general public education on social assessment. It lacked the strength and mandate to have a major input into social or natural resource policy, and ultimately to survive in the face of political disfavour. Other Australia states have established units. The Queensland Government followed Western Australia in establishing and disestablishing a unit for social assessment. The Social Policy Directorate in New South Wales advised the Government on social policy objectives. The Directorate produced material on public consultation techniques, and was involved in establishing social assessment for the Sydney 2000 Olympic games.

In the United States, social analysis has remained as largely an 'add on' or separate section of environmental impact assessments and sometimes is not included at all. Social assessments usually focus on economic, demographic, health and safety variables (though the latter may not be considered as part of the 'social' category). However, efforts of the group known as the Interorganizational Committee on Guidelines and Principles of Social Impact Assessment are changing this status. Their purpose was to develop a document to assist public and private sector agencies and organisations to comply with the social impact assessment mandate of NEPA, a mandate that up to that point (1994) lacked specific direction. The President's Council on Environmental Quality, the Executive Branch oversight committee for NEPA, now seems to be on the verge of formally adopting these guidelines (revised and republished in 2003).

Successful institutionalisation of social assessment requires a strong legal basis for the process throughout the project, programme and policy cycle. Taylor and Dale (2001) point out that clear, unambiguous mandates and rigorous enforcement (auditing) are essential. Most legislative requirements for social assessment exist through legislation requiring EIA (Taylor and Dale, 2001). Here, the definition of 'environment' used plays a crucial role in integrating the consideration of social impacts. Issues to consider in national institutional development include:

- give social assessment an equal legislative position to bio-physical assessment (see also Case study 1.1)

- development agencies or units with social assessment designations and provide mechanisms for integrating social assessment findings and recommendations with decision-making processes

- apply social assessment with clear roles at different levels of government (central, state or regional, local)

- treat social assessment as a beneficial planning tool not an administrative hurdle

- support participatory approaches and avoid domination of technocratic, product-oriented approaches

- pay attention to strategic social assessment for policy formation and resource (land use) planning.

## Regional planning

Integrated regional policy and planning strategies are necessary to facilitate and coordinate social assessment. Sound social policy as part of employment strategies and business development programmes, and the delivery of social services at a regional level, will also assist social assessment work. Regional policy and planning can play an important role in mediating differences between national and local goals. This task is particularly important where priorities for development set in a region rich in natural resources may be very different from those set in metropolitan centres. For instance, a regional framework for natural resource policy and the management of change can provide social policy guidelines for the region. Associated efforts would include employment strategies and local enterprise development for resource-dependent localities facing cycles of boom and bust. This framework could accommodate different perspectives on important natural resource policy issues. An example would be resource sustainability, where the use of a stock resource might be used as a step towards viability in a struggling community if other more sustainable developments were initiated as well.

In New Zealand, elected regional councils play a key part in natural resource planning and the implementation of the Resource Management Act (1991). But they have variable, and usually very limited, ability in social assessment and therefore in undertaking an integrated approach. In a few cases, regional government has provided the institutional basis for social assessment work. They have convened steering groups including relevant members of parliament, senior government officials and developers, to deal with a particular development or set of developments. Steering groups can initiate social assessment work, including local task groups, and articulate a balance between regional and national social costs and benefits. They have been involved in social monitoring and the allocation of social development funds levied from a project. Coordination of different social assessments for one region can also be carried out at this level, such as assessments of a series of irrigation schemes that will reallocate water resources and create land-use change.

Without a regional focus there will be little appreciation of cumulative effects of many changes, and inadequacies in more local or specific responses. In Case study 6.1, for example, there was simultaneous social assessment work on several energy projects at different phases of development, on an industry closedown, and on hill country farming systems facing financial difficulties.

### Case study 4.1  Coordinated regional assessment of social change

*In Taranaki, New Zealand, in the late 1970s and early 1980s, regional government was involved in the social assessment of impacts arising from of the construction and wind down of several major energy projects. At that same time, the dairy milk processing industry in the region was being 'rationalised', with many small factories (producing butter and cheese) closing and new large factories established. Also, the meat-processing industry changed, with a large plant closed. Furthermore, withdrawal of subsidies for sheep farming meant that there were substantial changes for hill-country farmers as they faced mortgage sales and farm amalgamation.*

*Several social assessments were conducted in Taranaki as these different changes took place in the regional economy. In this social assessment work the regional planning authority, the Taranaki United Council, played a pivotal role. The Council was originally responsible for undertaking regional monitoring of social and economic change associated with the major energy projects using gas from the Maui field. This work was published in the Taranaki Energy Monitor. Later on, this report series included information about the closedown of the Patea freezing works and changes in the farming and rural services sector. An additional report was produced on the particular changes occurring in the hill country farming sector (Taranaki United Council, 1986).*

*The United Council also coordinated work to mitigate and manage the impacts of change across sectors. The impetus here came from the development levies that were available from the major projects and also from the practical need to coordinate social service responses to the needs of the region. Here social task forces were used to good effect to link monitoring, mitigation and management(see also Figure 4.3).*

### The local level

There are many interconnections between an effective social assessment process and actions of social development at a local level. Social assessment work has encouraged identification of local social development issues that require local social development, and backed up cases for such development with relevant information. The most obvious cases have involved the provision or strengthening of social services, especially in cases of rapid social change.

In some cases a community development worker is paid for out of project funds to support local capacity and implementation of the social assessment. The community development worker can provide and extend skills in public participation, facilitate new group networks and community action, and encourage flows of information between less powerful groups, decision makers and the general public (Conland, 1985:10).

Social development work carried out by a community worker within the social assessment process requires a good local and regional institutional base. For this reason local task forces and technical advisory groups have proven very effective. These task forces are generally convened by the social assessment workers and will include representatives of relevant agencies of central and regional government, the developer (either public or private sector), local government and public interest groups. Their tasks include information gathering and consultation, evaluation and guidance for social assessors, specific monitoring tasks, and coordination of community based organisations, NGOs and social services responding to change. Task forces are therefore very effective in bridging the gap that often occurs between research and action (Figure 4.3).

**Figure 4.3    Social assessment task force**

**Professional capacity**

*A research base for social assessment*

Social assessment undertakes and utilises social research in its process (Burdge, 1998). Early on in the development of SIA, Freudenburg and Keating (1985) made the point, that "extrapolation" about comparative cases with known impacts was a basic technique for anticipatory SIA. But they noted "the frequent failure to make use of this relatively straightforward technique may not be due to oversight, but to the fact that the previous knowledge is often not available. Scientists cannot extrapolate from guesses alone; they need valid, reliable, empirical data" (1985: 583-4). Their call for a stronger research base seems largely to have gone unheard with little research conducted with the specific goal of improving social assessment practice. On the other hand, it is sometimes very difficult to translate the social science literature into terms that facilitate its use or application to the SIA process (Taylor et al., 2003).

Research helps develop the conceptual framework for an assessment, as discussed in Chapter 5. We also show in later chapters how an assessment can draw on social statistics and other empirical data. Time series and trend analysis help develop scenarios of change for social impact prediction. Also important here to rigorous development of scenarios of change are comparative cases (Taylor et al., 2003). There are two major, potential sources of comparative cases: one is comparative cases generated through social research, the other is work carried out as part of any particular assessment. So assessments can both use and generate comparative cases. Burdge originally developed and published in 1977 a diachronic model to characterise the production of comparative cases in and for social assessment (Burdge and Johnson,1998). Taylor et al. (2003) point out this model appears to have had only limited recognition and use in SIA, and develop it further to emphasise the importance of social research in social assessment, using:

- similar cases from one place to develop scenarios of social change in another place

- monitoring and evaluation data from one case in another case elsewhere

- longitudinal research on a similar (repeated) impact source in the same place

- research in another place that has not experienced the same impact source so that general processes of social change are distinguished from impact-related change.

As should be expected from the tension between research and action identified in Chapter 2, social research is often not well directed or applied to social action. Neither, unfortunately, is there incentive for practitioners, or their clients, to get off the 'treadmill' of applied, action-oriented work and build data bases that accumulate the experiences of specific cases, especially through social profiling, monitoring and evaluation.

*Training and professional development*

A strong legal mandate and good research are insufficient to support social assessment practice without training and professional development (Taylor and Dale, 2001). Despite progress in training and professional development internationally, there is a sense that social assessment still lags behind the other natural resource professions. A coordinated programme to build capacity should include the transfer of existing skills and experience through university and professional courses, and the support of professional organisations and networks. Training should include technical skills in areas such as qualitative data analysis, public involvement and facilitation, negotiation and mediation, community action research and specialist methods such as the use of geographic information systems. In addition, there is a need to build social assessment into training for other disciplines to overcome the fragmentation of training in environmental science and resource management programmes, and the gap between academic training and the practical application of skills. In addition to university programmes, professional networks such as the International Association for Impact Assessment (IAIA) on the international level, or national networks such as the New Zealand Association for Impact Assessment, make invaluable contributions to capacity building (Taylor and Dale, 2001).

*Capacity for gender analysis*

As with other aspects of social assessment, gender analysis should take place at all stages of the project cycle. Early in the analysis, there should be consideration of strategies for mitigation and management that respond to an explicit consideration of gender issues. Monitoring and evaluation should specify a gender analysis component. The analysis should also feed back into strategy and the development of further projects, programmes or policies. This can include more gender specific goals and objectives, planning processes including communication and participation, and new management systems. The result should be practical steps to meet the needs of women, such as improved individual and family health, living and work conditions, or income generating activities. It should also include wider strategic needs such as participation in policy and decision-making.

A specific examination of relative power between men and women can be useful to a gender analysis and development of the institutional basis for social assessment. Differences in power can be social-cultural, economic and political in nature. Of particular interest is the extent to which women participate in different levels of decision-making in society. For example, there may be varying involvement of women as developers, lawyers, local councillors, members of the judiciary and tribal leaders. It is noticeable that women often take on an important role acting as community organisers and advocates for environmental protection. In many cases, however, this is a relatively powerless position with regard to the assessment process.

There are a number of factors that affect participation in environmental decision-making. Gender analysis asks which factors affect levels of participation. For instance, men and women might favour particular modes of participation. There may also be particular constraints or incentives influencing their participation. These can include the type of participatory process being used, the timing of activities and the technical skills required. Also of interest are the types of community-based organisations and NGOs that take part in an assessment. It is useful to consider the leadership, roles and responsibilities of such groups and the extent to which they represent women or men. Sometimes specific mechanisms might be needed to ensure there is active participation by women, such as gender sensitive language, raising of awareness, advocacy for women and the mobilisation of women's organisations in the participatory process.

SOCIAL ASSESSMENT

*Guidelines development*

As noted above, a group in the United States, headed by Rabel Burdge, produced in 1994 and updated in 2003 the first guidelines for social assessment used internationally (The Interorganizational Committee on Guidelines and Principles for Social Impact Assessment, 1998). Their primary focus was on good practice principles and practical guidance for SIA in U.S. government agencies but they have been used much more widely. These guidelines contained:

- a discussion of the legal mandate for SIA under NEPA

- a basic model for SIA, which provided clear outline of the various stages of project/policy development from planning through to de-commissioning

- a matrix of 30 variables for assessing social impacts

- steps in the process including scoping, description of base-line conditions, projection and prediction of effects, and monitoring and mitigation

- suggestions for public involvement including feedback on social impacts.

A working group of the International Association for Impact Assessment addressed the production of international guidelines for SIA (Vanclay, 2002) as outlined in Case study 1.2 in Chapter 1. A key problem identified by the group was that guidelines are most useful when specific to application of social assessment in a particular institutional context. Furthermore, any guidelines require backing up from initiatives for capacity building, including institutional development and legal mandates, professional development and training and applied research and data bases. Examples are guidelines developed for social analysis of projects by multi-lateral agencies such as the World Bank (www.worldbank.org) and Asian Development Bank (www.adb.org), including guidelines for gender analysis and guidelines for forced resettlement, guidelines for projects developed by Shell International Exploration and Production B.V. (1996), and national guidelines developed as part of an institution building project for social assessment in Malaysia (Baines and Taylor, 2002). The Malaysian experience showed that guidelines:

- should assist practitioners and potential clients to recognise how social assessment is applied in a variety of settings, not just to projects

- should be written with audiences in mind, such as agency administrators or NGOs

- must strike a balance between the needs of those who require more detailed advice on approach and method, and those who are capable of applying general principles in a variety of specific situations - the balance between standardisation and flexibility.

As there is an established literature on social assessment methodologies there is no need to recreate this material in guidelines. An outline of topics that might be included in guidelines is provided in Table 4.3.

**Table 4.3      Broad outline of topics for guidelines development**

The domain of social assessment - context for the guidelines
The audience/s for the guidelines
Expected application of the guidelines - project, programme, plan or policy
The legal mandate for social assessment in the particular context
Procedural requirements, including provisions for external audits or review
The project/programme cycle - specific requirements for:
    scoping
    assessment of alternatives
    impact reporting
    monitoring
    mitigation and management
    evaluation
Typical social impact variables to consider in this context
Data specific issues for SIA in this context
Likely participants in the SIA and means of participation
Specific interests - including gender and indigenous peoples
Specific content - such as provisions for relocation
Specific sectoral requirements

## CONCLUSIONS

A clear process for social assessment has evolved and it can be applied throughout the project-programme cycle. Our approach in this chapter is to elaborate and encourage a process of social assessment that is anticipatory, and closely integrated with the formulation and implementation of resource management policies. The goal is to reduce uncertainties about social change, avoid mistakes that have been identified through past experience, and maximise social benefits and minimise costs of change, while paying attention to the distribution of these costs and benefits.

## SUMMARY

The social assessment process is one of research, planning and management to deal with the social change arising from intended and current policies and projects. The process involves social analysis, public involvement, monitoring and adaptive management of change. The objectives are to promote and maximise cooperation, coordination and communication among participants representing affected communities and groups, public agencies and the private sector.

Key components of the process are:

- scoping

- profiling

- formulation of alternatives

- projection and estimation of effects

- monitoring, mitigation and management

- evaluation

The process will ideally be proactive rather than reactive. The initiative for the process can be taken by the developer, or change agent, in response to formal requirements or for the purpose of socially informed management. The initiative can also be taken by groups affected by change, or by public agencies or other agencies advocating on their behalf. Where possible, the need for a social assessment process should be anticipated in the context of natural resource policy. All the phases of a development from design and planning, through construction/implementation, to operation and finally closedown should be recognised.

The process involves public agencies at the regional and central government levels. This process should also involve participants at the local level, including individuals, community groups and organisations, professionals such as community workers, and local government. However, the institutional basis for social assessment needs development and support, along with improved professional capacity.

# CHAPTER FIVE

## The issues-oriented approach

### INTRODUCTION

Social assessment has considerable potential as a basis for more proactive and applied social science. Yet it is often still hindered by problems with approach and methods that at times seem almost endemic to the field. In this chapter we describe an approach to the collection, organisation and validation of data that transcends many of these problems, an approach that embraces each phase of the assessment process described in Chapter 4.

The practitioner of social assessment is usually beset with time and money limitations, leading to a reliance on the use of secondary data. Much of the data available for analysis of the more crucial social variables are qualitative in nature, and therefore do not lend themselves to use in quantitatively-based techniques of projection. Yet qualitative data are considered by some decision makers to be less 'scientific', less reliable, and less valid than such 'hard' data as expenditure for goods and services, population change, number of jobs, or new houses. These problems with data are often exacerbated by an unwieldy 'laundry-list' approach, where investigators attempt to research almost every facet of community life to be affected by a plan or project.

The issues-oriented approach to information presented in this chapter has been used by the authors in a variety of cases, ranging from the preliminary identification of social issues arising from early planning of large coal developments and reservoir construction to the social analysis of land-use change by the US Forest Service, from assessment of the impacts of the 'farm crisis' and the reduction of rural social services in Western agriculture to agricultural planning in developing countries. It has been used to analyse different scales of social change, from major resource developments to local decisions in a small village. As the term issues-oriented implies, the analysis is guided by issues raised both by those with knowledge of the assessment literature and citizens affected by the proposed change. This approach is in contrast to encyclopaedic ones embracing comprehensive studies of social change. Major advantages of the issues-oriented approach are the time and money savings of focussing on 'what matters' to enable informed and timely decisions.

### APPLICATION OF THE ISSUES-ORIENTED APPROACH

The issues-oriented approach is iterative and adaptive (see Figure 5.1). That is, it is a dynamic approach that can at any time both accommodate additional data while also providing information at any stage of the social assessment. The techniques used to gather and analyse information are adjusted if necessary over the assessment, to deal with new information and increasing understanding of impacts.

## Figure 5.1    The issues-oriented approach

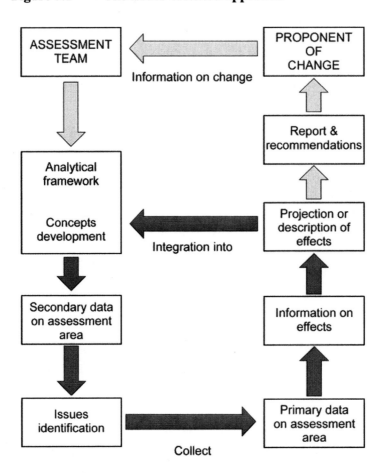

The approach assists social assessment practitioners to work constructively in an interdisciplinary team. It combines well-established methods of inquiry into a sensible scheme that permits individuals without strong social science backgrounds to become effective members of the team. While social assessment is usually most effective when carried out in a team context, the approach can and has been used successfully by an individual practitioner. Probably the most important reason for using a team is that a team can bring together a range of skills, experience and viewpoints. Also time restrictions are more easily overcome. This diversity is important because the social issues being considered usually cover a range of concerns from 'economic' to 'environmental' to 'social'. In addition, the assessment may require a range of data gathering and analytical work. In fact, in the United States, the interdisciplinary team approach is a requirement of NEPA.

## Analytical framework

The first major task of the assessment team is to form an analytical framework for the social assessment (Figure 5.1). This framework responds to initial information on the proposed change. It is based on a set of concepts that provides a mental guide to the assessment, to give direction to the work and ensure that the ultimate description of impacts is as comprehensive and cost effective as possible. The framework is developed from the experience and theoretical backgrounds of the assessment team utilising perspectives from a number of disciplines. However, it will usually be integrated using sociological or social anthropological concepts.

In the early stages of the assessment, the analytical framework will include information about the planned change and literature on the impacts of such change in similar social settings elsewhere. The iterative approach requires that the framework be continually modified throughout the assessment by the process of analytic induction (described below) as further information becomes available.

## Data gathering and public involvement

The next major task of the issues-oriented approach involves the application of the framework to the assessment area. Initially, this task will comprise a review of literature and search for secondary data on the assessment area. Although there is an emphasis in the issues-oriented approach on the use of qualitative techniques in field research, quantitative data are also used wherever possible in the assessment, particularly at this point. The collection of these data should begin as early as possible in the assessment, usually being initiated during any scoping work and extended for profiling. Secondary quantitative data might include information on the population or land uses, for example. Secondary qualitative data are also important, including historical information and life histories (biographies), and are often available for local communities. The collection and use of secondary data are discussed in more detail in Chapter 6.

A major objective of social assessment is to determine the validity of all social concerns raised. The test for identification of issues, and ultimately the final description of social impacts, will come from fieldwork. Fieldwork is an integral part of the approach. Without it, a practitioner would face considerable difficulty identifying and verifying social data and issues. Note here, as discussed in Chapter 4, social issues can be considered in respect to both actual and anticipated effects. Fieldwork allows the assessment team to identify the most critical points upon which decisions about change will ultimately rest. The identification of key issues involved in this work will not be achieved satisfactorily, and as early as possible, without close collaboration with the social groups affected. Therefore, fieldwork is also essential because it is participatory, involving the people most affected in the anticipation of issues that concern them.

Many of the field methods used follow closely those of anthropological fieldwork, which is known as ethnography. They include networking, in-depth and semi-structured interviewing, and participant observation. The issues-oriented approach to social assessment is in essence a participatory process for the practitioner as well as the stakeholders. Public or interest-group meetings precipitated by the planned action will involve the practitioner from the assessment's inception. The assessment itself is also likely to involve meetings and activities that are initiated as part of the fieldwork. All these activities will in turn allow opportunities for observing how a community operates, especially in response to change (see Chapter 8).

The establishment of a set of field contacts and identification of social networks are integral to the approach. In ethnographic or community research, access to the field can be a problem. However, in social assessments, access to the 'field' can come at a variety of points. Most often, initial access is obtained through local leaders and professional people, who are incomers due to the location of their work. These incomers may have astute observations about their community but not the depth of knowledge of a true 'local'. Interested and affected parties concerned about community change will accommodate the needs of a social assessment, especially if it is seen as relatively independent from the agents of change.

The primary challenge for the social assessor is to ensure that all social groups and sub groups are approached and their concerns recognised. It is especially important to ensure that relatively vulnerable, powerless, or less vocal groups have a say.

Formal surveys, usually a costly, time consuming research technique, should be used for collecting data in a social assessment only when absolutely necessary. For example, a full survey of households, employment, income, and expenditure might provide a detailed quantitative profile of a locality, but is it necessary? Existing data, such as census or official employment data might suffice. Nevertheless, a critical issue identified during fieldwork may require a survey approach. For example, employment might be a key issue in the establishment, or closing, of an industry, so additional data to that included in the most recent census or other official statistics may be necessary for the assessment. Interviews within employer and employee networks might yield much useful data to expand on and fill the gaps in the official statistics, yet unanswered questions could still remain. Perhaps the research team finds evidence of a recent increase in part-time work for women. A survey of employers on their particular patterns of employment would then yield crucial data about this issue. The use of surveys in social assessment is discussed in more detail in Chapter 6.

**The framework is iterative and adaptive**

We emphasise that an iterative process does not proceed in a step-by-step way leading to a 'final' report. As shown in Figure 5.1 by the bold arrows, the process builds on itself by revisiting any of the key components. The process is also adaptive (follow the grey arrows), as at any point new information can be assimilated. For example, new government policy may override some aspect of the planned change, a new 'opposition' group might emerge, or market prices for an industrial product might change causing a slowing or diversion of plans.

Similarly, information can be extracted or reported at any point in the assessment. For example, in the early phases of an assessment of a reservoir project, the developer may require preliminary information on issues for a new settlement to house the workforce. Initial information on the workforce might be provided for the early scoping and profiling work. In turn, workforce projections might be modified by the developer in response to issues raised, and the whole assessment has to adapt to new scenarios. Apprehensions and opinions then alter as the affected community is informed about possible impacts. As a result, land prices might rise or fall, new leadership might emerge in a local group, or school leavers might change their attitudes about future job prospects in the district. The social profile then needs to be adjusted.

The overall thrust of the issues-oriented approach outlined here is directed towards an ongoing process of impact assessment and management. It provides information throughout the project-programme cycle. The information is applied to the assessment of effects as necessitated at different stages of the cycle, including implementation, and the mitigation and adaptive management of impacts. As the analytical approach progresses, numerous iterations may be necessary as illustrated below in Figure 5.2. Normally, reporting on the assessment process will follow a period of synthesis, as reflected in scoping reports, preliminary and full assessments of effects, and monitoring and evaluation reports.

This dynamic approach to analysis in a process for planning and managing change subsumes more narrow approaches, ones often bounded by regulation or procedure. The tendency in the US under NEPA, and in a number of other countries, is to use impact assessment just prior to project proposals and more rarely for policy change. Critics have noted that in this way social assessment is a relatively autonomous, if not disconnected, component of the assessment process, or as Burdge (2002) puts it, the "orphan" of the assessment process. Case study 5.1 illustrates a departure from this approach, using the analytical approach emphasised here. It also illustrates the application of social assessment to a policy setting.

*Case study 5.1  Social assessment applied to integrated research and policy formation*

*This case study (Samya et al., 2003) illustrates the integration of social assessment into a research setting focussed on improved environmental and health outcomes. The study was sponsored by the US Environmental Protection Agency under the title: Social Impact Assessment of Human Exposure to Mercury Related to Land Use and Physicochemical Settings in the Mobile-Alabama River Basin (Agreement no. R827168-01-0). Impetus came from concerns about a disconnection between basic research in the sciences and their policy ramifications. Research results can remain in scientific journals, unknown to agency officials struggling to formulate effective remedial environmental actions, or in the case of 'hot button' issues, results are lost to inaction from issue polarisation and political stalemate.*

*The research centred on factors contributing to mercury getting into the food chain. Mercury is a heavy metal having toxic effects on humans, with fish consumption being a primary path of exposure. An interdisciplinary team of University of Alabama investigators in the fields of biology, geology, environmental engineering, and the social sciences conducted the study along the Mobile-Alabama River Basin in the Southeastern US. The purpose was to determine factors contributing to mercury getting into the aquatic food chain and to translate findings into public concerns and policy implications. Social assessment and public involvement processes began at the onset of the research and continued until after its completion. The objective was to facilitate the linkage of the research to resultant policy through:*

* *obtaining information and other assistance from key stakeholder groups and minimise polarisation over issues*
* *translating bio-physical research outcomes and policy alternatives into different stakeholder implications, so as to inform the decision process prior to major policy initiatives.*

*Main streaming the research findings into the policy arena though social assessment and public participation processes turned out to be important and timely for at least two reasons. Researchers found high levels of mercury in some fish, with hypothesised variables of no or slow water flow, and high organic matter and sediment load being contributing factors. However, a key issue developed with regard to the standard of risk for mercury consumption. Alabama's standard was twice as high as those set by the World Health Organization, the US Environmental Protection Agency, most other states, and Canada. Under the Alabama standard, few fish in the study exceeded the danger level, as opposed to the case of the less-lenient standard. This case study also demonstrates the application of consultative social assessment to policy formation in its own right, not as an adjunct to environmental assessment (see also Case study 8.6).*

## THE CASE FOR ANALYTIC INDUCTION

Analytic induction is at the heart of the issues-oriented approach. While the term might sound difficult and will not strike a familiar note with most people, the process has been used by theorists as diverse as the psychiatrist Sigmund Freud, the physicist Albert Einstein, the historian Arnold Toynbee, and the naturalist Charles Darwin. It has also been used by astronomers, investigative journalists, the fictionary Sherlock Holmes and his real-life counterparts.

Most of the emphasis in the physical sciences these days is on the logical model of deductive reasoning, the drawing (deducing) of specific expectations from general principles. (If it is cloudy, we deduce that it will rain soon.) But induction is the logical model where general principles or conceptions are developed from specific observations (It is cloudy while it rains; clouds must cause rain.)

In practice, of course, investigators use both processes, moving back and forth from principles to specific cases and from cases to principles, and actually modifying the principles to take account of cases that do not 'fit' or support prior principles. (It is cloudy, so we deduce that it will rain, but it does not always rain when it is cloudy - only when the wind is from the southwest. Therefore, the principle must be that rain is caused by moisture-laden clouds brought in by south-westerly air flows.)

The emphasis on deductive, hypothesis testing approaches in the social sciences parallels that of the physical and natural sciences. There is a neglect of inductive, theory-generating approaches. One can speculate as to the reasons for this neglect. Perhaps the testing of theories or hypotheses by looking at the 'hard facts' seems more scientific or rigorous. The emphasis on quantification certainly must contribute to the bias towards deduction. While it is difficult to start with raw numbers as a basis for a theory, it is easier to predict (deduce) the direction of the numbers (if not the magnitude). For example, census results that reveal a decline of population in rural areas can be logically extended (deduced) to infer a trend of future rural depopulation. But it is more difficult to construct a theory (induct) from census results to account for such trends and their possible reversal or cyclical movements over time. A broader approach is required.

**Analytic induction and social assessment**

How do the inductive techniques relate to social assessment? Most would agree that the projection of future conditions is an uncertain proposition at best for any of the sciences. But in social assessment there has been a paucity of guiding theories and concepts. Add to this the mix of different levels and types of data common to the assessment process (i.e. heavy reliance on secondary data in both quantitative and qualitative forms) and a good case can be made for explication of the inductive process.

Analytic induction as part of social assessment is more encompassing and systematic, however, than simply the direction of thought that induction and deduction indicate. Briefly stated, the induction process involves looking at the most immediately available data for an area or community, and formulating a conceptual framework or model to account for what one sees. Then another look is taken at additional data to see if the original model can predict or account for these data as well. If there are inconsistent findings, then the investigator goes back to the drawing board to rethink his/her scheme and modify it so that the discrepancies can now be explained. This process of looking and revising continues until the researcher is able to account for all or most of the data gathered (Figure 5.2).

**Figure 5.2**     **Analytic induction applied**

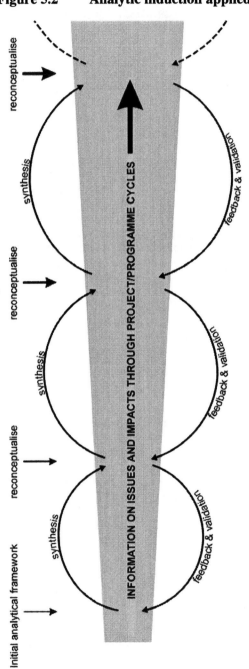

As an example, suppose that a community is adjacent to a coal reserve and a social assessment is undertaken of a proposed development of large-scale mining. The community is largely agriculturally based and has a population of about 2,500. A small but steadily increasing tourist industry contributes to the local economy. The area is attractive to tourists because it is a seashore community with a relatively mild year-round climate. Having had some experience projecting social effects on similar projects and being familiar with the literature on the area, your initial deduction is that the social impacts of the mining project will be considerable. You foresee a rapid population build-up, with local services and institutions (e.g. transportation, educational facilities and social support) being overwhelmed, and a rapid increase in housing costs, with resulting shortages of affordable accommodation. You predict a displacement of farmers off their land and away from their traditional lifestyle. Balanced against these social costs are the stimuli to the local economy brought about by the additional demands for goods and services, the fact that displaced farmers will get monetary compensation for their land (or have substitute lands made available), diversification of the local economy, and, of course, any regional or national benefits derived from the coal production. Most significantly, you suspect that since the community affected is relatively small and of limited resources, the people will be unable to mobilise much resistance to the proposal or be effective advocates for the mitigation of adverse effects, despite their concerns.

The preliminary investigation ('scoping') indicates that the initial expectations about probable social effects are largely supported by the data. But after further public participation you find a surprising and somewhat inconsistent result. Attendance at the community meetings is high and reservations about the proposed development are unusually well articulated across a large variety of well-organised local groups, especially for a community of this size. There does not seem to be much resignation in the face of a concerted campaign by mining interests and government energy officials to 'get the project rolling'.

How can one account for your initial conception of a passive community versus the reality found in the field? After reviewing profile data, attributes that appear to distinguish the area from others in similar 'boom town' situations are its seashore and mild climate, and the budding tourism industry. You reformulate your social assessment framework accordingly: there will be unusually active opposition to coal mining because this resource use is perceived by the tourism industry as aesthetically inconsistent with the atmosphere of a seaside resort. Opposition will also be strongly reinforced by farming families who see their stable, agriculturally based lifestyles threatened.

The process of public participation continues and the data keep coming in. But there are other discrepancies that your re-conceptualisation does not seem to handle well. Although there is much opposition to the mining, some community spokespersons consider that the project does have merits, in spite of what appear to be large social (and economic) costs to the area. Leaders from different segments of the community form a liaison group charged with determining how the town and area's interests can best be promoted; this is hardly a passive community!

You take a closer look at the town's infrastructure by analysing the yellow pages in the phone book (a frequently overlooked data source) and are surprised by the diversity of goods and services offered for a place this size. The town has twice the number of doctors, three times the number of lawyers, and one and one-half times the number of accountants to be expected for areas with its size of population.

Thinking that you may now have a clue as to what makes this community different, you interview several of the opinion leaders who have emerged during the public involvement process and ask them to account for the diversity. The respondents tell you that many of the people have been drawn to the area for its 'lifestyle'. They like the mild climate and proximity to the sea, and they came for these reasons, even though they may have 'done better professionally' elsewhere. You again revise your initial framework and description of issues to account for the diversity of services in this area, the active community leadership and diversity of opinion.

You now anticipate that given the apparent vitality of the community there are individuals and groups who will effectively oppose parts of the proposal not deemed in their interest, work to manage and mitigate others, ensure that benefits of employment and expenditure are obtained locally, and have some control over their futures.

**Analytic induction as part of the larger process**

Of course, analytic induction is not usually the sole technique at our disposal for making specific types of projection or formulating scenarios. Analytic induction can be the basis for organising a framework of assumptions and understanding about a community or area under analysis. Data are usually already available on a population, such as information on its age-sex composition and trends. There will be information about a development project, such as the new jobs likely to arise (numbers and types, education and skills required), and related economic information. This is the type of information from which projections of trends can be made (using various population multipliers, for example). Furthermore, as the body of social assessment literature has developed, much more information is available about comparative cases where communities have gone through various types of change resulting from different actions and plans (Taylor et al., 2003). These accumulated experiences and an expanding understanding about how communities respond to change will assist in improving the accuracy of future projections.

In the analytic-inductive strategy all of the different data and the resulting conclusions derived from the various techniques of projection are entered into the 'sleuthing' process. Discrepancies from expected results are noted and the necessary adjustments in interpretations are made. This strategy continues to provide information throughout the social assessment process, including monitoring and evaluation phases.

It might be contended: "isn't this what most of us do all the time anyway, only we don't give the process this fancy name, analytic induction?" The approach is indeed what most problem solvers do, or should do. But there is a further important point to be made in the explicit recognition of this approach. Analytic induction is a very powerful tool in establishing the validity of conclusions from an inquiry, whether the investigation is in the realm of physics and astronomy, solving a crime, journalistic reporting, or social assessment. It is the basic modelling process in all the sciences. This recognition helps counter the notion by some that inductive procedures used in the social sciences are 'soft', lacking in rigorous methodological development, and of dubious validity. In fact, these methods usually have a strongly developed system of triangulation for the testing of the data, as described by Hill (1984).

## SOFT-SYSTEMS METHOD AND SOCIAL ASSESSMENT

A fruitful method that some social assessment practitioners have utilised is known as soft-systems methodology. The methodology is used in a variety of strategic contexts, from the analysis of social policy reforms such as health restructuring in New Zealand, to the planning of agricultural development projects in isolated Pacific Islands. Soft-systems methodology features an attempt to capture the essence of 'wholes'. The method was developed as a way of problem solving for complex technical systems, where previously the 'hard' systems approach was applied to complex social problems and found to be wanting. This need is accounted for by the fact that 'hard' systems thinking focuses on a precisely detailed problem situation, e.g. how can we land a person on the moon? With complex social problems, however, there may be a multitude of needs to meet. The notion of 'problem' has to be replaced with that of 'problem situation'. As Warren et al. (1992) tell us, "the distinction is an important one because 'problem situations' are seen to be a collection of unstructured problems." Conversely "... the existence and definition of a structured problem implies a 'solution' exists". A key implication of this view is that rather than there being problems to be solved, there are conditions to be ameliorated.

Checkland (1981) offers what appears to be the most flexible approach to soft-systems analysis. His approach is dynamic and interactive, reflecting the notion that change in any part of the system will affect other parts of that system. Accordingly, the approach will require backtracking and iterations in order to be effective (a conceptual technique that bears a striking similarity to the one outlined in this chapter.) Checkland (1981: 63) argues that the approach is at its most effective when it is used as a framework, "...rather than a cookery book recipe". The methodology involves two kinds of separate activity as shown in Figure 5.3.

**Figure 5.3     Soft-systems methodology, after Checkland (1981)**

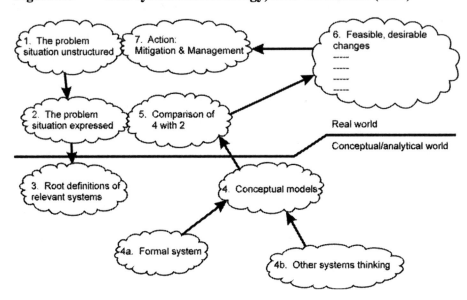

Checkland (1981: 163) explains that stages 1, 2, 5, 6 and 7 are 'real world' activities involving the 'problem situation' and those below the dotted line (stages 3 and 4) are 'systems thinking' or conceptualisation activities. Checkland points out that the stages are not necessarily followed sequentially when using the approach. In principle, a start can be made at any point in the method, and indeed he suggests that those using the approach should be working simultaneously on different levels of detail at different stages of the process.

As one becomes familiar with the soft-systems approach, as outlined by Checkland and other writers (e.g. Jackson, 1982; Jackson and Keys, 1984), the similarities with the analytic-inductive process for social assessment becomes clear. Both the soft-systems methods and issues-oriented social assessment allow a shift to a more interpretive perspective, the integration of qualitative and quantitative data, and the involvement of a full range of participants and interest groups in the analytical process.

In Figure 5.4 the social assessment process (as described in Chapter 4) is redefined in the light of the soft-systems philosophy and methodology. The main aspect of this redefinition is the distinction between 'real world' activities in the process and 'conceptual' or 'analytical' activities. In this way the analytic-inductive approach is overlaid on the general social assessment process 'steps', tackling a difficulty that has persisted in the separation of these two key elements. The separation of the 'real world' activities of the process and the 'conceptual' is arbitrary. They are continuously linked in the iterations that can be expected to take place in the course of any assessment work.

The redefined social assessment process is initiated, in a soft-systems terms, with the problem situation unstructured (1), which is labelled in Figure 5.4 as profiling. The identification of issues (2) and conceptual framework (3) include the testing of various conceptual models that drive the analysis. The estimation of effects (4) and formulation of alternatives (5), use techniques such as comparative studies (4a) and scenario construction (4b), which closely approximates the identification of 'feasible and desirable changes' emphasised in the soft-systems approach. The social assessment iterates back into action to implement changes (6), actions to improve the problem situation and implement the most feasible and desirable changes. These changes are monitored (7a) and evaluated (7b), with that information feeding into mitigation and management (7) and then back to the problem situation (1).

**Figure 5.4      The social assessment process redefined**

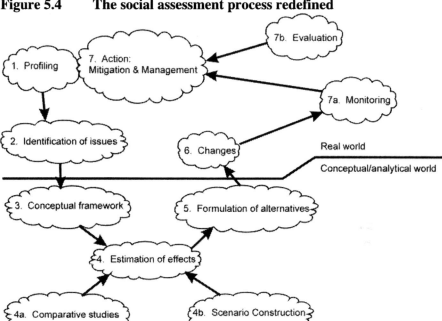

## THE CONCEPTUAL FRAMEWORK

As can be seen, the issues-oriented approach is guided by a framework of concepts in the analysis and management of social change. Driven by this framework, the process of analytic induction ensures that the collection and analysis of data will focus on those issues considered to be critical to the decision, plan or change in question.

The basic components of a conceptual framework will be useful in a variety of contexts of social change. While the framework we use is informed in general by the basic theoretical concepts outlined in Chapter 3 (level 1 in Table 5.1), we consider three other levels of concepts (levels 2-4 in Table 5.1), each level leading to greater engagement with affected people.

**Table 5.1    Levels for the application of theoretical concepts in a social assessment**

| Level of abstraction and least engagement with affected people | Elements of the conceptual framework | Related activities |
|---|---|---|
| Level 1 | Overall theory of environmental sociology (Chapter 3) | Development of overall approach and methods for a social assessment case, participatory/ consultative planning |
| Level 2 | Concepts of resource communities and sustainable development (Chapter 3) | Literature review, case analysis, comparison communities |
| Level 3 | The social universe approach to social profiling (Chapter 6) | Collection and analysis of social data, especially secondary data, for social profiling |
| Level 4 | Bases for understanding community and sets of interests (Chapter 8) | Fieldwork and consultative research to identify issues and effects, and strategies for mitigating and managing them |

The theoretical notions of environmental sociology and participatory planning inform the basic approach that we take. Then particular aspects of the sociological theory on social change will inform our overall understanding of a specific case. For instance, the body of theory on resource communities will inform any social assessment that might involve rapid demographic change in a community due to the use of natural resources. Within the context of the analytical approach proposed here, this part of the conceptual framework usually evolves mainly from literature on existing research and case studies. Organising variables are then required to guide the synthesis and analysis of secondary data in particular. Finally, an understanding of basic characteristics and dynamics of a community will inform, and be informed by, consultative fieldwork.

**Macro and historical concepts**

In any conceptual approach to a social assessment, an historical and macro perspective is useful. As argued in Chapter 3, events such as the construction of a new industrial plant or the closure of a traditional rural industry do not take place in isolation. They are usually part of an ongoing, macro process of economic restructuring and technological change. So any social changes are integrated with the wider changes occurring in any industry.

In an 'ideal' approach, as proposed by Burdge (1998: 15), the conceptual framework is based on, i) one or more 'control' studies of communities similar to the ones being analysed but without the proposed change, ii) comparative studies of communities affected by similar changes, and iii) studies of the community in question as it moves through a particular set of changes (Taylor et al., 2003). The reality is, of course, that the social assessment analysis can seldom, if ever, benefit from such a complete set of data. Existing literature and data, and new studies, are used as they become available. Unfortunately, the necessary research base to generate this type of information is often absent. Furthermore, in the absence of an analytic-inductive process, the social assessment often fails to make the best use of data available.

Any social assessment should build a critical inquiry into the extent to which similar patterns of social change have arisen at different times, places and in different social, economic and cultural environments for different types of change. Where these patterns have been investigated sociologically, the results are incorporated into the conceptual framework of the current impact assessment.

It should be noted that in any particular social context, different sets of historical processes may be operating at the same time in several places. While the local impacts of these changes may be assessed separately, the combined regional effects also need to be assessed. The origins of change can be traced to the same macro forces; hence, it is vital for those undertaking the social assessment to understand and account for these forces and to establish a social assessment process that deals with cumulative change and includes a strong predictive capacity.

Social change is sometimes seen in terms of a change in demand for social infrastructure, such as housing or public transport (although these variables are not always well considered). It can also be seen simplistically in terms of social organisation, such as a single community cop (police officer) being replaced by a modern police station, or a one-teacher school changes to a large school, or a local shopping centre is swamped by a nearby shopping mall. But these overt changes can also be viewed in a more complex and encompassing way that embodies an established range of social science concepts. For example, social change can be analysed in terms of such processes as globalisation, urbanisation and attendant social differentiation.

Without delving into the massive sociological literature and debates about these analyses of social change, let us simply note that a satisfactory conceptual basis is not always immediately available for much social assessment work. For example, consider a small 'rural' town in which a large new workforce is located. The town may have increased dramatically in numbers, perhaps two or three fold, so it is by definition more 'urban' from a sociological perspective. But the town may still be relatively isolated and located in a rural area, dependent in the longer term on its rural hinterland once the short-lived project is completed. Social networks may show urban characteristics for newcomers, yet old timers may remain a close-knit, distinctive group. In this example, uncritical distinctions between rural and urban could result in a simplistic conceptual framework.

The aim is not to provide the ultimate theory on social change but simply to use theories of society and social change to focus a pragmatic analysis within an analytic-inductive approach. The framework develops generally from the theoretical perspective of environmental sociology, to provide an interdisciplinary perspective of environment-society interactions, and a participatory and enabling process of assessment. Other concepts such as those found in resource community studies provide a basis for developing a macro, historical perspective in an assessment. They also provide the basis for comparative studies. Further concepts focus the collection and analysis of data for a social profile (see Chapter 6), and provide an understanding of communities and sets of interests within them as a basis for consultative fieldwork (as discussed in Chapter 8).

## CONCLUSIONS

One suspects that a large part of the negative reaction to social data by decision makers is due to the confusion between numbers (i.e. quantified variables) and the certainty of data or findings. The analytic-inductive process, and its explicit recognition as a formal method, can overcome the alleged inconsistencies or differences between quantitative and qualitative data and techniques. The reliance on numbers and the bias for them reflects, in fact, ignorance as to the role of numbers in scientific inquiry. The essence of what constitutes 'scientific information' is not directly the ease with which a variable can be translated into a precise unit of measurement, but rather the fact that scientists can agree as to what the units are and subsequently use these to replicate and test the results of the original inquiry. If the results are the same, the 'experts' agree that the results are 'true', and the conclusions become accepted as part of scientific knowledge until refuted by subsequent testing. In other words, what is 'scientific' depends on the consensus of experts and the approach that they adopt, not directly on the numbers or related preciseness of measurement.

Validation procedures incorporating a logical analysis of data in both numeric and qualitative forms, through analytic induction as a formal, systematic methodology, provide a basis upon which expert consensus can rest. It is not the numbers that make data valid under the analytic-inductive process, but rather the logical integration of data from different sources and different methods of analysis into a single, consistent interpretation. In fact, the integration of qualitative data with quantitative data to determine consistency of results (and to account for inconsistencies) adds power to the analysis. And the power of the analysis usually does not rest on the refinement of the measures when dealing with social data and making projections from them. If enough inferences drawn from the data are consistent with a particular interpretation (and the remainder can be explained) then the findings can be considered robust or valid.

# SUMMARY

An issues-oriented approach to collecting, organising and validating information for social assessment is anticipatory, i.e. it aims to identify issues for development at an early stage so that they can be resolved, or conflict reduced. The approach is efficient and effective, because the focus is on key issues affecting different stakeholders, rather than on high cost and time consuming comprehensive community studies.

The approach is also adaptive; in particular, the process of analytic induction to be used and the concepts developed within it are flexible. Concepts can be broadened, narrowed, adapted according to demands arising from the assessment process, or from the field, or from changes in the proponent's scheme. Furthermore, it is interdisciplinary. It can be attempted by practitioners with any disciplinary background, including a layperson, but is usually done by a team. All issues are assumed to be at least as social in nature as they are ecologic or economic. The approach assumes that participation by the interest groups affected can be as important as either academic or technical contributions. The approach is eclectic. There is no theoretical/ideological or methodological preference. It is assumed that a range of concepts and methods will be applied at any time. Fieldwork should include both qualitative and quantitative methods in order to establish the validity of any issue.

Conceptual frameworks provide 'intellectual maps', for social assessment. They help to identify the boundaries for social analysis, assist in the identification of key variables and provide a direction for the whole process. The framework has its foundation in theories for environmental sociology, draws on resource sociology and emphasises the historical background and processes of economic and technological change in which a social assessment is conducted.

The approach is responsive. At any stage of the assessment information can be extracted for a particular need. It provides an efficient means of organising information by concentrating on issues that are likely to arise. Like with soft-systems methodologies, there is an emphasis on 'feasible' changes. Thus, potentially costly mistakes in the formulation or implementation of a project or policy can be identified and avoided. Social and economic costs are reduced over the life of the planned change and benefits are enhanced.

# SOCIAL ASSESSMENT

# CHAPTER SIX

## Secondary data and surveys[1]

### INTRODUCTION

The last three chapters discuss sources and uses of information for the social assessment process. This chapter will focus on the use of secondary data and surveys; the next chapter (7) deals with economic data; and the final chapter (8) concludes the discussion of techniques with an examination of consultative methods, which form the core of an issues-oriented approach.

In social assessment the aim of gathering data from the various sources available is not to obtain as much information as possible but to gather as little as is necessary. As we have seen, social assessment should be issue driven, focussed on a particular problem or change with potential social significance. Although this priority given to issues does not deny the role of theory development or testing in relation to a wider set of social problems or research questions (see Chapter 5).

As with any data gathering or research work, the first step after identification of the main issues is to develop a plan for the collection of data. In a social assessment this planning should occur at the scoping stage (as discussed in Chapter 4). This basic step will ensure that the primary objectives of focus, relevance and validity for data collection are fulfilled.

At the scoping stage, the main sources of existing or secondary data can be identified and collection initiated. It is sensible to carry out some of this work while contacts are made to identify key people, groups, public agencies or other actors in the assessment area. This information helps in the scoping work itself, for example, by setting boundaries for the analysis, and becomes the basis for the profiling work and any baseline studies that will follow. Secondary data are employed throughout the different phases of the assessment process, as key sources of information about the social context and social changes in that context.

Regardless of the comprehensive nature of existing data, new or primary data will be required at each phase of the assessment. The principal techniques used to obtain primary data in social assessment are participatory. They include interviews and meetings, along with observation in the study area. (These techniques are presented in detail in Chapter 8.)

---

[1] We are grateful to Gerard Fitzgerald, Fitzgerald Applied Sociology, Christchurch, NZ, for input to the section on secondary data in this chapter. We suggest authorship of the chapter should be cited as Taylor, Nick; Goodrich, Colin; Fitzgerald, Gerard and Hobson Bryan.

Where necessary, surveys may also be undertaken. Surveys are most useful in the later stages of the assessment, to gather specific sets of data that have been identified as needed through the scoping work, the initial efforts at social profiling, and the review of secondary data. Surveys can provide specific information to establish the baseline of change as well as for estimating potential impacts, e.g. gauging community reaction to a proposal. They are also sources of primary data for monitoring of change once it is occurring.

## Conceptual framework: variables for the social profile

Any social assessment will require some preliminary description of the community to be affected by change. Although a number of frameworks can be used at this early stage of the assessment, we propose a simple one based on the following descriptive categories:

- how people are dispersed within, and use, the landscape (population/land-use)

- how people organise to meet their needs (social organisation)

- how people think (attitudes, beliefs, and values)

- people's customary modes of behaviour (lifestyles)

- health (physical and mental)

- economy (exchange of goods and services).

The descriptive categories are presented in more detail in Table 6.1. The use of these descriptors to comprise the 'social universe' will assist the study team, which may be composed of people without extensive social science backgrounds, to develop their initial conceptual framework. It is critical that the assembled team, comprising a variety of expertise, have a shared conceptual grasp of what constitutes the social realm during data collection, and a simple, easily explained starting point for disaggregating the data once it is collected.

**Table 6.1      The social universe approach to social profiling**

| Descriptive categories | Variable details |
|---|---|
| Demographics and Land Use - the extent to and manner in which people populate an area and how they use the landscape | Reflected in the number of people in the area, their sex and age ratios, settlement patterns and their historic bases, land uses both urban and rural |
| Social Organisation - the ways people organise to meet their needs | Reflected in such social institutions as family, education, politics, religion, and leisure, and the ways people organise to provide infrastructure and essential services, e.g., garbage removal, fire and police protection |
| Attitudes, Beliefs, and Values - the ways people think, world views | Reflected in reactions to proposed actions, cultural standards, fears, perception of risks, what people think is important about their community and way of life |
| Lifestyles - the ways people live | Reflected in work patterns, leisure and recreation behaviour, how and where people practice their religion, networks and visitation patterns with friends and family |
| Health and safety - physical and mental health | Reflected in patterns of health and illness, and includes direct health effects of pollution, job-associated illnesses and injuries, as well as indirect effects from such causes as traffic congestion and stress from rapid change |
| Economy - the manner and magnitude of the exchange of goods and services | Reflected in a range of indicators which measures the economic well-being of a community or region, includes unemployment, changes in employment, per capita income, expenditure and business activity |

The social universe framework in Table 6.1 is most useful in the initial research for the social profile, providing a basis for gathering and organising the necessary data. In setting up the data collection, the study team can employ 'brainstorming' to select variables and identify 'in-house' data, published and unpublished documents, library resources, official records and similar sources of information. These sources of data are discussed in the light of issues emerging from the scoping analysis, and initial tasks are set for data collection. This team approach can then be employed again at appropriate stages in the iterative process discussed in Chapter 5.

The social profile is an important part of the social assessment because it establishes the baseline conditions upon which a change will take place. In describing baseline conditions, however, care has to be taken to avoid assumptions that a community is a static entity. Any descriptive categories reflect, in fact, parts of a dynamic social system. Historical data and evidence of social trends should therefore be gathered wherever possible. The key variables in the final profile should describe a dynamic social context before, during and after any major new change being assessed. Burdge (1998: 43) takes a similar approach with his well-known list of 26 social assessment variables, which are focussed on typical areas of change within the social universe.

# SECONDARY DATA

As emphasised above, secondary data are usually an important part of any social assessment, especially in developing the social profile. In this section we provide an introduction to the use of secondary data based on our practical experience. Although the detailed sources and types of information will vary among countries, the basic approach will generally apply. Other useful discussions are provided by Branch et al. (1984: 274-278) and Burdge (1998: 22-25).

Briefly, secondary data are items of information that the researchers did not collect themselves. They are therefore typically collected for other purposes. Secondary data fall broadly into two categories: descriptive (e.g. words, pictures, maps) and quantitative (i.e. numbers like official statistics).

Reasons for using secondary data and include the following:

- these data are often easy to obtain, many in a computer readable form or available on websites (a lot less effort is required to access them than when collecting the information yourself). Using such data can therefore save a lot of time, especially where there are tight deadlines as is often the case with social assessments

- the use of secondary data is often very cost effective, especially when compared to doing interviews, surveys and observations (i.e. someone else has already paid for the data collection)

- the data often refer to the whole population of the area of interest, and are therefore more complete for statistical and general analysis than any you could generate yourself

- they can be the only source available and there is simply no time or resources to gather extensive primary data for the assessment work

- official statistics, by definition, have a stamp of credibility.

Examples of the utility of secondary data for social assessment include:

- producing a demographic profile, i.e. determining what the population is like, especially compared with an area in the past, and with other populations in other areas

- preparing an historical background and social trends for an assessment area

- finding one's way around a district (mentally and physically), i.e. maps, etc.

- assessing the availability and use of infrastructure and social services such as schools

- assessing housing and accommodation availability, prices, etc.

- examining the types of businesses operating and the state of the local economy (see also Chapter 7)

- gaining insights into the day to day events and happenings in a community

- locating contacts, groups and networks in the community (i.e. who's who?)

- identifying general community resources to change

- making a comparison with what has happened in similar areas under similar circumstances.

**Useful data at the initial stages of an assessment**

At the initial stage of a social assessment, during a scoping exercise, it is often best to start with descriptive information, such as maps and photographs, travel guides and visitor information, written histories, local and regional newspapers, 'yellow' and 'white' pages' or business directories, and, most importantly, previous studies including other social research or needs assessments. Much of this initial information is available on the internet using popular search engines and searchable sites, taking care to check validity.

After this initial work, more detailed quantitative information is researched. There may be many useful sources. The first, most obvious and readily available of these sources is a census of population and/or dwellings, yet the use of census data in social assessments is often surprising limited.

**Census data**

Most countries carry out a national population census (such as the Census of Population and Dwellings carried out five yearly in New Zealand). A census provides the most comprehensive set of social data available for a country, usually down to regional and community levels. The data are usually highly reliable, being derived from a rigorous survey of 100% of the population in every area, and the type of data is generally consistent between censuses.

Census data are usually provided at a number of levels, from the national level to state and regional, provincial or district, cities and towns, suburbs, villages and localities, down to the smallest 'building blocks' used. This layered system of building up the data also lends itself to mapping using geographical information systems, some designed especially for this purpose. A census system also has the potential to be transposed to additional boundaries, such as administrative areas of local government, tribal areas, and catchments of social service organisations such as health boards or schools.

These different levels of aggregation, and desegregation, will require maps and knowledge of the census system before the information can be accurately interpreted and presented in a social profile.

The most immediate value of census data at the early stages of a social assessment is for the production of demographic and historical profiles (i.e. the demographic and land use category of the social universe). In addition, they can provide extensive baseline information on the human resources and standard of living of communities or particular segments of the population, and can provide insights into how they have changed through time. However, the utility of census data ultimately depends on the user's familiarity with the material available. There are many possibilities to explore such data creatively, and to present the information obtained in association with that obtained from other sources. For this reason it is important for the practitioner to become familiar with the census data sets and the services provided by the census agency in a country.

The following are some of the census variables typically available at the regional or district level:

- numbers of residents by sex
- age groups by sex
- ethnic origin by sex
- marital status by sex
- occupations by sex
- employment status by sex
- industry of employment by sex
- income by sex
- social welfare payments by sex
- household composition
- dwelling type or building materials
- tenure of dwelling or house lot
- occupancy level of dwellings
- various appliances in dwellings

Census agencies, economic planning agencies and social welfare agencies often produce a range of reports based on their country's census data. Apart from saving the researcher time, these sorts of profiles often include useful comparative statistics and calculated indicators such as dependency ratios, labour force participation rates, and indices of social-economic status. These profiles may be available on agency websites and also from libraries, where time series are useful for historical work and trend analysis.

Examples of some of the demographic variables typically used in profiling an area are shown in Table 6.2. Of course, following the emphasis in this book on an issues-driven, approach, it is important to develop a list particular to every assessment, avoiding a formulaic approach.

**Table 6.2    Examples of variables for the demographic profile**

| Variable | Typical measure used |
|---|---|
| Total population | Number |
| Population change between recent census | Percent |
| Population by sex | Percent |
| Number of children under 15 years | Number and % |
| Number of people over 65 years | Number and % |
| Ethnicity, all groups | % |
| Education level | % |
| Personal income under a figure set as 'low' for the population | Number and % |
| Personal income under a figure set as 'high' for the population | Number and % |
| Household income, grouped | Number and % |
| Main industry groups | Number and % |
| Main occupational groups | Number and % |
| Number gainfully employed in the labour force | Number and % |
| Number of households | Number |
| Average size of household | Number |
| Number of 'large' households | Number and % |
| Dwelling type (such as building or roofing material) | Number and % |
| Dwelling water supply, toilet type | Number and % |
| Access to transport types | Number and % |

As mentioned above, care is required when combining data from the profile census sources since the population base for the tables may vary or the categories used for the variables may not be consistent.

**Other official statistics**

Official statistics are usually available through a statistics agency. For example, Statistics New Zealand produces comprehensive sets of official statistics in a wide number of topic areas in addition to the Census. The range and availability of these data sets are described in various departmental service guides. In addition, a Directory of Official Statistics lists the information collected and held by various government departments and agencies. Many of the statistics are available on the official website (www.stats.govt.nz). In the United States, a wide range of data is available from the US Census Bureau (www.census.gov) the official resource for social, demographic and economic statistics. The site includes news releases, a subscription service and a search facility. The Australian Bureau of Statistics (www.abs.gov.au) provides a statistical summary for Australia, its states and territories, and current key economic and social indicators.

Some of the most frequently used statistics in social assessments are economic performance data, employment and unemployment, social welfare recipients, household income and expenditure, industry sector censuses such as agriculture, manufacturing and retail, business statistics, credit and development loans, health statistics, education and school rolls, property valuations, housing starts, police and justice (offences), environmental management information such as planning consents, information on community facilities, transport (vehicle registrations) and physical infrastructure, and visitor numbers.

## Other sources of secondary data

The following are examples of sources of secondary data that often prove to be very useful once fieldwork starts at a local level:

- maps provide an immediate guide to geographical factors, settlement and infrastructure such as railways or roads, halls, hospitals and churches

- public relations offices and information centres, especially citizens advice bureaux, community resource centres and community directories

- local council/county offices, especially if there is a local planner or official who has an eye for background information or local social profiling or monitoring. It is important to identify early on any development projects and other sources of social change documented by the local council, or lodged with them

- local employment offices and training agencies

- schools and pre schools

- local housing, real estate and accommodation agencies

- local and regional libraries

- public and private museums

- community centres and notice boards

- tribal organisations and records

- local hospitals, medical centres and health agencies, public or community health services

- energy supply agencies (for up-to-date indications of migration in and out of the community)

- newspapers, community newsletters, radio and local TV

- Automobile Association offices and guides

- business directories and Who's Who publications.

A summary of local sources of secondary statistical data is provided in Table 6.3.

**Table 6.3     Illustrative local sources of secondary data - statistics**

| Type of data | Typical source of data |
| --- | --- |
| Local population change | Records of births and deaths, school rolls, new connections/turnover, e.g. for energy supply gives up-to-date information on people migrating in and out |
| Employment and unemployment by industry | Employment Service district offices |
| Land use and agriculture | Agriculture extension service, rural credit organisation |
| Education | Education agency, school boards, school offices |
| Crime | Police, justice agency, courts |
| Health | Health authorities, health service providers |
| Housing | Housing agency, community housing organisation, tenants' organisation, land agents/realtors |
| Other accommodation | Tourism organisation and visitor information centres, occupancy surveys, visitor guide |
| Land availability zoning etc | Local councils, district and regional plans, building permits, resource permits and consents |
| Property valuations | Land agents, valuation agency, local councils |
| Transport and traffic | Traffic counts, vehicle registrations, accident records |

A summary of local sources of secondary descriptive data is provided in Table 6.4. These sources are pursued as the social profile is built up in more detail.

Table 6.4          Illustrative local sources of secondary data - descriptive

| Type of data | Typical source of data |
|---|---|
| Commercial activity | Telephone books, business directories and Who's Who publications, local council/county offices, visitor guides/booklets, newspapers |
| Community and social services/ clubs and local organisations | Community directories, local councils, libraries, Dept of Social Welfare district offices, councils of social services, Citizens' Advice Bureaux |
| Land ownership/location and use | Extension service, farmer organisations, real estate agents/realtors |
| Historical information on social and economic change | Local councils/county (official histories), local libraries, tourist and visitor guides, local museums, historical society |
| Recreation | Local council/county recreation officer, outdoor recreation centres, sports clubs and organisations, visitor information centre, community surveys |
| Tribal community and issues | Tribal authorities and councils, elders, local government tribal agency |
| Social issues and needs | Schools, health clinics and community health workers, community resource centres and local service providers |
| General community activity | Newspapers, local radio, noticeboards, regional TV |
| Previous community surveys | Usually cover recreation, present and future local issues and needs, social services, planning issues including school projects) |

## Data for gender analysis

Gender differences in social-economic characteristics, economic opportunities and societal roles are inherent in most societies. These differences are recognised in social profiles of people and communities assessed for change. This gender analysis is then applied to assessing effects. For instance, in assessing a project the workforce, the construction workforce might typically involve men whereas the operational workforce might largely involve women. Implications for the local economy, families and community activities will probably vary during construction and operation. Patterns of work can also affect participation in the assessment process such as the time of day chosen for community meetings.

Information on the gender division of labour and other activities is recognised in an activity profile. This method employs a simple matrix approach to describe activities of men and women with respect to a number of variables (types of activities). The matrix is completed as far as possible with secondary data and then used as a guide to identifying and filling in any data gaps. The nature of the activity is described as fully as possible, and should include typical hours per day and week and also seasonal variations if applicable. An age dimension can be added to this matrix if required, by splitting each cell in the male and female columns. Typical variables used in preparing a matrix for the activity profile include:

- the type of paid work that is done, including the nature of the work, the skills required, levels of employment, levels of pay

- the type of unpaid work done in households, such as child rearing, cleaning, tending to sick relatives, household management

- the type of work done in family businesses and farms

- voluntary, unpaid contributions to community activities

- education and training activity

- leisure and entertainment activity.

A further focus of gender analysis is on access to and control of resources. There are a number of attributes to resources and again are assessed initially using a simple matrix. Once again, the assessor first completes the matrix with available data and then undertakes any necessary research to fill in the gaps. Typical variables used in preparing a matrix on access to resources include:

- ownership of land and buildings

- control of household resources such as food, fuel and clothes

- access to and control over household cash income

- access to credit

- access to education

- access to information

- access to free time and leisure

- access to political decision-making, from voting to acting as representatives.

## Use and presentation of secondary data

The use and presentation of secondary data are important. Used poorly, these data can confound those who have to read and draw on a social assessment to make decisions. Generally, secondary data can be used in two ways: absolutely, that is without recourse or reference to other information, or by comparisons. Much data derived from census and other statistics, including quantitative indicators (such as age profiles, dependency ratios, rates of home ownership, unemployment rates, average incomes) only become meaningful when used with a reference point (e.g. the whole population, the regional population, rural population, the population over time), or when details of more than one local area or population are compared.

The application of the material will lead the assessment team to decisions on presentation of the findings. A useful approach is comparative presentation in graphs and charts combined with some description or summary of the main observations from the data. Detailed tables and long commentaries should be avoided. User-friendly graphics, statistical software and spreadsheet programmes available for personal computers allow for considerable creativity with both analysis and presentation of data. It is good to use the 'keep it simple' rule though, avoiding complex graphs. A social assessment report should have good readability so it is accessible to all stakeholders.

Examples of some presentation styles are provided in Case study 6.1. These examples include bar graphs to display information, such as age-sex structures. Used in a stacked form they can also display comparative trends such as changes in unemployment or size of population. Pie graphs are useful when presenting information in categories, such as the types of employment or industry groupings in the workforce of a study area.

### Case study 6.1   Chatham Islands profile

*In 1989, the New Zealand Government made a comprehensive review of its administration and economic assistance to the remote Chatham Islands (Taylor Baines and Lincoln International, 1989). Aspects of resource, social and cultural development, and the impact of suggested changes in government policy were examined during the review. The review was completed in 10 intensive weeks of work by a 13-person team. The scoping work was undertaken in the first two weeks, with preliminary field research and community consultation in the second week. A comprehensive profile of the people, dwellings and economic activity of the population had to be in draft form by the end of the first week, to help guide the fieldwork. The profile was then refined into appendix material for the final report while the rest of the review proceeded.*

*Then, in 2002 the Chatham Islands Enterprise Trust, established after the first review to administer a development fund and facilitate social and economic development on the Islands, commissioned a review of development ten years on from the original review (Taylor Baines, 2003). The review team worked closely with the local community to evaluate change and propose ongoing development initiatives. The team used a range of statistical and other secondary data to provide reports on key sectors such as fishing, farming and tourism, as well as social and community issues.*

*Data for these profiles were drawn from existing statistics and reports, especially census data. These data were displayed in graph form to take to the field for ready reference, and were also displayed in graph form in the final report. Some examples are data on the age-sex structure of the population which related to community issues of community viability and the impact of no secondary school on the islands (Figure 6.1), and types of home heating, which related to the expense of electricity generated from costly imported fuels (Figure 6.1). Tenure of dwellings showed considerable variation from the general New Zealand figures (Figure 6.2). For purposes of comparison, there are graphs for the total New Zealand population for each variable.*

**Figure 6.1    Illustration of age/sex graphs**

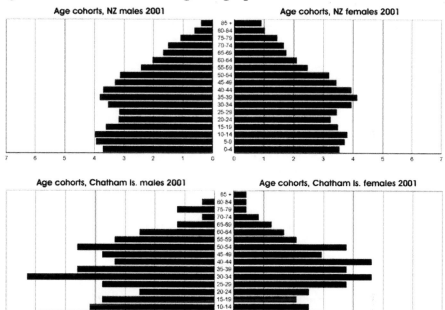

**Figure 6.1    Illustration of bar graphs, home heating**

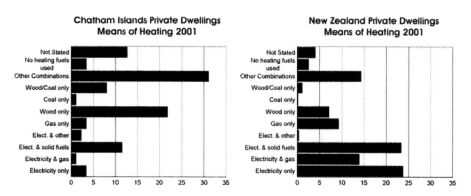

**Figure 6.2      Illustration of pie graphs, household tenure**

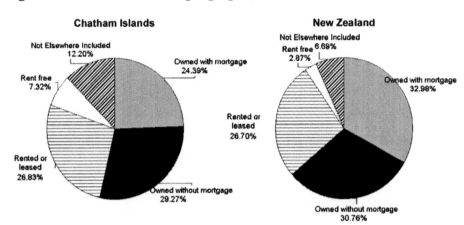

Presentation of social data via thematic maps is a useful way of showing the spatial distribution of social characteristics of a study population. Thematic maps are used to help assess community social needs and services, for example, mapping variables such as percentage of the population over 65 years, average household incomes or housing types. Some countries have thematic mapping systems that work with their census data on personal computers. Key features of the social structures and the distribution of resources of neighbourhoods and communities can be seen by glancing at such maps (Figures 6.3 and 6.4). In these two examples, the maps show the distribution of solid-fuel heating of households in the city of Christchurch, New Zealand. One map shows the distribution of the proportion of houses that burn coal, and the other map shows the houses that burn wood. It is easy to see that coal burning is most common in the older, eastern suburbs reflecting older house types (with open fires) and lower social-economic status. Whereas wood burning is concentrated in the newer, western suburbs and areas of higher social-economic status. These maps can assist with the strategic development of resource policy, such as air quality management programmes, where low-income households are assisted to convert away from solid fuel heating to reduce serious winter air pollution (Baines et al., 2003a).

## COLLECTING AND USING SURVEY DATA

This section considers the use of data obtained through survey research. Surveys use a number of techniques for collecting social data. Questionnaires are most commonly used in survey research, but other techniques - such as systematic observations, content analysis, delphi methods and option scoring - are also acceptable variations within the use of surveys.

**Figures 6.3** **Illustration of thematic map, Christchurch homes burning wood**

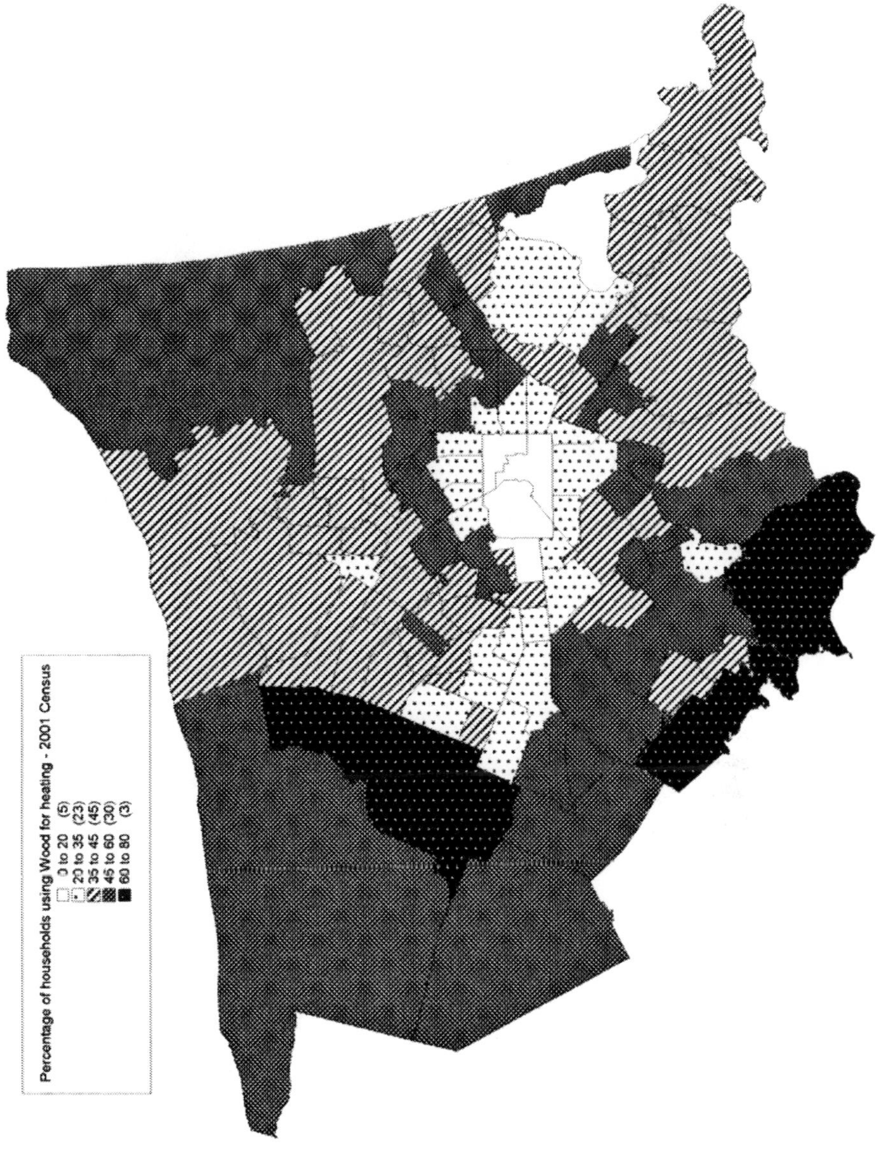

Percentage of households using Wood for heating - 2001 Census

0 to 20 (5)
20 to 35 (23)
35 to 45 (45)
45 to 60 (30)
60 to 80 (3)

**Figures 6.4** **Illustration of thematic map, Christchurch homes burning coal**

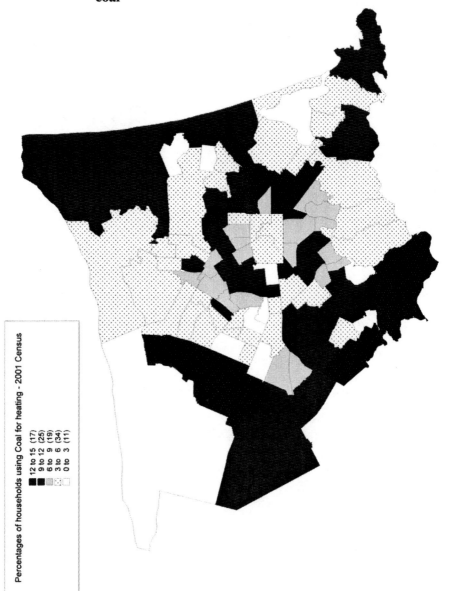

Surveys are characterised by a structured or systematic set of data that is known as a variable by case matrix. What this means is that the researcher collects information about the same variable or characteristic for at least two cases and normally for many more. The most simple and familiar example of this matrix is provided by those reporting on political polls when they tell us that x% of a given population will vote for y party. Table 6.4 provides another example.

**Table 6.4      Example of a variable by case matrix**

|  | Individual respondents (cases) | | | |
|---|---|---|---|---|
| **Variables** | **1** | **2** | **3** | **4** |
| Sex | Female | Male | Female | Male |
| Age (in years) | 42 | 53 | 49 | 23 |
| Years in present job | 4 | 14 | 1 | 2 |
| Number of dependants | 2 | 4 | 0 | 1 |

Surveys are therefore investigations in which systematic measurements are made over a series of cases, yielding a matrix of data. The variables in the matrix are analysed to find any patterns.

Marsh (1982) argues that the subject matter must have a social context. Following the logic of Chapter 3, this limitation is not an unnecessary constraint for practitioners, allowing that the subject matter has to be 'socially significant'. Thus, topics for a survey to collect social assessment data might include, for example: the enumeration of physical housing stock, household equipment and means of transport, social services, physical and other infrastructure, savings and credit, and recreation resources.

A common criticism of questionnaire-based research for social assessment is that the techniques and analysis involved tend to be technocratic and manipulative. This criticism can be countered if the survey is considered as just one, albeit commonly used, method of obtaining social information, especially if the technique is used within the analytic-inductive approach as suggested in Chapter 5.

The poor reputation that survey research has acquired is not normally levelled at the method per se but at its application. There are two major problems. The first arises from a common belief that a survey is the easiest and most appropriate way to obtain social data. However, the social assessor should address some questions before conducting or commissioning survey research. Most importantly, is a survey the most appropriate research method to use, given the nature of the problem, the availability of other types of data, and the cost effectiveness of alternative methods? Here the common constraints of time and money experienced in most social assessments are particularly important to consider.

Another problem stems from the misconception that one does not need any special training to conduct social surveys. As with any skilled enterprise, the more competent the practitioner the better the result. If a survey is the most appropriate means of gathering data for a social assessment, the individual or assessment team involved should have the requisite knowledge and skills. If they do not, they should seek advice and help from those who do. These skills are normally held by staff of organisations involved in survey implementation and analysis, e.g. government or private sector research units, social science departments in universities, social-survey firms and consultants.

## The process of survey research

It is not possible or relevant to provide a complete 'how to do it' for surveys in this chapter. Therefore, what follows is a brief overview to alert practitioners to some of the potential, and the pitfalls, of this method. Excellent volumes exist and provide a review of the use of surveys. References are given below where appropriate.

An important consideration for social assessment is that a survey, whatever form is chosen, must be considered in the overall context of the assessment. Very seldom will the survey provide sufficient information in itself to resolve the questions asked. Hence, in line with Chapter 5, it is always appropriate to see the survey as only one way of adding to the information to describe, understand and elaborate upon the nature of the problem addressed. Use of surveys is issues driven, like any other applied research technique used in a social assessment. Surveys are used when, and only when, they are the most appropriate device for obtaining certain types of information as defined by the issues at hand. It is not a simple task to decide on what is the most appropriate research device within any prescribed context. The following simplified flow chart of the survey research process helps the social assessor to make such decisions.

The research process, within which a survey is developed, can be reduced to four basic stages:

| I | II | III | IV |
|---|---|---|---|
| Defining the problem & data needs | Developing the research plan & questionnaire | Implementing the research plan | Analysing & interpreting the findings |

*Defining the problem* (I)

In social assessments a definition of the survey research problem and a statement of the research objectives is normally found within the survey brief. However, these briefs are often poorly formulated or lack sufficient detail. Given the narrow definition often applied to social assessments (note the number of times a lay person will use the term 'survey' in place of the term 'assessment') it is not surprising that a 'survey' may even be prescribed in the original brief for a social assessment. Energy devoted at this point to clarification of what is required of the assessment is never wasted. Such clarification could require consultation with key actors located within the assessment framework, including the proponent of change and representatives of the stakeholders. Ideally, decisions to undertake a survey, and the nature of that survey, should happen after full scoping and some analysis of secondary data.

Once the research problem is defined and sources of data relevant to the assessment are reviewed, the practitioner is more confident about what is required to fill various information gaps. Decisions are then possible about the best ways of filling these gaps, with surveys considered along with the variety of other research techniques available. It should be remembered here that surveys can provide both qualitative and quantitative data, and the selection and design of research methods will be guided by the issues, and the process of triangulation.

Another consideration at this stage is the political context of the assessment and the probable use of the findings. If, for example, the results are to be presented at formal hearings alongside the contributions of the other sciences, questions of comparative validity and credibility become important. Such hearings may require the presentation of formal tables, lots of numbers and the inevitable 'to two decimal places'. A practitioner constrained by these sorts of parameters must respond accordingly. This potential for adaptation in research methodology is an advantageous, flexible aspect of social assessment. Hence, the choice of types of data and the best methods for their collection, analysis and presentation will depend on the context of their final use.

*Development of a survey research plan and questionnaire* (II)

The preparation of a survey has now moved from Stage I to Stage II of the survey research process. Further decisions must be made about the detailed survey techniques for obtaining information. These decisions will again involve the type of information needed and how it is most easily obtained. It is assumed here that a survey is deemed the best way to provide this information, so the next task involves identifying the survey population.

Normally the target population will be obvious from refinement of the research problem as the assessment proceeds. If this definition is not clear then perhaps further work is necessary using secondary data or consultative techniques.

A survey population is usually too small to poll all members. Thus questions of sample size and representativeness are considered at this point. All things being equal, the larger the sample the smaller the expected error in results. Past a certain point, larger samples yield diminishing returns because as the size of the sample increases so too does the survey cost. De Vaus (2002: 80) tells us that "... required sample size depends on two key factors: the degree of accuracy we require ... and the extent to which there is variation in the population in regard to the key characteristics of the study". He provides a very useful discussion of how to satisfy these requirements.

The next task in the survey process is to establish the sample. There are two broad types of samples: probability and non-probability. In a probability sample, each person in the study population has an equal chance of appearing in the sample, whereas in a non-probability sample this is not the case.

Most surveys are of the probability type as this allows the researcher, as far as possible, to provide sets of findings that are relatively free of systematic patterns of error or bias. There are five main types of probability samples and the choice between them will depend on the desired level of accuracy, available funds for the survey, the quality of the sampling frame and the method by which the data are to be collected. These sample types are: simple random sampling, systematic selection sampling, stratified sampling, cluster sampling and multi-stage sampling. Details as to the elements of each of these types are found in virtually all texts on social research techniques.

There are sometimes situations where the application of probability sampling techniques is either impossible or unnecessary. In these instances non-probability techniques are employed. Examples of such techniques include availability sampling - also known as haphazard sampling - 'typical' people sampling, quota sampling and purposive sampling. Weisberg and Bowen (1977: 26) provide a useful summary of the relative advantages of the various techniques (see Table 6.5 adapted from Weisberg and Bowen).

**Table 6.5      Types of samples**

| Sampling Method | Advantages | Disadvantages |
|---|---|---|
| *Probability* | | |
| Simple random sample | Sampling error (accuracy) can be estimated | Interviews too widely dispersed; need list of total population; periodicity, expensive |
| Systematic sample | Convenience, accuracy can be estimated | Lists often out of date; periodicity, expensive |
| Stratified sample | Guarantee adequate representation of groups; usually decreased error that can be estimated | Sometimes requires weighting, expensive |
| Cluster | Accuracy can be estimated | Increased error - can be estimated , less expensive |
| Multi-stage | Lower cost than simple random sample for large populations; lower error than cluster; accuracy can be estimated | Higher error than simple random sample; more expensive than cluster |
| *Non-probability* | | |
| Haphazard sampling, typical people and purposive sampling | Available sample, focussed, inexpensive | No necessary relation to population - no estimate of accuracy; middle class and other bias possible |
| Quota sampling | Willing respondents, inexpensive | No necessary relation to population - no estimate of accuracy; middle class and other bias possible |

Before leaving this discussion of sampling, it is important to be aware of the problem of non-response. For a variety of reasons some people in a sample will either refuse to be part of a study or cannot be contacted through any normal means. The size of the non-response group is normally in the range of 10% to 40% of the sample. Opinions differ as to the importance of this non-response group but as far as possible the researcher should attempt to ascertain whether or not there is a systematic basis to the non-response. If, for example, one is studying the degree to which various ethnic minority groups adapt to 'mainstream' culture, only to find very high non-response rates from some groups, then techniques are needed to address this problem. The rule of thumb here is that the higher the non-response rate the more important it is to ascertain whether or not the non-response has a systematic basis, i.e. whether a definable section of the sample is refusing to take part.

Once the sample is established the next major issue to resolve is the method for collecting the data. There are three common survey techniques: postal questionnaires, telephone questionnaires and face-to-face interviews. There are also some more specialised techniques including the increasingly popular use of web-based questionnaires. Table 6.6 provides a summary of these techniques. The decision as to choice of survey method will normally be based on a variety of factors including time, money, the type of information required, the limitations of the method.

Postal questionnaires have an advantage in that they can be administered over a large number of respondents at relatively low cost. Disadvantages of this technique include the inability of the respondent to clarify questions and the fact that there is no opportunity to ask back-up questions or record unsolicited comments. The most frequently cited disadvantage of postal questionnaires, however, concerns poor return rates, with under 50% often noted. Around 75% returns are considered good in most circumstances. There are well-tested methods for increasing return rates and Dillman (2000) and Graetz (1985) give valuable accounts of these. Personal follow-up, usually by telephone, is often useful but the time spent can soon nullify the advantages gained from using the post in the first instance.

Telephone surveys have the obvious bias of excluding all those without access to telephones or who have unlisted telephone numbers. Such surveys are very useful for locating large dispersed populations relatively cheaply, and the technique offers the opportunity for interaction between questioner and respondent while providing a measure of anonymity. Dillman (2000) provides a useful guide for this technique.

Face-to-face (personally administered) interviews have the advantage of enabling a greater degree of interaction between the interviewer and the respondent, but necessarily involve higher costs than either of the other two techniques in terms of time, travel expenses, and labour. Well-trained interviewers are essential for the application of this technique.

At this point it is necessary to construct the questionnaire. Too often, insufficient effort is expended constructing questionnaires and many surveys fail to deliver for want of the necessary skills in questionnaire design. There are five factors to consider:

- the selection of topics about which questions will be asked

- the construction of the questions

- whether the questions provide useful information for analysis and presentation

- the layout of the questionnaire including the order of the questions

- a plan for analysing the information that the questionnaire yields, such as expected tabulations.

# Table 6.6    Types of social survey

| Technique | Uses | Advantages | Other Aspects |
|---|---|---|---|
| Postal Surveys: Written questionnaire sent to respondents for reply by post. Sometimes questionnaires are picked up by hand, providing an opportunity to clarify questions and check replies. | Cover large populations. Do allow more questions to be asked. Design is a specialised activity. | Anonymity, time for respondents to consider their replies. No interviewer bias. | Openended questions are usually avoided in favour of closed and multiple choice questions. Poor response rates a serious issue, might require telephone followup. |
| Telephone surveys: Interviews conducted by telephone, often with a team of interviewers. | Can cover large populations relatively cheaply. Useful if a limited number of questions are involved. | Less expensive and better response rates than postal. Provide a rapid return/results. Allows some interaction. Retains anonymity. | Usually produce results that can be entered and analysed directly, especially if sampling is completed carefully. |
| Structured Interviews: Face-to-face between the interviewer and interviewee. Can include both closed and open questions, use of flip cards and similar devices. | Useful for smaller study populations, where high response rates are needed, and open questions are useful. | Provide an opportunity for some interaction between interviewer and respondent. Allow an opportunity to collect qualitative data. Provide reliability and consistency in putting questions and filling responses. Usually have a high response rate. | Increased costs of survey, may require considerable transport resource, especially in rural areas. Reliability reduced if more than one interviewer is used. An interview team will require good training. |
| Delphi: A panel of individual experts or key people answer series of confidential questionnaires until a consensus emerges. The process is iterative, taking place over a number of rounds of surveying. At the end of each round, the results are summarised and recirculated, thereby increasing the amount of information available, and facilitating a consensus. | Used mainly for forecasting, developing strategy, identifying outcomes, preferences and perceptions of current and future situations. Helps identify future issues, problems, opportunities etc. Very useful for complex or unstructured problems. | Brings variety or perspectives and expertise to bear on a problem or issue; because of anonymity in questionnaires participants are free to respond as they feel and the effect of personality and status is removed. Information and insight grow with the process. | Participants may not be representative; problems of dropout and non response in time frame set. Method requires high level of technical expertise and integrative skills which may be hard to obtain; dependence on technical experts for summaries and overviews; consensus may not be possible. Requires a skilled researcher. |
| Option Scoring: List of options and/or problem statements developed into a questionnaire. People then asked to indicate choices or rate/rank issues, within a set of constraints, in terms of importance for their neighbourhood or group. | Can be done at meetings or through postal questionnaires to get community preferences. Requires care with regard to representativeness of sample, methodology and the presentation of options/issues. | Increases understanding of constraints in planning, links planners and the public, and can reach people who may not usually participate. | The problem and options definition is in the hands of planners. Other options and problems may be overlooked in the design. Community therefore should have input into the definition of the options early in the process. Danger of low response rates in questionnaires. Requires lot of preliminary work and expertise to administer surveys. |

Addressing these areas requires skill and experience so money spent obtaining advice at this stage can provide good returns. A range of excellent books and manuals designed to assist the practitioner exists, including Oppenheim (1970), Weisberg and Bowen (1977), Sudman and Bradburn (1982), Statistics New Zealand (1995), May (2001) and de Vaus (2002).

*Implementing the survey* (III)

Once the questionnaire is constructed the next task is to pre-test (or pilot) it out in the field. Pre-testing is essential no matter how the questionnaire is administered. Pre-testing allows for checking and further development of the questionnaire in 'real world' circumstances.

Pre-testing will help resolve inevitable consideration of the scope and length of a questionnaire. A useful rule of thumb in designing the questionnaire, and indeed, in any information-gathering process, is to keep in mind that the aim of data gathering is to gather only as much data as necessary. The practitioner should resist the temptation, or external pressures, to ask questions not directly related to the information required for an assessment. A major function of the pre-test is to ascertain whether the questions 'work' and the language used is appropriate for the purpose.

Pre-testing will also help to identify logistical issues, including how long the questionnaire will take to conduct. There may also be issues to consider about where to conduct the questionnaire (for example at home or at work), and when, including the best good time of day, the effect of weather on surveys conducted outside, or even when is the best time of the year or season. Other logistical issues include who will administer the questionnaire, transport required, and checking or quality control.

*Analysing, interpreting and presenting the findings* (IV)

The final stage of the survey research process involves the retrieval of information, its analysis and presentation. Consideration of these aspects of the research should have been planned for from Stage II (developing the research plan) of the research process as set out above and discussed in the references cited.

A crucial consideration in the analysis and presentation of survey information for social assessment is that it must always be appropriate to the needs of the client and the communities of interest. In an important way the findings 'belong' to all concerned parties and unless there are specified constraints they should be accessible to and understandable by all. Survey findings might be included in general assessment reports, or sometimes in a separate report. Clients, or respondents, may sometimes specify the final shape of such a report or indeed the production of interim reports that present survey results in the course of an assessment. Effort spent checking style and format is worthwhile, including an explanation of the survey research problem, the methods employed to obtain data, the methods employed to analyse data, an interpretation of the survey findings and, where appropriate, conclusions drawn from them. Care is necessary to clearly label graphs, tables and illustrations relating them to the survey source. A summary is useful as a feedback device to the study population, and as an addition to other social assessment activities that might be undertaken, such as meetings and workshops. In short, a mass of survey data should not be presented in numerous, complex tables with little explanation.

## Case study 6.2  Examples of surveys used in social assessments

| Type of survey and sampling method | Example of the method |
| --- | --- |
| *Simple random Administered by interviewer* | *The Tongan outer islands development project included a rapid rural appraisal and social design study to prepare integrated development plans for agriculture on the isolated Niuas Islands. The social assessment drew on both secondary and primary data sources to develop a social profile of the islands in a relatively short space of time. Due to a lack of secondary data on living standards a short, sample household survey was conducted. The survey obtained information on demographics, household income and expenditure, and household building materials and facilities. One person in every fifth house was interviewed in Tongan by a local interview team. In addition to the survey, in-depth interviews with farmers and woman, plus village meetings, provided detailed information on development issues.* |
| *Purposive quota Administered by interviewer* | *As part of a study of the impacts of options for wastewater disposal, either continuing to go into an estuary or to build an ocean outfall, in Christchurch, NZ, a survey was undertaken of people engaged in recreation activity in the estuary and beach areas. In addition recreation activities and counts were carried out by observation and mapped. Altogether 188 people were surveyed. They were chosen in a random, purposive sample. Initially, people were approached at random when they were actively involved in recreation in the study area. These people were approached, asked if they were willing to participate and then interviewed. Types of recreation activity represented in this sample were monitored as the numbers of respondents built up. Groups that were lightly represented in relation to observed recreation patterns were targeted to build up response numbers, adding the purposive dimension to the sample.* |
| *Purposive/random Administered by interviewer* | *A study analysed actual impacts of several solid waste management facilities in New Zealand, with comparison to the impacts originally projected. It included structured interviews with nearby residents, who were selected in decreasing numbers radiating out from each site. The interviews obtained information on the experience of individuals with the facility. Initially respondents were asked an unprompted question about the impacts they noted. Then they were asked prompted questions for those impacts they did not identify. For each impact the person experienced, a set of additional question explored those experiences. In addition, recreational users and local businesses were interviewed using separate questionnaires (Baines et al., 2003b).* |
| *Universe Self completed* | *As part of the social assessment of relocating an inter-island ferry terminal from an existing port town, a survey was conducted to profile the workforce, obtaining information about demographics, job types, skills, home location, and means of travel to work. The questionnaire was delivered at work to all the workforce and they were asked to return it to a drop-off box. While the employer assisted in conducting the survey, respondents were assured of confidentiality by the researchers.* |

# CONCLUSIONS

A social assessment will require a variety of data, and several techniques and typical sources for obtaining these data are described in this chapter, covering secondary data and social surveys. These techniques are part of a research process elaborated upon throughout this text, so they are used within an iterative framework. Emphasis is placed on data that is focussed on the issues identified in an assessment.

There is a tendency to polarise the choice of data collection between so-called qualitative and quantitative techniques. Adopting this dichotomous view is unfortunate as it has the tendency to assume one or another type of data is best. Very seldom is this the case but rather the combination of the two broad forms, guided by the research issues, will normally yield the best information. The process of triangulation elaborated in Chapter 5 is facilitated by the application of findings obtained from diverse research techniques.

Ultimately the usefulness of secondary data depends on the form in which they are available, the trends they show, their reliability and accuracy, the extent to which they aid in triangulating or checking the validity of other data, the insight sought from the data, and the imagination and ingenuity of the researcher.

Surveys constitute only one possible aspect of the social assessment research approach. When applied appropriately they can be a powerful tool for obtaining relevant information. It is important to remember that survey techniques are only one part of the methods available for collecting social information and, wherever possible, the practitioner should blend a variety of techniques to reinforce their understanding of the research problem.

A final consideration is that the presentation of the information must be appropriate to the needs of the client and also the interested and affected parties. The findings 'belong' to all concerned parties and unless there are specified constraints they must be accessible and understandable to them.

For most assessments secondary data and surveys are complemented by consultative, 'hands on and feet wet' involvement with the people affected by change, as discussed in detail in Chapter 8.

## SUMMARY

This chapter introduces techniques for social assessment that are focussed on and relevant to the issues-oriented approach. Early information on issues, the study area, sources of information and likely needs for the collection of new, primary data will be obtained in the scoping phase of work.

At this scoping stage secondary data, in particular, will be used. Secondary data are often relatively inexpensive to obtain, and save valuable time otherwise spent in primary research. These data provide basic geographical and historical description, are the basis of demographic profiles, and can often provide an indication of changes over time if a series is available.

Census data are the most common source of statistics used in social assessments, and they can provide a comprehensive picture of many assessment areas. Other official statistics are also important along with many other sources of secondary data, both formal and informal. Social surveys should only be used after all the other available sources of information are pursued.

Survey research should be preceded by a thorough definition of the problem and the issues for which data are needed. If a survey is considered necessary, then the research plan is developed, including a selection of the sample required of the target population, and the techniques to be used, such as mail or phone surveys or personal interviews. Particular attention is required in the development of a questionnaire, including the selection and phrasing of questions, layout and ease of analysis. Pre-testing or piloting of a questionnaire is an important step. If an assessment team does not have the necessary skills to conduct either secondary data searches or a social survey then they should consider bringing those skills in.

# CHAPTER SEVEN

## The assessment of impacts on the regional and local economy[2]

### INTRODUCTION

This chapter is an introduction to techniques for assessment of impacts on the local and regional economy. Economic impacts that arise from planned or actual changes are an important part of the issues found in most social assessments. At a regional level, assessment of economic impacts is crucial to resource policy and decision making. Resource management legislation often places emphasis on regional level resource policy. Such policy design requires a range of information about both social and economic change. Furthermore, local economies are inevitably affected by and linked to change at the regional level. Policy and decision makers will require information about economic change at both levels.

These assessments of economic impacts are often undertaken in conjunction with a social assessment Economic impacts discussed in this chapter are directly related to the nature of the planned or actual change, and to the social characteristics of the affected area. The discussion does not extend to the analysis of costs and benefits at a national level, or to the analysis of the financial viability of a project or programme. Neither does the chapter include discussion of non-market valuation techniques. These include hedonic pricing, contingent valuation or choice models used to estimate "willingness to pay" for public goods, and the travel-cost method, which may be used to help calculate money measures of benefits for recreation activities.

Projects, programmes and policies need to be considered at the level of the regional economy because regional economic systems provide the overall setting for local economies. Regional patterns of resource use, employment and processing provide the context for change. In an assessment of the economic impacts of change, the main factors that usually need to be considered are the nature and level of capital investment, including the technology involved, the size and character of the workforce, and the requirements over time for raw materials and infrastructure such as transport, energy, health, education and social services. The characteristics to note in the area being studied thus include the nature of the existing industry, workforce, employment, infrastructure and its capacity to expand, social services such as housing, health, training and education, and the formal and informal provision of social welfare services.

---

[2]    We are grateful to Dr Geoff Kerr, Lincoln University, for leading authorship of this updated chapter. We suggest authorship of the chapter should be cited as Kerr, Geoff; Bryan Hobson; Taylor, Nick and Ruth Houghton.

In the discussion of impacts on the local economy, small business is highlighted as a major element in many communities. Many of the flow-on effects to local employment caused by a change in the regional economy are likely to have an impact on small business units.

There are established techniques for analysis of change in the regional and local economy. However, there are often difficulties assessing such change because of a lack of substantive regional, local and business-level economic data. Limits to data make the task of regional and local economic assessment difficult if it is to advance beyond general description.

# THE REGIONAL ECONOMY

## Types of regional economic impacts

Economic analysis is extremely useful for predicting social impacts at the level of the regional economy. Direct economic changes are usually fairly obvious but other changes may not be. Because the economy, society and environment form part of a complex system, effects may occur elsewhere in the system. Input-output analysis provides a method for identifying and predicting the scale of non-direct effects, referred to variously as flow-on, knock-on, trickle down, or ripple effects.

While regional analysis focuses on economic impacts, social and environmental factors may be addressed as well. For example, use of input-output models to identify pollution emission implications of proposed changes. The types of changes that can be addressed are diverse. They include evaluations of plan changes, alternative land uses, impacts of tourism, business closures, infrastructure projects, and changes in economic conditions (such as the prices of agricultural produce, or economic growth).

In order to differentiate regional economic changes it is useful to classify them into direct, indirect and induced impacts. Direct impacts are those that arise because of the immediate requirements of a development project, including direct purchases and labour employed on the project itself. In the case of a tourist resort project, for example, direct impacts include the revenue (also known as turnover or output) obtained from guests, the employment of people to operate the resort, and the net income (profits or value-added) accruing to its owners.

Indirect impacts result from the increased production of goods and services necessary to maintain and operate the development. In the case of a tourism resort, indirect impacts would arise from the production of inputs required to run the resort, e.g. publicity, food, transport, laundry services, etc. Of course, each of these inputs also has its own indirect impacts, e.g. laundry services require inputs of construction, electronics, transport, labour and chemicals, etc.

Induced impacts are the increases in economic activity caused by increased spending resulting from the extra income earned directly and indirectly as a result of the project. The induced demand for goods creates further jobs and income in a flow-on effect.

## Techniques for assessing regional effects

The full regional impacts of change can only be determined after consideration of indirect and induced, or flow-on, effects. Different tourism projects, for instance, have different impacts in terms of regional employment and income creation because they require different inputs of skills, labour, capital and infrastructure. These may be available in the region or they may need to be imported. A project that relies more heavily on regional inputs will usually have greater regional income and employment-creation effects. Further, regionally produced inputs may have differing import contents, and therefore different indirect effects. Alternative projects may provide additional income to sectors of society with different propensities to consume within the region, and therefore have different induced effects.

### Multipliers

The flow-on effects of the initial project are called multiplier effects. Multipliers are used to compare the size of these effects with the size of the initial impact. Type I multipliers are the ratio of direct plus indirect effects to direct effects, while Type II multipliers are the ratio of direct plus indirect plus induced effects to direct effects.

A simple illustration of multipliers for a tourist resort is provided in Figure 7.1. Suppose $100 is spent on accommodation at the resort. Some of this $100 stays within the region, while some immediately flows outside for goods and services. Suppose all inputs are purchased outside the region, except for food, which is purchased from a local retailer for $25. Other inputs, from outside the region, cost $50 leaving $25 in profit for the local hotel owner. Direct revenue of $100 has thus created direct income of $25 in the region.

Indirect regional impacts include the $25 revenue earned by the local food retailer, of which $12 is paid to local market gardeners for vegetables. Indirect regional income is the $5 accruing to the food retailer, and the $6 accruing to the grower. Direct revenue of $100 has created direct plus indirect regional income of $36 and direct plus indirect regional output of $137.

**Figure 7.1    Direct and indirect economic impacts**

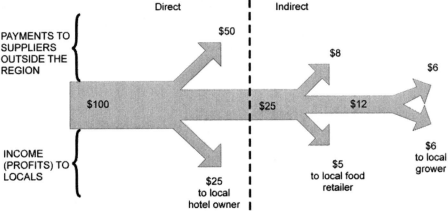

Direct plus indirect (Type I) multipliers for this example are:

Revenue      1.37  ([$100 + $25 + $12]/$100)
Income       1.44  ([$25 + $5 + $6]/$25)

Induced impacts result because of the $36 of increased local income, some of which will be spent within the region.

There are many different types of multipliers used so great care must be taken in their interpretation. Some of them include only indirect impacts while others include induced impacts as well. Some multipliers are used to describe changes in chosen variables on an absolute basis (employment per dollar spent), while others are used on a relative basis (indirect plus direct employment per direct employee). Small, open economies have relatively small multipliers. New Zealand's Type I output multipliers (126 industries) range from 1.30 (public order and safety) to 2.67 (owner-builders), with mean 1.85 and median 1.86. The larger, less open, United States economy has Type I multipliers (91 industries) that range from 1.25 (owner-occupied dwellings) to 3.20 (gas production and distribution), with mean and median of 2.05 and 2.03, respectively. Because small regions are very open to trade, regional multipliers can be much smaller than national multipliers, as discussed later.

*Multipliers and estimates of benefits*

Multiplier effects are often quoted by developers and public officials in attempts to promote the economic benefits of proposals. Benefit-cost analysis (BCA) is also undertaken to determine the worth of projects, programmes and policies. Benefits and costs are estimated using market prices, net of indirect taxes and subsidies. Only direct costs and direct benefits are used in BCA and most projects are required to meet a target rate of return, such as the 10% rate used by the New Zealand Government, to gain approval. The use to which these different measures of worth are put is often confused; sometimes the measures are presented as alternatives, sometimes only one is presented, and in other cases they are added in an attempt to measure 'total' benefits.

Benefit-cost analysis does not address distributional objectives; it is concerned only with measuring changes in social welfare, usually by national income. On the other hand, multipliers are applied to a variety of economic objectives, commonly including income, output (sales) and employment. The income multipliers include the direct income effects measured in BCA, so they cannot be added to the output of BCA. The multiplier measures are greater than the BCA measures, so they are often favoured by prospective developers. Economists may, however, shun the use of multipliers as measures of benefit. Their main reason for holding this view is that, unless special circumstances exist, these additional effects are simply transfers from one part of the economy to another (see Eckstein, 1958; McKean, 1958; Gittinger, 1972 for further elaboration).

Multipliers become important where there are market imperfections, when the wage rate does not represent the real cost of labour, for example, where there are distributional objectives, or where multiple objectives are important.

Distribution of wealth, particularly among geographical regions, is a common concern of policy makers, as are issues such as environmental quality and employment. Multiplier analysis provides a method for comparing how alternative proposals fare on these criteria.

It is possible to include these matters in benefit-cost analysis, but only after explicit trade offs between objectives have been made (i.e. 1 job = $X, or 1 job at M = y jobs at N, or 1 job = Z tonnes of emissions). Given the ways in which these trade offs should be made have not been explicitly agreed upon by society, decisions are generally made in the political arena. Multipliers provide another way of informing politicians about a range of outcomes that depend on decisions that they may make.

Although multipliers are a useful way of summarising some of the impacts that concern society, they should usually be presented alongside a BCA and in association with full social and environmental assessments, so that decisions are not made on a limited set of criteria.

*Input-output analysis*

Multipliers can indicate aggregate changes in the regional economy but they do not indicate in which industries the changes occur. More specific information on the interconnections within an economy is required to identify specific changes. This type of information can be summarised using input-output models. Input requirements from each industry to all other industries are placed in a matrix.

The matrix has sectors to describe household demands from each industry, imports to each industry, and so forth.

A section of the United States 1999 ten-industry matrix is shown in Table 7.1. It shows that the agricultural industry, for example, annually required $48.3 billion of inputs from the manufacturing industry. A simple, complete hypothetical matrix is shown in Table 7.2 (Butcher, 1985).

**Table 7.1    USA 1999 inter-industry transactions (US$million)**

|  | Agri-cultural | Mining | Other industries | Total inter-mediate | Total non-intermediate (GDP) | Total commodity output |
|---|---|---|---|---|---|---|
| Agricultural | 67179 | 87 |  | 244583 | 32640 | 277223 |
| Mining | 348 | 31951 |  | 204630 | -54230 | 150401 |
| Construction | 3232 | 4082 |  | 226544 | 839829 | 1066373 |
| Manufacturing | 48321 | 15400 |  | 2337774 | 1677639 | 4015413 |
| Transportation, communication and utilities | 13253 | 12204 |  | 736882 | 617365 | 1354247 |
| Trade | 14602 | 3682 |  | 489408 | 1189977 | 1679385 |
| Finance, insurance and real estate | 19250 | 37582 |  | 1020399 | 1626867 | 2647267 |
| Services | 9826 | 6541 |  | 1578163 | 2365728 | 3943891 |
| Other | 178 | 31 |  | 85089 | 1053278 | 1138367 |
| Noncomparable imports | 67 | 2052 |  | 74771 | -74771 |  |
| Total Intermediate | 176256 | 113612 |  | 6998243 | 9274323 |  |
| Value added | 103000 | 48145 |  |  |  |  |
| Total Industry Output | 279256 | 161757 |  |  |  | 16272566 |

www.bea.doc.gov

To enable use of this information, it is typically assumed that each industry is homogeneous, showing constant returns to scale. In other words, all firms use the same technology, and unit costs of production are the same regardless of the number of units produced. This assumption implies that marginal and average input requirements are identical. Thus historical data may be used to predict the outcome of potential changes. In some instances it is possible to use knowledge about technology differences to avoid this assumption.

**Table 7.2    A simplified input-output matrix ($m)**

| From/To | Farming | Agri-cultural services | Freight | All other industry | Household consumption | Other final demand | Total Industry |
|---|---|---|---|---|---|---|---|
| Farming | 110 | 1 | 1 | 600 | 90 | 198 | 1000 |
| Agricultural services | 10 | 1 | 0 | 3 | 0 | 6 | 20 |
| Freight | 30 | 2 | 5 | 133 | 20 | 10 | 200 |
| All other industry | 500 | 5 | 104 | 6734 | 2000 | 657 | 10000 |
| | | | | | | | |
| Labour | 150 | 10 | 40 | 1530 | 505 | 600 | 2835 |
| Other primary inputs | 200 | 1 | 50 | 1000 | 220 | 490 | 1961 |
| | | | | | | | |
| TOTAL INDUSTRY REQUIREMENTS | 1000 | 20 | 200 | 10000 | 2835 | 1961 | 16016 |

Indirect and induced effects of a change in demand for any industry may be calculated using matrix algebra. Industry requirements are summarised by the technical coefficients matrix (Table 7.3, derived from Table 7.2). This matrix can be interpreted as: every dollar of farming output requires direct inputs of $0.11 from farming, $0.03 from freight, and $0.15 of labour.

**Table 7.3    A technical coefficients matrix**

| From/To | Farming | Agricultural services | Freight | All other industry | Household consumption | Other final demand |
|---|---|---|---|---|---|---|
| Farming | 0.11 | 0.05 | 0.01 | 0.06 | 0.032 | 0.101 |
| Agricultural services | 0.01 | 0.05 | 0 | 0 | 0 | 0.003 |
| Freight | 0.03 | 0.1 | 0.025 | 0.0133 | 0.007 | 0.005 |
| All other Industry | 0.5 | 0.25 | 0.52 | 0.6734 | 0.705 | 0.335 |
| | | | | | | |
| Labour | 0.15 | 0.5 | 0.2 | 0.153 | 0.178 | 0.306 |
| Other primary inputs | 0.2 | 0.05 | 0.25 | 0.1 | 0.078 | 0.25 |
| | | | | | | |
| TOTAL | 1 | 1 | 1 | 1 | 1 | 1 |

Mathematical manipulation of the technical coefficients matrix yields the Leontief inverse matrix. Table 7.4 reports the agriculture column of the USA 1999 ten-sector Leontief inverse matrix. The Leontief inverse matrix shows the total increase in output from each industry for a unit increase in direct demand for any one industry. Adding up the column of coefficients yields the Type I multiplier for that industry. The Type I multiplier for USA Agriculture is 2.307. A unit increase in agricultural sales increases sales in the whole economy by 2.3

units, comprised of increases in sales from agriculture (1.337 units), mining (0.023 units), construction (0.029 units), and so on. When the input-output matrix has been augmented by the inclusion of household expenditures, the Leontief inverse matrix takes account of extra take home income as well as inter-industry demands and provides the larger Type II multipliers.

**Table 7.4       Column of Leontief inverse matrix (USA, 1999)**

| From/To | Agriculture |
|---|---|
| Agriculture | 1.337 |
| Mining | 0.023 |
| Construction | 0.029 |
| Manufacturing | 0.41 |
| Transportation, communication and utilities | 0.11 |
| Trade | 0.104 |
| Finance, insurance and real estate | 0.151 |
| Services | 0.13 |
| Other | 0.014 |
| **Total (Industry output multiplier)** | **2.307** |

www.bea.doc.gov

Because of rapid technological changes, economies of scale in some industries, and data limitations, input-output analysis can never give an entirely accurate picture of the impacts of particular actions. However, input-output analysis should not be discarded because of this potential inaccuracy. This type of analysis may be accurate enough for many purposes, especially those requiring measures of orders of magnitude, and the analysis could theoretically be applied using marginal rather than average data.

We will not go into the mathematical techniques for manipulating input-output matrices to obtain multipliers (see Richardson, 1972 or Miller and Blair, 1985), but will concentrate on the applicability of the method for determining regional or local, rather than national, impacts of particular actions.

*Regional input-output analysis*

A major problem when applying input-output analysis is the massive data requirement. The enormity of assembling the information to construct the transactions matrix is illustrated by the time taken to produce national tables. For example, the final 1996 New Zealand tables were not published until 2002. The information obtained in the most recent input-output tables is therefore well out of date when published. The analyst should therefore be wary of placing too much weight on the tables as a source of information.

The position with regional data is no better. Governments rarely produce regional input-output tables. Notable exceptions include Canada and Finland, although the Canadian provincial tables (www.statcan.gc.ca) apply to regions larger than many countries. The New Zealand government is currently evaluating the merits of producing official regional tables (Statistics New Zealand, 2003). There are also many cases where academics and the private sector have developed regional input-output tables to meet specific industry and community needs. Typically these regional tables are not constructed from primary data, but are modified from national tables to represent better the distribution of industries within the region. The time taken to make the required amendments to national tables means that regional tables are more out of date at production than their national level counterparts.

*The GRIT method*

Generating regional input-output tables (GRIT) is a technique developed at the University of Queensland that uses existing national level data. The method assumes that if a regional industry produces less than the national industry in relation to total regional output of all industries, then it will be unable to meet regional demands for its products. So products will have to be imported from other regions. Technical coefficients are adjusted downwards. The regional multipliers associated with that industry will therefore be smaller than national multipliers. If an industry is very dominant in a region, it is assumed that all extra output is exported.

Because regional economies are more 'open' than national economies, regional tables derived in this way tend to overestimate within-region coefficients. In other words, GRIT assumes similar within-region trading patterns at national and regional levels, but we expect that, the smaller a region is, the more likely trade will occur across its boundaries. Clearly the assumptions made by GRIT are ad hoc and there is no theoretically defensible way to obtain regional tables from national tables. This issue is analysed further, and other approaches to estimation of regional tables are canvassed, by Richardson (1972), Miller and Blair (1985) and Hewings (1985).

Improved regional tables could be constructed by collecting primary data on inter-industry transactions within the region. This data collection is usually not done for two main reasons: firstly because of the expense involved and secondly the difficulty of collecting the data, even if it is affordable. The smaller a region, the more identifiable are the operators within an industry. Then commercial sensitivity of the information necessary to produce input-output tables causes reluctance among many firms to provide it voluntarily.

Constructing regional input-output tables from scratch requires knowledge of either physical flows of products or their values, within and between industries. If local industry outputs are known (unlikely), and technology is known or standard (also unlikely) then inter-industry transfers may be calculated. Whether locally required inputs are locally sourced will, however, also have to be known, as would the distribution of household spending. Information on the latter may be obtained from household surveys, but the former would probably be extremely difficult to obtain. It is these problems, apart from the expense involved in obtaining such information, which has led to the development of methods for producing regional and local models from national data.

The prime requirement when applying GRIT and other methods for generating regional input-output tables is a local industrial profile, in terms of output by industry. This information is often not easily obtained for the area of interest. Or changes since statistical data were collected may limit its value. If technologies are similar across regions, employment in each industry may be a suitable proxy for levels of output. Employment information is usually readily obtained, at low cost, for small areas.

## Case study 7.1 Economic impacts of tourism development

*A series of studies undertaken by Butcher and associates (Butcher et al. 1998, 2000, 2001, 2003) into the impacts of tourism in New Zealand communities illustrates some of the uses of regional input-output studies. Butcher and colleagues developed regional input-output models for several small communities using the GRIT approach and utilising superior information they had available from detailed community studies. In each case the authors generated multipliers for employment, output, value-added and household income. Combined with survey-based information on tourism expenditures, the multipliers allow prediction of community impacts. Direct effects and multipliers are summarised in Table 7.5.*

**Table 7.5        Direct tourism impacts and tourism multipliers**

|  |  | Akaroa | Westland | Kaikoura | Rotorua | Christchurch |
|---|---|---|---|---|---|---|
| Direct effect | Employment (FTE) | 160 | 810 | 327 | 3500 | 10970 |
|  | Output ($m) | 17.3 | 82.4 | 27.9 | 310 | 1103 |
|  | Value-added ($m) | 6 | 43.9 | 11.8 | 126 | 376 |
|  | Household income ($m) | 3.9 | 23.7 | 6.8 | 83 | 244 |
| Type II Multiplier | Employment | 1.08 | 1.11 | 1.21 | 1.39 | 1.46 |
|  | Output | 1.11 | 1.19 | 1.3 | 1.49 | 1.75 |
|  | Value-added | 1.15 | 1.19 | 1.38 | 1.59 | 1.98 |
|  | Household income | 1.1 | 1.17 | 1.32 | 1.51 | 1.81 |

*Akaroa, Westland and Kaikoura are all remote and smaller than 10,000 people, whereas Rotorua is a regional centre of about 50,000 people and Christchurch is a city of around 300,000 people. Tourism multipliers are low for the small, isolated communities, which can expect little in the way of flow-on effects from the tourism industry, typically in the 10% to 30% range. Because of their broader economic bases, multiplier effects are somewhat larger in Rotorua and*

*Christchurch. While direct tourism sales (output) per direct employee are similar in each location ($90,000 - $110,000 per Full Time Equivalent - FTE), the difference in multipliers creates larger differences in total employment impacts. Whereas Rotorua requires only $63,000 of tourism spending to generate a full time job in the region, Akaroa requires over $100,000 of spending to create a single local job after multiplier effects are accounted for.*

*The richness of regional input-output models as a planning tool is illustrated by Table 7.6, which shows the location of jobs generated by tourism in each of the local economies.*

**Table 7.6      Tourism-generated employment**

|  | Akaroa | Westland | Kaikoura | Rotorua | Christchurch |
|---|---|---|---|---|---|
| Accommodation | 33% | 27% | 25% | 33% | 20% |
| Restaurants & cafes | 40% | 24% | 27% | 40% | 38% |
| Activites | 11% | 19% | 28% |  | 9% |
| Other | 6% | 30% | 7% | 11% | 5% |
| Retail | 9% |  | 13% | 16% | 14% |
| Travel | 2% |  |  |  | 13% |

*These studies grouped industries somewhat differently, so the compilation of "other" varies by location. However, it is apparent that the location of tourism-generated impacts can differ significantly between locations. In Christchurch, only 20% of employment occurs in the accommodation industry, while that industry accounts for 33% of employment in Akaroa and Rotorua. Restaurants and cafes are significant beneficiaries of tourism, accounting for up to 40% of FTEs.*

This case study provides an indication of the impacts of a single industry and how they vary by location. Knowledge of these and other impacts can be important for planning infrastructural developments to meet projected future changes, such as a downturn, or growth in the tourism industry. This type of approach is just as useful for comparing the impacts of different potential developments within a region, or the best uses for scarce resources. For example, Ford et al. (2001) compare benefits from alternative water uses in a region of New Zealand, as shown in Table 7.7. If water were the limiting factor in community development, then sheep and beef farming would yield considerably greater community benefits than alternatives such as electricity generation or horticulture. The same models used to generate Table 7.7 can also be used to help identify the location of impacts within the community from each of the alternative water uses.

Table 7.7        Total impact per 1000 m³ of total water used

|  | Employment (FTE) | Value added ($m) |
|---|---|---|
| Electricity generation and supply | 0.1 | 0.011 |
| Meat processing | 0.4 | 0.019 |
| Dairy processing | 0.4 | 0.023 |
| Sheep/beef farming | 2.2 | 0.1 |
| Dairy farming | 1 | 0.048 |
| Horticulture | 0.5 | 0.015 |

These sorts of assessments assist the political process of decision making about alternative policies and projects, where economic factors will often dominate the decision criteria used. Case study 7.2 illustrates the backdrop and associated political forces that can come into play for analytical work, in this case determining the value of sporting events in a politicised context.

*Case study 7.2  Assessment of multipliers for sports fishing tournaments*

*Major sport fishing tournaments have gained widespread popularity in the United States since their inception in 1967. With the growth of major sponsoring organizations such as Bass Anglers Sportsmen's Society (which has been purchased by ESPN, the major sports television network in the United States) and its competitor Operation Bass, tournament fishing has become institutionalised. Bass fishing tournaments have in fact proliferated across the country. It has been estimated that well over 100,000 'local' fishing tournaments are held in the United States annually, in addition to the two dozen or so major events hosted for professional anglers. It is now possible for a growing number of anglers to earn good livings out of prize money and fees for product endorsements.*

*Supporters of tournament angling note that fishing and boating industries have boomed with this boost in fishing interest. New technologies have been developed creating products sold to a much larger angling base than ever before. Greater efforts have been directed to the management and enhancement of fisheries to met demand. The development and expansion of tournament fishing around the world, extended to saltwater species, has significant economic implications for cities and communities hosting such events, not to mention generating support for clean waterways and good fish habitat. Communities vie to host the events in expectation of their economic benefits, including payments to attract major tournaments because of their perceived economic and promotional value.*

*Critics of the sport's ascendancy have raised concerns about the future of fisheries in the face of significant increases in fishing pressure. Although the tournament industry promotes live release of fish, the sheer magnitude of participation has caused crowding and limited angling opportunities on some waters. Anglers are also faced with limits on availability of quality fishing waters due to the end of the dam building era and reservoir creation, reduction of fish habitat in aging reservoirs, and non-point pollution.*

*Some state agencies have sought to impose restrictions on tournament activity through imposing special fees, taxes, and requirements for permission to hold tournaments. Large tournaments have even been banned on certain lakes, and communities that have become popular bases for tournament fishers have debated over cost/benefits of hosting tournaments in their localities. Area anglers complain that boat ramps are largely unavailable to non-tournament anglers, with as many as two hundred boats being launched and taken out during some events.*

*As the voices of skeptics became louder, the major tournament organisations sponsored a series of socio-economic impact studies though the University of Alabama from 1987 to 2000 to answer certain critical questions. What exactly were the economic benefits of tournament events? What was the promotional value of these events in economic terms? And how did these balance against the costs, economic and otherwise? The assessments revealed that the impacts were significant, with direct expenditures of contestants, accompanying family and friends, tournament officials, and spectators being three-quarters to one million dollars US for each major event during the year. The end-of-the-year 'Classic' pitting the best anglers in the country against each other attracted from 20,000 to 30,000 spectators at weigh-ins and associated events, and yielded direct expenditures over the six days of activity between twelve and fifteen million dollars US.*

*Economic multipliers for these events depended on location and size of the business area, with the larger the area, the larger the multiplier. However, it soon became apparent that the Chambers of Commerce promoting these events for their cities were claiming high multipliers, while critics of tournaments were able to obtain calculations of low multipliers. Though the investigator relied on a credible University Center for Business Research to generate multipliers, all stakeholders seemed satisfied if multipliers were given as a range rather than as an absolute figure. Thus, for example, a figure of twelve million dollars in direct expenditures could be expressed as generating from twenty-four (using a multiplier of 2.0) to thirty million dollars US (using a multiplier of 2.5) of economic benefits to the area.*

## THE LOCAL ECONOMY

Our approach to the assessment of change in the local economy is based on experience gained by the authors in New Zealand and the USA, and also in a number of other countries including Pacific Islands countries such as Tonga and the Cook Islands, and Asian countries such as the Philippines and Malaysia. This experience points to the important relationships between the regional economy and local economies, and the cycles of change experienced at a community level (as discussed in Chapter 3). It also points to the need to assess changes to small businesses in particular, including farms, when considering implications of change for the livelihoods of individuals and households.

## Characteristics of small businesses

Small businesses are a major contributor to employment and economic activity in many countries. They are a particular feature in rural areas. Devlin (1984) estimated there were about 100,000 small-business units (excluding fishing and farming operations) in New Zealand, employing 54% of the private work force. The contribution, according to Devlin, to Gross Domestic Product (GDP) by small firms (on a value-added basis) ranges from 32% to 50% of value added to GDP.

The distinguishing features of small business are their small number of employees, as well as their structure, ownership and style of management. The size of businesses can be categorised by numbers of staff. Although the number of staff of a small business will vary by sector, many will have just 1-5 employees. Generally, small businesses will have less than 50 staff.

### Structure and ownership of small businesses

The structure and ownership of small businesses are important distinguishing characteristics. Many small businesses are operated by their owner, or the owner and members of their family. They tend to play a dominant part in the financial affairs of the owner/manager and the family of the owner. As such businesses grow, however, the means of ownership tends to change from sole trader and partnership agreements to limited liability. Under sole trader or partnership arrangements, debts of the business become a personal liability of the owner. As they grow, they may move to the structure of a limited liability company. Thus the limited liability company, as the term implies, limits the personal indebtedness of the owners.

Despite the fragility of new small businesses, their ownership and management tends to be stable in the longer term. Eighty percent of firms studied in one survey had been in existence for more than five years; and 75% of the managers had been with the firm for more than five years as well. In the same survey, it was found that 53% of the businesses had been established for 20 years or more, and managers in 41% of the businesses had been with the firm 10 years or more (Houghton et al., 1986b).

Owners and managers in small businesses tend to stay in their business and their community, in contrast to larger firms or organisations, such as banks, government agencies or large rural service firms. A regional centre will therefore experience more changes in the membership of the business and administrative sector of the population because of this career pattern than will be the case in smaller towns. Thus the business community in larger towns is likely to be more flexible and adaptable to change than in very small towns.

The local business operator often plays an integral role in the life of a small community. In some rural areas, males still predominate in rural businesses but in many places woman play an active part in business operation and ownership. In the social life of the community, the business owner/manager is likely to hold

148

a position of high status because of the status of the respective business; because the influence of a manager on local employment is respected, and/or also because of personal qualities that are important to the community, such as leadership and initiative at a time of change. The business owner/manager is likely to be involved in community organisations and serve as an elected representative on local committees.

As the owner or owners personally manage small businesses, decision making is close to the community. Thus decisions in the day-by-day operation are heavily influenced by confidence in the future of the business as well as in the local economy. The confidence of business managers can be an important element in an assessment of the local economy. Willingness to hire people, or spend money on development are indicators of the ways in which the local business sector is likely to respond to change.

Consumer spending patterns are an important influence on small business and the local economy and these patterns vary by sector over time and resource cycles. This influence is illustrated by a study of spending patterns of forest sector households in rural New Zealand (Gold and Houghton, 1985). Although forestry households had a lower annual income as well as lower annual expenditure than other households, they spent proportionately more in the local area and consequently were an important element in the local economy. In this sort of instance, an assessment of changes in the forestry workforce would need to take account of the flow-on effects to local businesses in addition to any assessment at the regional level.

*Typical issues relating to impacts on small businesses*

The distinctive characteristics of small businesses will influence the way in which the local economy and community in which they are located will be affected by change. In particular, a social assessment should consider how constraints faced by small businesses limits their ability to take advantage of opportunities for development, or, alternatively, they might be more affected by negative effects than larger ones.

Small businesses face a number of problems and some are endemic, especially to new businesses, which are prone to high failure rates and susceptibility to a take-over. Problems include:

- poor management skills in one or more functional areas of the business, lack of a sound budgeting system and poor cash planning, with insufficient time or resources to plan effectively. The potential payoff for longer term planning often does not seem to justify the effort. Owner-managers are 'close' to the business so the 'formality' of a written plan does not find favour, at least until the business seeks credit approval

- the inability of small businesses, individually, to influence their markets, which are often poorly defined. Insufficient or nonexistent marketing and related planning characterise such operations, due to time and resource constraints. Much marketing is by 'word of mouth'

- a lack of public sector recognition or support. Compared with larger enterprises, local businesses face obvious constraints in lobbying central government, and government economic policy and legislation are usually orientated to the activities of large-scale enterprises, unfairly disadvantaging smaller ones

- the lack of the full range of specialist services available to large-scale enterprises. When support services must be sought from outside the business, such as specialised training or communications technologies, these may be unavailable or not affordable

- difficulty raising finance from traditional sources because of 'high risk' stereotyping, compounding the problems of a limited asset base

- dependence on a single large client or industry, and therefore vulnerability to any changes invoked by the client. This problem is especially important in many resource communities dominated by a single major industry

- dependence upon one person (the owner, or their family). If anything adverse happens to the owners, the business quickly reaches a crisis situation

- the immediate and seriously disproportionate consequences of failure to the owners of small businesses and their employees compared with the owners or shareholders of a large enterprise, where adverse results are usually dissipated over a larger number of people.

Many governments provide assistance to small businesses, either through central government agencies or regional government. Multi-lateral organisations and NGOs are also active in this regard. Efforts to encourage the small business sector and to overcome the sorts of issues identified above, are often organised and implemented at the local level. Examples include development of a local business association, a tourism promotional organisation of operators who advertise their area together, or a micro-credit scheme. Local business resource centres and development boards also offer advice, training and sometimes funding for business initiatives.

**Methods for gathering data on small businesses**

Data on small businesses are often not available in standard statistics or in other sources of secondary data such as public company reports. It is therefore useful to consider some techniques for gathering primary data on the local economy, especially to develop information about small businesses as part of a social profile.

Small businesses analysed as part the local economy for a social assessment are likely to be located in a small community or neighbourhood, possibly one that is very close knit. The analyst will need to develop a close rapport with the respondents, and build the confidence and co-operation of the business operators to assist with compiling the necessary data. This cooperation requires someone with professional business knowledge to establish credibility with the business community under study. Early contact with local business representatives or their association is useful at the scoping stage. A point in favour of such cooperation is that businesses may be able to use the information from a social assessment for other purposes, such as developing a local strategic development plan, or for promotional activities of the local business community.

Suggestions for topics that might be covered in a survey of small businesses are listed in Table 7.8. Particular questions should be drafted after considering their usefulness in the assessment, and the ease of data processing (see discussion of surveys in Chapter 6). A few well-phrased questions are likely to gain a higher return rate than a lengthy, 'academic' questionnaire (see Case study 7.3).

**Table 7.8    Examples of topics for a small business survey**

| Variable | Typical data collected |
| --- | --- |
| The main business activity | Activity by sector or sectors |
| Age of business | Number of years since it was established<br>Years current manager has operated this business |
| Employment in the business | Number and of employees, full-time, part-time<br>Number and of employees, male and female<br>Number and of employees by length of employment |
| Skills required by the business | Number and of employees by their training and/or principal skills<br>Skill needs, current and anticipated |
| Changes in employment | Change in number of employees over the last five years<br>Anticipated changes in employees in the next five years |
| Size of the business | Typical number of clients - with seasonal variations<br>Annual sales turnover for last tax year or set of accounts<br>Factors that increase and decrease the level of business activity |
| Credit requirements and use | Amount of long and short-term debt last tax year or set of accounts<br>Current level of debt servicing<br>Expected new credit needs |
| Future of the business in the local economy | Perceptions of the current business climate Views on future business climate<br>Plans for the business |

Surveys of local businesses for social assessment will usually have insufficient respondents for a detailed statistical analysis, with analysis limited to basic tabulations and cross tabulations. Qualitative data from business operators will add to the picture of a local economy.

Early dissemination of the results to the respondents and any local business grouping, with clear reference to the protection of individual confidentiality, is often necessary and helpful. A useful technique is to give participants a progress report from the research. It may also be useful to hold a meeting so that local public agencies and the community can learn about the survey results. In this way information and issues can be clarified and verified. In some cases data collection and analysis may be done in conjunction with a local committee; if this is the case it will ease the problem of gaining co-operation. This collaborative approach requires careful preparation so that the analysis and reporting procedures protect the confidentiality of the respondents.

### Case study 7.3   Assessment of impacts on local business centres

*A series of social assessments examined the potential effects of new and expanded shopping malls on existing commercial centres in the greater Auckland urban area, New Zealand. These assessments considered both the functional amenity of centres, in terms of the range of services they offered and their ease of access, and also their social amenity. Here social amenity included the social and community services found in close association with retail activity, the provision of places for leisure, recreation and socialising, and a sense of community or belonging (Taylor et al., 2003). Data for the social assessments came from studies of retail spending, surveys of residents, and interviews with providers of social services and community organisations.*

*To assess impacts on local businesses close to the proposed mall developments, semi-structured interviews were undertaken with the business operator or manager. The short (one-page) interview form included questions on the age of the business and the operator's length of ownership, the number of employees, the main business activity and perceptions of the business climate in the area. These interviews were generally conducted in the business facility, where a one-page form on a clipboard facilitated the process for the interviewer. However, the business operators were also shown plans of the proposed development and associated changes such as traffic proposals. Semi-structured questions followed based on a series of key words (see Chapter 8) to identify impacts and possible mitigation options. These impacts included traffic, parking, noise and visual effects of a mall, in addition to impacts on the local business area. Findings were reported back through community meetings and open days.*

*Analysis of social impacts showed there are reasons from a social or community perspective to base new retail development in and around existing centres so long as there is a process for managing impacts and change. This approach enables people and communities, including business operators, to provide for their social and economic well being. It enhances commercial centres as focal points for social life, and community activity and identity, within the wider urban environment, and allows for the rational development of urban infrastructure such as transport systems.*

# CONCLUSIONS

The costs and benefits of a project or planned change are often assessed at the level of the regional economy, which provides an effective comparison with any national analysis. A number of techniques are available to investigate changes in the make-up of a regional economy, drawing on both secondary data and survey research.

Knowledge of the different types of economic impacts is an important part of a social assessment. This information is likely to be of great assistance to decision makers and assists in the determination of opportunities and impacts created by projects. For example, in deciding whether forestry or tourism is the better industry for a depressed region to be developing, the number of jobs created in total is likely to be an important factor, especially if financial returns (the direct returns to the developer) are similar for each resource use. It is also important to identify how great the demand for health, education, transport, recreation, and other services will be should any project proceed.

The businesses likely to be considered in the study of a local economy, when undertaking a social assessment, will often be based in a small community or neighbourhood. Major new industrial or infrastructure developments, or restructuring of existing industries, can have considerable effects on these local economies.

Any failure, or decline, in small businesses directly and seriously affects the owner(s) and employees in contrast to larger enterprises, in which ownership and employment are dispersed over a number of activities and people. Furthermore, the success or failure of a small business is closely associated with the vitality of the local community in which these businesses are based. Where there are very large numbers of small businesses, as in major urban centres, the interaction between the community and the businesses is more diffuse and less personal. The viability of a smaller rural community is, in contrast, directly related to the local economy, which is, in turn, highly dependent on the success of small businesses.

## SUMMARY

The regional economy is an important level of analysis for resource policy and decision making. Regional economic impacts can be direct, indirect and induced. There are a number of techniques available to assess them. These are primarily multipliers and input-output analysis, including the GRIT method. These techniques are usually limited by the availability of suitable secondary data.

The regional economy also provides an important context for the local economy. At this level the assessment usually focuses on small businesses. The basic features of small businesses include, the size of turnover, number of employees and the structure of management and ownership. Most such businesses are conservatively managed and are long established in local communities.

The viability of small communities can depend heavily on the vitality of small businesses, especially in cases where one large industry dominates the business sector. Business owners and operators play a key part in the community social structure. Their operations are an important source of employment and diversity in the economy.

Research on the regional economy and small businesses often requires the collection of original data. Where surveys of businesses are conducted, it is important first to build up a rapport to ensure confidentiality of data, and later to report results back to the respondents.

# CHAPTER EIGHT

## Community-based and consultative techniques[3]

### INTRODUCTION

Community-based and consultative techniques are an integral part of the participatory approach to social assessment advanced in this book. These techniques are vital to the process of analytic induction and the triangulation and validation of information that take place in the assessment process (Chapter 5). The techniques are also important in the establishment of a participatory orientation and in enabling practice, as discussed in Chapters 2 and 3.

This chapter looks first at the philosophical and ethical basis of a participatory approach, considers the concept of community that guides community-based assessment, and provides a number of techniques.

**Participatory social assessment and the practitioner**

In addition the methodological need to be empirically strong, there are other important reasons for using community-based and consultative techniques. Practitioners of these techniques believe that people have a right to help make decisions about changes that affect them and their lives. In addition, these practitioners recognise that such decisions and their outcomes are only as good as the process by which they are generated  The aim, therefore, is a more technically competent, democratic and ethically robust process of assessment.

For the practitioner, this approach involves a personal recognition that one's own viewpoint, and one's style of decision making, may not be compatible with those of people who are proponents of change, affected by change or otherwise involved in the assessment. Some, often holding considerable power or key positions, may see public consultation and community involvement as an unnecessary impediment, or a threat to their own positions or agenda. Therefore, social assessments sometimes contend with, or challenge, the existing order. There is, however, an implicit assumption here that the practitioner has a mandate to promote constructive change, and community or individual development and empowerment.

There are some personal challenges for the practitioner in adopting a participatory approach. In anthropology it is considered vital for the ethnographer/field researcher to recognise and come to terms with their own cultural conditioning. For the psychologist or psychiatrist acting as a facilitator of personal change, it

---

[3]  We are grateful to Gerard Fitzgerald, Fitzgerald Applied Sociology, Christchurch, NZ, for input to this chapter. We suggest authorship of the chapter should be cited as Fitzgerald, Gerard; Taylor, Nick; Goodrich, Colin and Hobson Bryan.

is accepted that it is important to first recognise and accept one's own psyche and behaviour. It is also vital and healthy for the social assessment practitioner who wants to work in a consultative way to scrutinise where they are 'coming from', or their orientation, as discussed in Chapter 2. The values of practitioners are inevitably shaped by their own cultures, perhaps grounded in philosophical and ethical systems, or religious belief. Inevitably these values will be challenged by consultative and community-based research, and contradictions may emerge for them in the course of an assessment.

## A basis for enabling practice

The community-based and consultative approach acknowledges the right of interested and affected people to react to and have a say in the changes proposed. It means that the social assessment practitioner takes the opportunity to listen to people at the community level, on such things as their perception of that community, its preferred futures, problems, and current issues. This information can then be communicated to the main agents of change (such as a project developer) and incorporated into planning for and managing change.

Participatory social assessment requires active contributions from interested and affected groups and communities in defining the issues of importance to them, not simply a regurgitation of generic social impacts assembled from the literature and other commentators. These contributions require that the public is adequately informed through appropriate channels and protocols, and given adequate time to digest the information and prepare responses. As Franklin (1991) proposes with Franklin's Fulcrum: "Although there are no guarantees, the potential for public acceptance of your project is directly proportional to the amount of control you are willing to relinquish, and inversely proportional to the walls behind which you try to hide".

Community-based and consultative techniques help to redress imbalances (injustices) caused by a lack, or tight control, of information on the processes and factors influencing social change. Such imbalances are redressed by facilitating the timely distribution of information to all stakeholders and by providing for interactive questioning by them. The social assessment practitioner can also enhance this information flow by drawing on experience from previous cases.

At the community level, groups are empowered when the social assessment practitioner shares information about the planned change and responses to it. By also sharing information on how things work locally, the practitioner can help demystify decision-making processes and structures, and thereby encourage more effective participation. When members of a community have a greater sense of their own rights, the value of their own experience and how this can be used, the issues surrounding a development or proposed change can be considered more fully. This participation results in a rational and fair approach to considering benefits and disadvantages of particular proposals, and creates opportunities for 'win-win' outcomes (Case study 8.1).

*Case study 8.1   The tale of two petrol (gasoline) stations*

*Two petrol stations in Christchurch NZ were typical of many of the old-style stations providing a mechanical service and selling petrol and other oil products. Both stations were located on secondary, arterial routes from the suburbs to the city centre, and adjacent to small, local shopping centres. Modern, larger, complexes that have new layouts, self-service pumps and 'convenience' stores have largely replaced these local stations at strategic sites.*

*Each of the two stations took a different approach to development. One gained planning permission back in 1972 to locate on its current commercial site, adjacent to ten local shops on the corner. A planned extension of the station included removal of these local shops to make a complete corner site. As a result, there was considerable opposition to the plan by the tenants of the shops, and the local residents. There were many submissions in opposition by individuals, as well as the local residents' association. The local council refused planning permission for the extension and the Planning Tribunal turned down the developer's appeal, believing that the shopping centre would have remained viable (Skelton, Decision C24/91: 9). The developer pulled down the shops anyway but was unable to extend the station, leaving the site still empty in 2004 and residents angry in a loss-loss stalemate.*

*The second petrol station is also sited on a corner adjacent to local shops, and the plan was to extend it onto three adjoining residential sections. There was also potential, however, to remove the shops along one side of the site in order to open it up as a complete corner site for the station. Mindful of the difficulties faced by other companies extending stations, including the case above, the developer decided to adopt an innovative approach including social assessment with community consultation.*

*The social assessment and consultation focussed on local residents and operators of the nearby shops in a scoping exercise aimed to identify key issues. Techniques used were mainly individual interviews and a meeting with the local businesses. The initial list of issues included increased traffic and changes in traffic flows, inadequate parking around the area, lighting, noise and hours of operation, the future of the mechanical workshop and landscaping. But the most vigorous and widespread concerns were over the future of the building containing five adjacent shops owned by the developer, and the potential impact of their loss on the rest of the small shopping centre. Locals saw the loss of these shops affecting the viability of the whole shopping area, especially in the face of major mall developments in nearby suburbs. Residents did not want to lose their local shops.*

*The assessment caused the developer to modify and strengthen their plans in several ways, some of which became conditions of the planning consent. These included comprehensive landscaping on all sides, restricted hours of operation, no noisy car wash, no natural gas on site, no access off the side road, and extra car parks available to the shopping area. In this case the application for planning emphasised the consultation with affected parties and permission was granted. Most importantly, the adjacent shops were retained, and their unkempt rear areas upgraded. The shopping area remains a dynamic centre serving local residents and passing traffic, with the expanded petrol station an integral part of it.*

The advantages of a participatory approach far outweigh the disadvantages. Advantages include:

- better information on effects, including the integration of social and bio-physical effects

- use of diverse local knowledge and the expertise of a variety of people, rather than exclusive reliance on 'expert' information

- a basis for negotiation or, if necessary, mediation, with fewer of the problems inherent in expensive hearings and litigation

- less apathy and antagonism among the public because people are not continually involved in processes with disappointing outcomes

- more focussed and useful formal processes such as public submissions and hearings

- wider sharing of responsibility for the project and its outcomes

- a sound basis for monitoring, mitigation and management of change in project/programme implementation.

There are some potential difficulties and disadvantages with the approach to manage, including:

- a danger of leading people on by promising more than can be delivered, and lack of clarity by a proponent of change about the possibilities for considering alternatives

- inflexibility of participants over the positions that they take

- the risk of lowest common denominator decisions, often caused by a lack of agreement among parties on decision criteria

- consultation overload on individuals, groups or communities

- differences in the scale and context of decision making previously experienced by individuals or community groups, compared with that of the current project or programme

- potential for 'squeaky wheels' - individuals or groups to dominate the consultation with their views

- the time required for consultation

- any failure to base consultation within a full social assessment process, or assuming that public participation is social assessment.

# THE CONCEPT OF COMMUNITY

Much consultation within social assessment takes place at the local or community level, including a range of consultative field work, issue identification and the organisation of impact mitigation and management. This assessment work requires having an understanding of the bases for human affiliation and social organisation, and thus for focussing the social assessment at the local level.

Social relationships within a community are a fundamental part of social life. The community is an important level of social analysis, intimate, yet large enough to contain distinct social groups. It provides a unit for historical, political, economic, demographic, and ecological analyses. Bases for social affiliation and interaction, which shape individual and collective actions, are described below. These bases are used for grounding fieldwork at a community level.

By understanding the various bases from which social relationships are forged, it is possible to explore the various separate and overlapping networks of individuals and groups (sometimes referred to as community stakeholders) and thus plan, conduct, and evaluate the consultative social assessment.

The suggested bases for social life at the local level are developed from sociological studies of community (Hall et al., 1983; Wilkinson, 1986), and from studies of resource communities and social assessments of change arising from resource development projects (Taylor et al., 2001). The bases are an analytical device and since they interact with or depend on each other are normally used in combination. Collectively, these bases help to explain patterns of affiliation and social relationships. They also help to explain the paradox of social conflict that is often found in contrast to social cohesion in communities.

The bases for affiliation and social relationships at the local level represent contexts from which individuals take subjective meaning for their social life. For example, the analytical category of kinship could have subjective meaning in terms of family, gender in terms of mateship, or proximity in terms of neighbourliness. The bases also provide a useful set of categories for social profiling.

### The bases for community

*Proximity*

A feature of many communities is the close proximity of people who live there. So proximity is usually an overriding basis for community. In some cases, proximity is obvious, although the exact community boundaries may not be. In many rural localities the only obvious sign of community may be a shared local facility, such as a small school, church, pub, or hall yet residents will be able to agree readily on clear social boundaries, often identified by geographical features.

For many, and especially indigenous peoples, there is a close spiritual link with a particular locality and its resources and other natural features, where they or their kin reside and forge their livelihoods.

The following two examples illustrate social boundaries based on proximity. Twizel, a town built in the early 1970s specifically to house a hydro construction workforce in the open, pastoral landscape of New Zealand's Mackenzie basin, has clear physical boundaries. It also had a specific economic and social purpose. Yet, as its function broadened from its original purpose to become a centre for the rural people nearby, the social boundaries of Twizel became less distinct. The town now offers services such as schools, shops and medical facilities, new forms of association, a new source of employment, and a base for tourism to a wider rural area. Similarly, the valleys of the rugged West Coast of the South Island have dramatic physical boundaries of rivers and mountains, and each had a distinct community. Better road transport, the closure of local mines and timber mills, the development of tourism and reorganisation of social services have blurred previous social boundaries so they are no longer so topographically focussed.

Cities also commonly contain distinct localities that reflect community. These areas can be marked by topography, major highways, types of housing and commercial centres. Like rural areas, however, communities in the city that were once distinct physically are often less distinct today, through urban sprawl and the influence of new features such as shopping malls that serve a wider area. Urban places of residence are often very different from places of employment, or places of education, recreation, sport, religious worship and other places where people associate.

*Social class*

Social class based on ownership of property is a clear basis for social affiliation and social separation in many communities. The divisions often occur between those who own and control land, resources, industries and businesses, and those who do not. Among the latter might be employees of the owners, or those lacking both resources and work (i.e. the poor). Hall et al. (1983: 84) demonstrate the use of social class as a key variable in understanding community formation.

A broad analysis of social class, status and power in community life will inevitably reveal a number of distinct social groupings, exhibited in type and location of housing, for instance, and differences in working lives and social life. In developing countries, some poor may be difficult to identify since they may not be included in many areas of public social life.

*Gender*

While sex refers to biological and universal differences between males and females, the concept of gender goes further to refer to the social difference between them. These differences vary between cultures and social contexts over time. Gender-based differences in social life include labour and work practices (including paid and unpaid employment), child rearing, and work inside the home. Project analysis has often focussed on the commercial activities of men, such as increased cash income for men's agricultural labour, but ignored the work of women and children, say collecting water or fuel wood. Indeed, a project may cause net positive impacts for the labour of one gender group and net negative impacts for another. In many places women remain in the subsistence economy, and women-headed households are often over-represented among the poor, thereby shaping and significantly limiting their social lives. Gender also shapes political processes and participation, including community leadership.

*Work*

Work is an important basis for community relationships. In rural areas, distinct social relationships are based upon activities such as farming, forestry, mining, tourism and fishing (Taylor et al., 2001). Sometimes a community is distinguished by the dominant type of work, as in a mining town or fishing village. When social relationships are forged around the work of males in particular, such as in logging or mining, the social life of women and families are also part of these occupational communities. In these communities a strong distinction often exists between the status of men's work, and women's unpaid work in the home, or in community organisations and social services. Work in the dominant industry might be very different from that available in the service or business sector, or from other less recognised industries such as outdoor recreation.

*Ethnicity*

Ethnicity represents the social and cultural identity of different groups. The concept can enlighten us about different cultural perceptions, values, behaviour, social organisation and social status. In New Zealand, for instance, there is a particular historical need to understand the concept of 'tangata whenua' (literally people of the land) for the indigenous Maori people in relation to all other ethnic groups. This sensitivity follows increasing recognition of the 1840 Treaty of Waitangi, between Maori and the British Crown, in shaping rights and participation in resource management.

Ethnicity is an important factor in the process of community formation in rural communities where there are ethnically diverse, incoming workforces. Ethnicity is also a key factor in rapidly expanding urban areas, where increasing demand for labour is met by migrating people of different ethnic backgrounds seeking economic opportunities in the city. Extended family relationships are important in this type of migration as a family in the new location attracts members from the home area (i.e. chain migration). These relationships form the basis for a variety of organisations and activities in the urban environment. Examples of recent emigrant groups in urban New Zealand bringing new forms of social life include people from the Pacific Islands and people from Asia.

*Kinship*

Kinship is a strong basis for social relationships and networks. Although Hall et al. (1983) note that in New Zealand settler society kinship does not always have the richness of European kinship systems, kinship is a principal basis for community relationships. In Maori communities, and for Maori living outside their tribal area, kinship and patterns of whanau (family), hapu (extended family) and iwi (tribe), are vital bases for social affiliation.

In many societies kinship is an important influence on the location of family homes. It shapes patterns of land ownership and the means of generating wealth and passing on wealth. Where wealth and land are handed down through male or female lines, kinship can reinforce patterns of class and gender.

*Age and length of residence*

Length of residence is important as a basis for social groupings in many localities. Age and length of residence are factors in the development of kinship ties, and the accumulation of property, wealth and social status. Where there are rapid population changes, as with an incoming project workforce, or even the seasonal movements of casual rural labour, there is a ready distinction to be made between 'old timers' and 'new comers'. Length of residence in respect to family or tribal affiliations has an ultimate expression in a place to stand, or have one's 'roots'. Different patterns of social life, employment or housing, can usually be found for youth, young couples, families with children, or the elderly.

In a discussion of the problem of gaining access to a rural community for social research, Hall (1987) draws a distinction between 'locals' and 'non locals' that social assessors find useful. He sees these two groupings as reflecting a 'focus of interest' rather than length of residence per se. Nevertheless, length of residence is clearly a factor since, in many places, being local implies that one has been born in a particular locality. But it also implies a distinction that ties back to ownership of property. Landowners tend to be local, and newcomers who own land, as well as the incoming spouses of locals, tend to be more readily accepted, at least as 'new locals'. In most rural localities both professional and working-class people, and people living in an area for reasons of lifestyle, are usually transients in the eyes of locals.

*Religion*

In many western societies, religion might appear to have a greatly reduced influence on modern community formation. But it is possible to identify localities, rural and urban, where different religious affiliation is a strong basis for community relationships, often linked to ethnicity. Places of worship can play an important part in community relationships despite decreased formal participation or 'church' going. Religious groupings often form an umbrella for a variety of social services and voluntary organisations, with activities ranging from the creative arts to employment creation, and with views varying from conservative fundamentalism to radical social action. Furthermore, a revival of religious participation in some places is a basis for strong group cohesion and identity.

## CONSULTATIVE METHODS

There are a variety of consultative techniques used in social assessment. The most important techniques used in a consultative approach typically fit under the heading of qualitative research. In its simplest form this research consists of personal interviews with individuals or small groups, as well as observation and participation in local activities and community life. This work may be supplemented by quantitative techniques such as surveys and use of statistical data. Fitzgerald (2003) provides suggestions for recording, handling and analysing qualitative data.

Other consultation techniques are summarised in Table 8.1, with further techniques for information sharing in Table 8.2.

### Interviews

Interviews in social assessment are usually dynamic, in contrast to the one-way gathering of data in structured or semi-structured surveys. Interviews are often the first time that community members have had direct contact with anyone working on the proposed change. Sharing of information on other groups and their concerns, providing insights on the way things seem to work locally, and advising on the formal processes that may be involved in the development are all part of the exchange. As noted, this activity can put the practitioner into the role of a change agent as he or she enters as a participant into the local society, a position that can create some dilemmas and conflicts.

Interviews give the social assessment practitioner opportunities to check information from secondary sources or information given by others (i.e. what has been referred to in Chapter 5 as triangulation). They also allow the practitioner to establish relationships with the community and its members, and to clarify and establish roles for the team. Interviews encourage community members and groups to participate in the decision-making process, to link up with other local groups and individuals, and to gain access to information and other resources.

Interviews are usually carried out with those people most closely affected by or involved in the project development, with members of the community or groups, and with service providers. Members of the community most commonly targeted for interviews are key actors in various aspects of community life, including formal and informal representatives of interest groups and organisations. Such people might typically be:

- local social service providers, such as teachers and school principals, preschool workers, public health workers and general practitioners, community police personnel, local clergy, social workers and community workers

- local community councillors and committee members, district and city council representatives and officials

- tribal or community elders

- representatives of a residents' association

- shop owners and business people, and their associations and promotion groups

- representatives of service clubs and other voluntary groups

- women's organisations

- sports and recreation organisers and leaders

- special interest group representatives (e.g. youth, disabled, elderly).

Valuable interviewees or informants can also include relatively new arrivals in the area, those with some social science training or interest, outsiders and 'oddballs'. Most social assessment researchers also find that casual and unplanned contacts can prove very valuable sources of information and insight. Such opportunities are valuable for verifying issues and checking information received elsewhere (Case study 8.2).

Interviews therefore allow the researcher to:

- observe people in their own environments

- gather information (using a semi or unstructured question format)

- provide information about the project, previous projects and their outcomes.

The sorts of information typically gathered include:

- assessment of present understandings about a proposal (and the extent of information distribution)

- insights into the structure of the community and how it works, its history, ecology, and economy

- identification of present and future issues, including project impacts, for the groups contacted

- identification of human and other resources available

- further contacts and entry into networks for further interviewing and discussion.

## Case study 8.2 Interviews

*Interviews were used extensively as part of an assessment of a proposed dam for hydro-electricity generation in the Clutha River valley, New Zealand. A key aim of the interviews, carried out in people's homes, was to identify and describe the interest groups and stakeholders present in the large, sparsely settled rural area of the valley. Communities in such areas lack obvious proximity, or settlement focus, and are instead characterised by patterns of social behaviour. Individuals interviewed identified activities, patterns of interaction, communication channels and support networks that were checked in subsequent interviews. The snowballing technique used to select interviewees included most residents of the valley and the key people providing services to them. This technique enabled the assessor to identify and profile local communities and describe important aspects of local culture. Population statistics and communication channels were later analysed using the boundaries identified.*

*Interviews also provided residents with information on the project, its parameters and organisational arrangements. Issues having an impact on each family and community, as well as their strategies for responding to these impacts, were thus identified. This interview work meant the assessment could include a description of the close interrelations between local communities, their social histories and structures, and local farming practices, and potential impacts on these, for consideration in the planning process.*

## Meetings

Participation in meetings is often an essential part of any community-based and consultative fieldwork. There are generally two types of meetings: those organised by local groups in which their concerns about a change are being discussed, and those facilitated in the course of a social assessment. Both types of meetings provide opportunities to observe participants while information is exchanged between the assessment team and local groups.

Discussions that take place at appropriately scheduled meetings throughout the assessment can contribute much to the different stages of the project. During meetings issues may be identified, data collection initiated, explained and facilitated, and findings validated. There are a number of different types of meetings and workshops that might be organised as part of a social assessment (see Table 8.1).

### Small group meetings

Small group meetings are often most successful when they are informal and only semi-structured. They generally enable the practitioner to do most of the things he or she would attempt during interviews, although this time it is with a group. While allowing observation of the dynamics of the group in action, small group meetings enable a better focus on specific issues and interests. They also provide a good opportunity for the group to do more in-depth questioning of the assessment team. The assessment can thus promote interaction between local interest groups by bringing their members together in small group meetings and by suggesting to particular groups new methods of functioning and interacting with others.

Opportunities to hold informal meetings occur frequently and should be seized upon if offered. Alternatively, meetings can be arranged through an intermediary or 'key actor'. This technique is illustrated with an example from fieldwork on a coal mine development project (Case study 8.3).

### Case study 8.3  Small group meetings

*Fieldwork was conducted to assess the impacts of a proposed new coal mine development on the West Coast, New Zealand. A short interview with the miners union president led to an invitation for the two researchers to meet four members of the union committee nearby. This meeting initiated a two-way exchange of information and allowed the miners to focus on issues important to them. Some of these had arisen out of the recent corporatisation (including many 'lay offs') of the government coal mining agency. These issues had important implications for planning the workforce of the new project. The meeting led in turn to a detailed guided tour of the mine, with an invaluable introduction to the traditional work environment of underground coal mining, (an environment that was likely to change dramatically with the new development) and an extended interview with managers of the mine.*

*Another valuable meeting took place at the instigation of the mayor of the local town, who was able quickly to bring together various borough council officers and a neighbouring county councillor to discuss local issues and early reactions to the proposal. The mining project manager was also present at that gathering. Other informal meetings included one with another mayor in the local pub.*

*Later in the assessment, informal neighbourhood and interest groups meetings were organised in the study area using intermediaries. These meetings allowed issues identified in the assessment to be elaborated upon, as well as options for their mitigation and strategies for their management to be initiated (including the idea of a community liaison group).*

Small groups are usually most effective when they involve five to ten people and have two people facilitating and taking notes between them. It is important to pay attention to the process of the groups, and there is ample guidance in the adult education literature. Good meetings are carefully planned and have a focus and clear objectives. They also set out ground rules for conduct during the meeting such as limiting discussion, dealing with conflict and encouraging creative and divergent thinking. These more structured, small-group meetings are often called 'focus groups'. The discussion in the meeting is usually focussed on the issues that have been identified during the scoping work of the assessment.

*Large and more formal meetings*

Large and more formal meetings or workshops need to be properly facilitated and representative of the community. They allow for:

• wide dissemination of information, providing that good use is made of audio-visual presentation methods

• observation of the community in action, especially the nature of major groups of interest and operation of power

• direct contact between the community and project and the chance to observe the interaction. Such contact usually requires the developers to deal directly with community reaction.

Workshop techniques designed to explore issues and options, and develop scenarios, are summarised in Table 8.1.

'Old-style' public meetings can present problems. They are usually too structured, often in favour of project promoters. There are bound to be hidden personal and group agendas revealed by some individuals in these meetings, making consultation and facilitation difficult. There is a great deal of potential for the meeting to be diverted from its main purpose, bogged in detail, dominated by 'squeaky wheels' or frustrated by confrontation.

*Case study 8.4 The use of formal meetings*

*An example of the use of meetings in participatory fieldwork is provided by a preliminary social assessment of lignite development in Otago and Southland in New Zealand. It soon became evident in this assessment that a large number of farmers could be directly affected by the proposed development. There could be important implications facing farmers and rural communities beyond the obvious direct effects of opencast mining and a new petro-chemical industry. Federated Farmers was the focal organisation representing farmer interests and officials wanted the study team to meet with their members. Consequently, meetings were held with people living on or near each of the nine coal deposits.*

*The selection of contact organisations for the meetings required sensitivity to the different areas. For instance, the team aligned itself with Federated Farmers in one area, but not in another area where farmers were highly independent or members of other organisations. Key people were used to invite members of the local communities and introduce meetings in the second farming area.*

*At each meeting the field team of three made a presentation using audio visual aids extensively. The proposed industry was described, as were issues identified in the study to date. Then discussion was lead by the team. Informal talks were held before and after the meeting and during supper. A short questionnaire was filled out by participants at each meeting.*

167

*Originally the team believed that most discussion would focus on the issues of land compensation and land rehabilitation evident during the round of initial, scoping interviews. But the discussion was, in fact, very wide ranging and provided a valuable information base for the assessment including the development of scenarios of change.*

*Meetings were also held in the towns and boroughs near coal deposits. Again, key contacts were used to organise each meeting. People with 'social interests' were specifically involved: the local county planning officer, doctor, health nurse, school principal, police officer, minister, business manager and union representative, for example. In the nearest city this approach was extended by holding separate meetings with people working in social-community development, and with business people. Other organisations, education, health, police, trades and local council, were approached individually. In these meetings key local social issues were identified and then the impacts of the proposed major industrial development was considered. For example, alcoholism, integration of newcomers and family welfare were all identified as key current issues that would probably be even more important given a rapidly expanding immigrant workforce in a town.*

*Two major seminars were held and were important foci for the assessment. These seminars were an opportunity for the study team to meet in a forum with local people conversant with the many topics included in the study. The seminars were important because they involved, as hosts, the two regional councils in the study areas. Seminar participants included representatives from local bodies, government agencies, interest groups, local experts and interested individuals. The first seminar concentrated on identifying issues, the second on revising and elaborating upon research needs and their scheduling. Each seminar began with a presentation by the assessment team and was followed by an afternoon of workshop sessions.*

*A relatively high profile was obtained through the media during the assessment, both in newspapers and radio. Reports about the assessment and meetings were included in local newspapers and monitored by the team. Radio reports were given on local stations and national networks. In addition, there were a number of stories carried about other aspects of lignite use and research. The consequent high public awareness of current issues and the work of the assessment team greatly assisted the fieldwork. In arranging meetings or interviews, for example, it was found that respondents usually knew something about the team and its work. The media reports also allowed feedback from the meetings and seminars to a much wider audience.*

## Liaison forums

Public meetings, especially the sorts of seminars described above, can develop into ongoing consultation forums that provide for regular liaison between community representatives and the project developer. The Waihi Liaison Forum is an example (Case study 8.5). These liaison forums can provide an important basis for ongoing monitoring and the mitigation and management of impacts.

### Case study 8.5 Liaison forum

*The Waihi Liaison Forum was initiated in May 1982 by the Waihi Gold Company Incorporated, the developers of the Martha Hill Project in the Coromandel, New Zealand. The Forum arose out of a perceived need by the Company and others to have structures "through which information about the project could be disseminated and feedback received so that the social consequences of the project could be ascertained and considered" (Drury, 1983: 27). The Forum was established early in the planning of the project as the main means of building and maintaining links with the community, and the fact that the Forum continued through the construction phase of the project is testimony to its success. The Forum was also seen as a means of overcoming the limitations of the one-off 'snapshot' gained by environmental impact reports, which do not capture the dynamics of the community nor the likely effects of any proposed change.*

*The Waihi Liaison Forum comprised representatives from most local groups and organisations from Waihi Borough and its environs. Meetings were open to the public. Forum meetings, which occurred about every two to three months during project planning, were run using usual meeting procedure rules but were informal enough to allow members of the public to contribute along with group representatives. Forum meetings tended to focus on a previously determined topic or issue area and speakers/experts from outside the study area were usually invited. Social and community impacts were well down the list of concerns for the community, at least until relatively late in the project development.*

*Naturally, conflict and some (warranted) cynicism surfaced, since the company, as both the organiser of the Forum and information giver, was able to exercise considerable control over the process. As some members of the local community and Forum were also keen to exploit the development for their own personal gain, the company, understandably, limited the dissemination of sensitive business information. Some critics of the Forum felt that it tended to soften valid and healthy opposition to the project, while others had trouble keeping up with the dynamic nature of the development process in a changing community. In any event the Liaison Forum promoted community development and clearly facilitated dialogue and discussion, as well as bringing diverse groups together for the first time.*

**Table 8.1     Consultative techniques: workshops/liaison groups**

| Technique | Uses | Advantages | Other Aspects |
|---|---|---|---|
| *Workshops, seminars* Typically one-day exercises looking at specific issues or wider, long term planning questions. | For planners, researchers, community members, politicians to come together to hear and participate in discussion on issues facing the community. | Most useful if focussed on a well defined problem or set of local issues. Can encourage participation in planning and bring together various groups for an exchange of viewpoints. Can take a variety of forms - from focussing on key speakers or papers to small group working sessions. Other techniques can be included. | Tend to favour joiners and those few who are willing and able to speak out. Formality can even discourage participation of those attending. Requires participants to have a block of time to devote to the exercise and costs can be off-putting. Also requires organisation of venue, speakers (if any), refreshments and equipment. Administrative support on the day may also be necessary. |
| *Liaison Forums and Community Committees* Organised ad hoc or semi- permanent group of representatives from community organisations, neighbourhoods, etc. who review, discuss, evaluate and advise on planned changes on behalf of the community. | Useful for project liaison, social monitoring, and providing feedback of information from experts to a community. Usefulness depends on composition and size of the group, its standing and relative power. Can advise on resource allocation, alert attention to problems, and muster expertise to manage change. | Can act as liaison between the various actors in the change situation - local and central government, developers, official agencies and community groups and grass roots. Brings best of local expertise and experience to bear. Can focus community concerns and responses. Depends on standing of the participants and the committee and their connections to key agencies etc. | May be seen as unrepresentative, as duplicating local councils (in small communities), as reinforcing unbalanced power structures, or as self seeking. May not be able to focus or muster community resources and expertise. Participants may have no real commitment. Membership can change a lot. |
| *Scenario Assessment* Proposals and their alternatives are assessed for their outcomes and impacts using scenarios. Groups assess the scenarios and the results are compared. Groups can be used to address only one scenario each. Can be extended using surveys, e.g. Delphi. | Used with groups to explore the impacts of alternative proposals and to educate the participants. | Helps in identifying and focusing on impacts. If only one scenario is assessed by each group, each scenario can be treated equally. Final analysis requires skill. Preferred scenario/s should be discussed in a second round. | Scenarios require careful preparation with inclusion of all relevant factors and assumptions. May be subject to bias of those who prepare the scenarios or contain incomplete information. Requires availability of information and willingness to share this out. |

| Technique | Uses | Advantages | Other Aspects |
|---|---|---|---|
| *Role Playing/ Simulation Games* People take on roles of others or various actors in the community or authority in a real, simulated or analogous planning situation. | In a group situation gives people the opportunity to appreciate the positions of others involved in the planning process and the constraints and influences on them. | Opens people up to other viewpoints, promotes tolerance, helps build empathy and provides skills. Enables options to be identified in a creative way. | Best seen and used as complement to wider programme of education and relation building. Requires careful planning and allocation of roles. Adequate information, briefing and extensive debriefing are critical to get maximum gain and to resolve difficulties encountered. A skilful facilitator is mandatory. |
| *Charette* An intensive planning exercise where a small group of participants spends a series meetings, often over several days, discussing questions relating to a specific problem, to reach a consensus view within a defined deadline. | Intensive, accelerated process of arriving at a solution or agreeing on decisions. Can facilitate good in-depth communication and relations. Often used for community visioning and planning exercises but these require follow-up to ensure there is implementation. | Aim for representative group. This involves careful selection. Pose the problem in terms the participants understand and relate to. Useful where you want to develop solutions to a specific problem, or resolve issues. | Requires blocks of time from the participants. Too many experts can inhibit discussion. Participants may not be representative of the community. A suitable venue, accommodation, childcare etc., must be funded. |
| *Issue scoping* A group process for impact scoping and assessment. With the help of a facilitator, small groups identify, list, then web and chain, social impacts. Stakeholders are identified for each impact or impact chain. Process can then be discussed and vacillated with the larger group. Requires main facilitator, assistants and venue. | Assists scoping and issues identification. Larger groups (separate or as part of larger group) can quickly identify and appreciate the impacts of a proposal or policy. Concerns are shared and particular group concerns noted for action or more detailed assessment. Helps set priorities and identify stakeholders. | Simple to run, interesting, easy to participate, and very productive in a short time. Helps groups with different backgrounds or disciplines prioritise issues and communicate these to one another and promoters of change. Aids in scoping, and focussing social assessment studies and responses to change. | Number of concurrent small groups limited by assistants or facilitators. May be difficult to coordinate in larger or plenary group. The process has to be managed to ensure everyone has a say and a few views don't dominate. |
| *Impact scoring* A group activity for assessing significance of impacts. The whole group is provided with information about a proposal or policy. This is discussed and impacts identified and listed. Smaller groups then score and order impacts according to their significance. The scores of each small group are used to provide an overall score for each impact. | Helps groups and individuals to identify and understand the impacts of projects etc., and identify their own priorities and values | Forces people to think about the situation of change, to discuss their assumptions, to recognise their own knowledge about an issue, area or situation, and to systematically consider impacts of change. | The larger goup must be broken into small groups (often limited to 3 persons each). Can be frustrating if it does not result in action on significant impacts or further participation in the decision-making process. |

## Other consultative techniques

A host of other techniques are available to stimulate and carry out community consultation and obtain community input to planning, decision making and management of change. Some of these techniques are mentioned elsewhere including community surveys, local information offices, project open days, talk-back radio, and simulation games (see Table 8.2). There are other techniques available in the area of Participatory Appraisal, sometimes known as Participatory Learning and Action (see, for example, Kumar 2003 for a comprehensive guide, and the notes series at www.iied.org). A number of publications provide overviews and details of on techniques. For Australian readers in particular, Sarkissian (1997) provides a handbook on workshops. For Canada and the United States, Roberts (2003) and Burdge and Roberston (1998) provide overviews and details of 'public involvement'.

**Table 8.2    Consultative techniques: information sharing**

| Technique | Uses | Advantages | Other Aspects |
|---|---|---|---|
| *Freephone/hotline* A telephone-based system where callers receive or give information on issues. Toll calls are paid by the sponsoring organisation. Could be manned or unmanned. | If manned, this system can be used to receive submissions, comments on issues etc. Issues are noted and followed up; individuals may be contacted further if necessary. If unmanned/automated, only basic information can be given or received. | Quick information system. Easy informal contact for callers, unthreatening for those who don't find it easy to participate or speak out. Can run in conjunction with public information campaigns. | Can become bogged down with calls unrelated to the issue; requires right staff; expensive if freephone service. Requires a systematic process for processing and analysing information obtained. |
| *Information Centres/Displays* Can take the form of a permanent office (e.g. shop with street access) or a mobile centre e.g. van or bus, where information is presented. Often held in a community centre or hall. | Useful for displaying and presenting information to the general public or specific target groups, and for getting informal reactions to proposals. Can be used to scope issues and setting up further activities. Tends to be used by larger organisations and projects. | Enables information to be accessed by large number of people at their own pace, to present information in an attractive and graphic form Provides a point of contact between proposers or researchers and the community. If mobile or moved around can be targeted for particular groups and communities. | Requires advertising, good location, availability of informed field staff, access to appropriate premises or vehicle and careful presentation of displays etc. However, they can be regarded by some as 'slick sell' of powerful interests and dominant viewpoints, and the proponent may think this technique is all they have to do. |

| Technique | Uses | Advantages | Other Aspects |
|---|---|---|---|
| *Radio (and Talkback)* Local radio including University and community access radio. | Used to prepare and present documentaries, discussion and talk-back programmes to increase community awareness of planning issues and responses to these. | Can give wide airing of issues affecting local communities by providing opportunity for direct public feedback and discussion. All viewpoints offered can be heard by all, and some will participate because the format usually provides for anonymity and is informal. | Tends to allow for only shallow, often 'hyped' discussion of single issues, and the audience gets lost or confused. Individual callers get very limited time to present their views, many of which are likely to be off the point. Programmes require good preparation, an informed presenter, and the cooperation of a community-minded radio station. |
| *Newsletters* Can take a variety of forms and be produced at what ever frequency is required. Mostly used by local authorities and established organisations and developers. | Used to feed information to interested individuals, groups and organisations, as a communication with wide or specialised audiences, to provoke discussion for feedback or further action and signal forthcoming events and activities. | Encourages and stimulates public and specific group awareness and involvement in planning and other matters. Keeps people over a wide area in touch with key happenings and feedback. Can easily provide a lot of focussed information to readers. | Tends to be only one way communication, susceptible to bias of the editor, and frequently aren't read by the recipients. Requires staff or team to produce and to have access to printing/copying facilities. Mailing and material costs involved. |
| *Internet websites* An information facility publicly available via computer and the 'web'. Sites with restricted access are called intranet. Can include current information and archives (files). Usually navigated from a home page with contacts available for followup. | Useful for providing information in summary form and also in detail, such as a draft impact report available for downloading. Can include pictures. | Makes a lot of technical information readily available to a computer user without having to obtain a copy of the original material. Easily browsed, often through a search facility. Can be updated as information is available. | Only available to people with suitable computers, phone-lines or satellite connections, with the ability to handle internet quickly, and people with the necessary skills. Mostly a one-way flow of information although short questionnaires and comments facilities are used. |
| *Newspapers* Community, local and regional newspapers, specialist magazines etc. Local newspapers are often prepared to include a special feature or information insert. | Can be used for advertisements, articles on planning, proposals, issues etc. Can incorporate limited questionnaires. Need to know about target audience and reading habits. Good source of information for research e.g. issues, activities, clubs and societies, key individuals and for gaining historical view. | Wide audience can be reached with advertisements and articles, and feedback can be received in letters to the editor. Excellent for covering community issues if at local level. | Depth of reporting can be variable and superficial, especially at community newspaper level. Limited utility of questionnaire data collected through newspapers. Requires development of a good relationship with the media and help in improving their coverage and knowledge of community issues. This requires a knowledge of the role of the media in the community. |

*Case study 8.6   Stakeholder involvement in policy formation*

*Case study 5.1 introduced the application of social assessment into integrated research and policy formation related to mercury in the food chain. The Mobile-Alabama River Basin where the assessment focussed (Samya et al., 2003), drains 70% of the state of Alabama, a region characterised by poverty levels ranging from 20-40% of county populations, low educational attainment, and lack of access to basic human services. The sport fishing industry is large in the state, and many residents depend on catching or buying fish from public waters to meet their nutritional requirements. Research findings of high mercury levels in fish had the potential of polarising stakeholders to nullify effective remedial policies. The primary challenge of the social assessment was to involve stakeholders having influence on policy into the research process, to avoid stalemate over issues and to translate bio-physical findings into their social implications and remedial policies. These premises guided the effort, stakeholders*
- *have the right to be informed and involved at the inception of a policy and decisions affecting them*
- *have equal standing in the assessment process*
- *can be a legitimate and vital source of information.*

*Accordingly, consultation in small group meetings, informal interviews and exchanges of information, a newsletter and telephone hotline about the research, angler participation in data gathering, and the use of resident expert knowledge were employed before and during the course of the bio-physical research. Stakeholders included a major utility company, a coal bed methane industry association, state health, environment, and fishery officials, environmental groups, and recreational and commercial anglers.*

*Early and ongoing involvement of stakeholders in framing dialogue about the research in terms of its social implications not only avoided issue polarisation, but constructive discussion and debate ensued with key stakeholders regarding both short and long-term remedial policies. Full knowledge and cooperation with state and industry officials about the research helped secure an invitation to present preliminary findings to a national 'Mercury Forum'. During the course of the project, dangerously high amounts of methyl mercury (i.e. mercury in its organic form) were found in people who consumed seafood out of the Gulf of Mexico. Since thriving recreational and commercial fishing industries are based on these waters, the issue dominated the news, and the Mercury Forum was held to inform policy officials and secure funding for additional research. Thus, mercury as a public health issue was expanded from coastal to fresh waters of the state, and funding opportunities generated to reach high-risk groups.*

*The continual push of bio-physical findings to social effects enabled researchers from diverse disciplinary backgrounds to interact effectively and work truly as an interdisciplinary team. Social scientists aided in data collection and bio-physical scientists explained the research in lay language to stakeholder groups. The project team received valuable information from scientists representing industry and state oversight agencies, as well as data collection assistance and expression of concerns by those who fished public waters.*

# CONCLUSIONS

Community-based and consultative social assessment involves the acknowledgement of the right of communities and their members to contribute to decisions affecting them. The social assessment practitioner is responsible for informing and facilitating a two-way communication process. The practitioner's role is therefore frequently one of a change agent, facilitating opportunities for community participation in the process of social assessment.

In particular, the techniques described in this last chapter require the practitioner to consider the importance of channels of information flow and questions of 'enabling practice'. We believe this enabling practice is essential to obtaining some 'middle ground' in social assessment, and in turning the field towards a proactive and integrated approach, as outlined throughout the book.

This book advances an issues-orientated approach to the process of social assessment, a process for research, planning and management of change arising from projects, programmes and policies. The approach is consultative in nature. Consultation with interested and affected parties is initiated during scoping, and continues through all other parts of the process. Techniques of consultation provide an important source of qualitative data about issues and effects, to complement quantitative data.

# SUMMARY

Community-based and consultative techniques are an integral part of the issues-oriented approach to social assessment. However, the practitioner needs to understand the bases for social affiliation at the local level, which include proximity, class, gender, work, ethnicity, kinship, religion, age and length of residence.

Consultative techniques provide qualitative information to augment quantitative and documentary data obtained through secondary sources and surveys. They often complete the 'triangulation' of information required to validate an issue. The techniques provide both a personal philosophical challenge and a technical challenge to the practitioner.

A variety of specialised, consultation techniques can be selected to add to the information base of the assessment, and to establish flows of information.

Techniques described include interviews, both formal and informal, with informants from groups involved in the process of change. These interviews are often carried out with key informants, using a networking approach for selection of interviewees.

Meetings are a further useful device. Small group meetings, discussion sessions and workshops are particularly useful. Larger meetings have limited use and can produce negative results. Ongoing liaison forums can be important for monitoring, and the management of longer term changes.

# REFERENCES

Asian Development Bank 1994. Handbook for incorporation of social dimensions in projects. Social Development Unit, Asian Development Bank, Manila.

Baines, James; Morgan, Bronwyn and Brigid Buckenham 2003a. From technology-focused rules to socially responsible implementation: an SIA of proposed home heating rules in Christchurch, New Zealand. *Impact Assessment and Project Appraisal, 21(3):*187-194.

Baines, James; McClintock, Wayne; Taylor, Nick and Buckenham, Brigid 2003b. Using local knowledge. Chapter 3 in Henk Becker and Frank Vanclay (Eds.), *Handbook of Social Impact Assessment, Conceptual and Methodological Advances*, Edward Elgar, Cheltenham.

Baines, James and Taylor, Nick 2002. Institutionalising SIA in rapidly developing economies - the Malaysian case. Paper presented at the 22nd Annual Conference of the International Association for Impact Assessment, The Hague, The Netherlands, 15-21 June.

Becker, Henk 2003. Theory formation and application in social impact assessment. Chapter 9 in Henk Becker and Frank Vanclay (Eds.), *Handbook of Social Impact Assessment, Conceptual and Methodological Advances*, Edward Elgar, Cheltenham.

Becker, Henk and Vanclay, Frank (Eds.) 2003. *Handbook of Social Impact Assessment, Conceptual and Methodological Advances.* Edward Elgar, Cheltenham.

Berger, P.L. and Berger, B. 1976. *Sociology: a Biographical Approach.* Penguin Educational Books, Auckland.

Bowles, R.T. 1981. *Social Impact Assessment in Small Communities.* Butterworth and Co. (Canada) Ltd, Toronto.

Bowles, R.T. 1982. *Little Communities and Big Industries: Studies in the Social Impact of Canadian Resource Extraction.* Butterworth and Co. (Canada) Ltd, Toronto.

Bradbury, J.H. and St. Martin, I. 1983. Winding down in a Quebec mining town: a case study of Schefferville. *The Canadian Geographer, 17(2):* 128-144.

Branch, K.; Hooper, D.A.; Thompson, J. and Creighton, J. 1984. *Guide to Social Assessment: a Framework for Assessing Social Change.* Westview Press, Boulder Colorado.

Brown, A.L. and Therivel, R. 2000. Principles to guide the development of strategic environmental assessment methodology. *Impact Assessment and Project Appraisal*, 18(3): 183-189.

Bryan, C.H. 1977. Leisure value systems and recreational specialisation: the case of trout fishermen. *Journal of Leisure Research, 9(3):* 174-187.

Bryan, C.H. 1979. Conflict in the great outdoors: toward understanding and managing for diverse sportsmen preferences. *Social Studies No.4,* Bureau of Public Administration, University of Alabama, Tuscaloosa.

Bryan, C.H. 1983. A social science perspective for managing recreational conflict. In R.H. Stroud (Ed.), Marine Recreational Fisheries, Sport Training Institute, Washington, D.C.

Bryan, C.H. 1995. Social impact analysis: principles and procedures. Ecosystem Management, USDA Forest Service, Washington, DC.

Bryan, C.H. and Hendee, J.C. 1983. Social impact analysis in U.S. Forest Service decisions; background and proposed principles. In E.V Maurice and W.A. Fleischman (Eds.), *Sociology and Social Impact Analysis in Federal Resource Management Agencies.* United States Department of Agriculture, Forest Service, Washington, D.C.

Bryan, C. H. and Taylor, C.N. 1987. Towards an outdoor recreation resource policy. *Policy Studies Review, 7(2):* 349-358.

Burdge, R. 1985. Social impact assessment and the planning process. *Planning and Public Policy, 11.* Bureau of Urban and Regional Planning Research, University of Illinois.

Burdge, R.J. 1991. A brief history and major trends in the field of impact assessment. *Impact Assessment Bulletin*, 9(4): 93-104.

Burdge, Rabel J. 1994 (revised 1998). *A Community Guide to Social Impact Assessment.* Social Ecology Press, Middleton.

Burdge, Rabel J. (Ed.) 1998. *A Conceptual Approach to Social Impact Assessment: Collection of Writings by Rabel J. Brudge and Colleagues, Revised Edition.* Social Ecology Press, Middleton.

Burdge, R.J. 2002. Why is social impact assessment the orphan of the assessment process? *Impact Assessment and Project Appraisal,* 18(3): 3-9.

Burdge, Rabel J. (Guest Ed.) 2003. Special issue on the practice of social impact assessment, Parts I and II. *Impact Assessment and Project Appraisal,* 21(2) and 21(3).

Burdge, Rabel J. and Johnson, Sue 1998. Social impact assessment: developing the basic model. Chapter 2 in Rabel, J. Burdge (Ed.), *A Conceptual Approach to Social Impact Assessment: Collection of writings by Rabel J. Brudge and Colleagues, Revised Edition*, Social Ecology Press, Middleton.

Burdge, Rabel J. and Robertson, Robert A. 1998. Social impact assessment and the public involvement process. Chapter 13 in Rabel, J. Burdge (Ed.), *A Conceptual Approach to Social Impact Assessment: Collection of writings by Rabel J. Brudge and Colleagues, Revised Edition*, Social Ecology Press, Middleton.

Burdge, R.J. and Vanclay, F. 1995. Social impact assessment. Chapter 2 in F. Vanclay and D. Bronstein (Eds.), *Environmental and Social Impact Assessment*, John Wiley and Sons, Chichester.

Butcher, G.V. 1985. Regional income, output and employment multipliers: their uses and estimates of them. Economics Division, Ministry of Agriculture and Fisheries, Wellington.

Butcher, G.; Fairweather, J. and Simmons, D.G. 1998. The economic impact of tourism on Kaikoura. Tourism Recreation and Research Centre (TRREC) Report No. 8/1998. Lincoln University.

Butcher, G.; Fairweather, J. and Simmons, D.G. 2000. The economic impact of tourism on Rotorua. Tourism Recreation and Research Centre (TRREC) Report No. 17/2000. Lincoln University.

Butcher, G.; Fairweather, J. and Simmons, D.G. 2001. The economic impact of tourism on Westland District. Tourism Recreation and Research Centre (TRREC) Report No. 26/2001. Lincoln University.

Butcher, G.; MacDonald, G.; Fairweather, J. and Simmons, D.G. 2003. The economic impact of tourism on Christchurch City and Akaroa Township. Tourism Recreation and Research Centre (TRREC) Report No. 37/2003. Lincoln University.

Casley, D.J. and Kumar, K. 1987. *Project Monitoring and Evaluation in Agriculture*. Published for The World Bank, The Johns Hopkins University Press, Baltimore.

Catton, W.R. Jr. 1980. *Overshoot: The Ecological Basis of Revolutionary Change*. University of Illinois Press, Urbana.

Catton, W.R. Jr. 1983. Social and behavioural aspects of the carrying capacity of natural environment. In: I. Altman, I. and J. Wohlwill (Eds.), *Behaviour and the Natural Environment*. Vol. 6 of The Human Behaviour and Environment, Advances in Theory and Research, Plenum Press, New York.

Catton, W.R. Jr. and Dunlap, R.E. 1978. Environmental sociology - a new paradigm. *The American Sociologist, 12:* 41-49.

Checkland, P. 1981. *Systems Thinking, Systems Practice.* John Wiley and Sons, Chichester.

Conland, J. (Ed.) 1985. *Social impact assessment in New Zealand - a practical approach.* Town and Country Planning Directorate, Ministry of Works and Development, Wellington.

Council on Environmental Quality 1978. Regulations for implementing the procedural provisions of the National Environmental Policy Act. Government Printing Office, Washington D.C.

Coup, Owen, et al. 1990. We are doing well, aren't we: a guide to planning, monitoring and evaluating community projects. Department of Internal Affairs, Wellington.

Cowell, Stuart; Lane, Marcus; Burke, Bronwen and Crisp, Rosie 2001. Social assessment and indigenous peoples: aboriginal verses bureaucratic agency. In A. Dale, N. Taylor and M. Lane (Eds.), *Social Assessment in Natural Resource Management Institutions,* CSIRO Publishing, Collingwood.

Cronin, K. 1987. Social impact assessment and social policy. *People and Planning, 41:* 8-10.

Dale, Allan; Taylor, Nick and Lane, Marcus (Eds.) 2001. *Social Assessment in Natural Resource Management Institutions.* CSIRO Publishing, Collingwood.

de Vaus, D.A. 2002. *Surveys in Social Research, Fifth Edition.* Allen and Unwin, Sydney.

Devlin, M. 1984. The status of small business research in New Zealand. Development Finance Corporation, Wellington.

Dietz, T. 1987. Theory and method in social impact assessment. *Sociological Inquiry, 57:* 54-69.

Dillman, Don A. 2000. *Mail and Internet Surveys: the Tailored Design Method.* Wiley, New York.

Drury, R.G. 1983. The Waihi liaison forum. *People and Planning, 27:* 8-9.

Duffecy, Jennifer and Pollard, Lisa 2001. The Western Australian Social Impact Unit 1989-1993: nicety or necessity? In Dale, A.; Taylor, N. and Lane, M. (Eds.), *Social Assessment in Natural Resource Management Institutions,* CSIRO Publishing, Collingwood.

Duncan, O.D. 1961. From social system to ecosystem. *Sociological Inquiry, 31*: 140-149.

Eckstein, O. 1958. *Water Resources Development: the Economics of Project Evaluation*. Harvard University Press, Cambridge.

Eggenberger, M. and Partidário, M. d R. 2000. Development of a framework to assist the integration of environmental, social and economic issues in spatial planning. *Impact Assessment and Project Appraisal*, 18,3: 201-207.

Ekstrom, B.L. and Leistritz, F.L. 1988. *Rural Community Decline and Revitalisation: an Annotated Bibliography*. Garland Publishing, New York, United States of America.

FAO Investment Centre 1992. Sociological analysis in agricultural investment project design. Technical Paper 9, Food and Agriculture Organisation of the United Nations, Rome.

Fitzgerald, Gerard 2003. Computer-based qualitative data methods. Chapter 10 in Henk Becker and Frank Vanclay (Eds.), *Handbook of Social Impact Assessment, Conceptual and Methodological Advances*, Edward Elgar, Cheltenham.

Fookes, T.W., Drury, R.G. and Mead, J.M. 1980. Intentions and practice of a social and economic impact monitoring project: a review of the philosophy, methodology and variables used in monitoring the Huntly Power Project. Internal Technical Paper No. 20. University of Waikato, Hamilton.

Fookes, T.W.; Drury, R.G.; Porter, D.J. and Tester, F.J. 1981. Alternative approaches to social and economic impact monitoring. Huntly Monitoring Project. Final report series No. 13. University of Waikato, Hamilton.

Ford, S.; Butcher, G.; Edmonds, K. and Braggins, A. 2001. Economic efficiency of water allocation. MAF Technical Paper 2001/7, MAF Policy, Wellington.

Forester, J. 1980. Critical theory and planning practice. *Journal of the American Planning Association, 46*: 275-286.

Francis, P. and Jacobs, S. 1999. Institutionalizing social analysis at the World Bank. *Environmental Impact Assessment Review*, 19(3): 341-357.

Franklin, Brad 1991. Community relations in support of remedial programs at historic low-level radioactive waste sites in Canada. Paper presented at the Meetings of the IAIA, Urbana-Champaign, Illinois.

Freudenburg, W.R. 1986. Social impact assessment. *Annual Review of Sociology, 12*: 451-478.

Freudenburg, W.R. and Keating, K.M. 1982. Increasing the impact of sociology on Social Impact Assessment: toward ending the inattention. *The American Sociologist, 17*: 71-80.

Freudenburg, William R. and Keating, Kenneth M. 1985. Applying sociology to policy: social science and the environmental impact statement. *Rural Sociology*, 50,4: 578-605.

Gittinger, J.P. 1972. *Economic analysis of agricultural projects*. John Hopkins University Press, Baltimore.

Glasson, J. 1999 . The first 10 years of the UK EIA system: strengths, weaknesses, opportunities and threats. *Planning Practice and Research*, 14,3: 363-375.

Gold, U. and Houghton, R.M. 1985. Bruce County forestry employees' household spending patterns. Business Development Centre, University of Otago, Dunedin.

Government of South Australia 1989. Planning Act Amendment Act, 1989: Environmental assessment amendments - major projects. White Paper, Adelaide.

Graetz, B. 1985. The potential of mail surveys. *Australian and New Zealand Journal of Sociology, 21(3):* 445-455.

Hall, R.; Thorns, D. and Willmott, W.E. 1983. Community formation and change - a study of rural and urban localities in New Zealand. Working Paper No. 4. Department of Sociology, University of Canterbury, Christchurch.

Hall, R. 1987. Te Kohurau: continuity and change in a New Zealand rural district: methodology. Unpublished paper, Department of Sociology, University of Canterbury, Christchurch.

Hawley, A.H. 1950. *Human Ecology: Theory of Community Structure*. Ronald Press Co., New York.

Hewings, G.J.D. 1985. *Regional Input-output Analysis*. Sage Publications, Beverly Hills.

Hill, A.A. 1981. Statement before the Committee on Environment and Public Works, United States Senate. Council for Environmental Quality, Washington.

Hill, R. 1984. Establishing validity in the social sciences: an empirical illustration. *New Zealand Science Review, 41(4)*: 59-62.

Hindmarsh, R.A.; Hundloe, T.J.; McDonald, G.T. and Rickson, R.E. (Eds.) 1988. *Papers on Assessing the Social Impacts of Development*. Institute of Applied Environmental Research, Griffith University, Brisbane.

Houghton, R.M.; Caskey, M.; Gold, U. and Wilson, A. 1986a. The local impacts of the Clyde Power Project, Upper Clutha Development 1981-1985. Business Development Centre, University of Otago, Dunedin.

Houghton, R.M.; Caskey, M. and Wilson, A. 1986b. Otautau business and employment survey. A report to the Southland and Wallace County Councils. Business Development Centre, University of Otago, Dunedin.

Howard, A. 1976. The great participation fallacy. *The Planner, 62(6)*: 163-164.

Humphrey, C.R. and Buttel, F.H. 1982. *Environment, Energy and Society.* Wadsworth, Belmont.

Humphrey, Craig R.; Lewis, Tammy L. and Buttel, Frederick H. 2002. *Environment, Energy and Society: a New Synthesis.* Wadsworth, Belmont.

Interorganizational Committee on Guidelines and Principles for Social Impact Assessment. 1994. Guidelines and principles for social impact assessment. US Department of Commerce National Oceanic and Atmospheric Administration National Marine Fisheries Service, NOAA Technical Memorandum NMFS-F/SPO-16.

Interorganizational Committee on Principles and Guidelines for Social Impact Assessment. 2003. Principles and guidelines for social impact assessment in the USA. *Impact Assessment and Project Appraisal*, 21(3): 231-250.

Jackson, M.C. 1982. The nature of "soft" systems thinking: the work of Churchman, Ackoff and Checkland. *Journal of Applied System Analysis*, 9:17-29.

Jackson, M.C. and Keys, P. 1984. Towards a system of systems methodologies. *Journal of the Operations Research Society*, 35 (6):473-486.

Johnson and Field, D. 1981. Applied and basic social research: a difference in social context. *Leisure Sciences, 4(3)*: 269-279.

Kilmartin, L., Thorns, D. and Burke, T. 1985. *Social Theory and the Australian City.* George Allen and Unwin, Sydney.

Krawetz, N.M. 1981. Intentions and practice reviewed with reference to monitoring prototypes. Huntly Monitoring Project. Final Report Series No. 10. University of Waikato, Hamilton.

Krawetz, Natalia; MacDonald, William R. and Nichols, Peter 1987. A framework for effective monitoring. CEARC (Canadian Environment Assessment Research Council), Quebec.

Kumar, S. 2003. Methods for community participation: a complete guide for practitioners. Intermediate Technologies, London.

Leistritz, F. Larry; Coon, Randel C. and Hamm, Rita R. 1994-95. A microcomputer model for assessing socioeconomic impacts of development projects. *Impact Assessment Bulletin*, 12(4): 373-384.

Leu, W. S.;Williams, W. P. and Bark, A. W. 1997. Evaluation of environmental impact assessment in three Southeast Asian Nations. *Project Appraisal*, 12(2): 89-100.

Lockie, Stewart 2001. SIA in review: setting the agenda for impact assessment in the 21st century. *Impact Assessment and Porject Appraisal*, 19(4): 277-288.

Lucas, R.A. 1971. *Minetown, Milltown, Railtown: Life in Canadian Communities of Single Industry*. University of Toronto Press, Toronto.

Marsh, K. 1982. *The Survey Method*. George Allen and Unwin, London.

McKean, R.N. 1958. *Efficiency in Government Through Systems Analysis*. Wiley, New York.

McPherson, J. 1985. Social impact assessment in New Zealand. *Impact Assessment Bulletin, 4*: 1-2. pp.261-270.

May, Tim 2001. *Social Research: Issues, Methods and Process*. Open University Press, Buckingham.

Miller, R.E. and Blair, P.D. 1985. *Input-Output Analysis: Foundations and Extensions*. Prentice-Hall, Englewood Cliffs, New Jersey.

New Zealand Social Impact Assessment (SIA) Working Group, 1988. Social impact assessment and social policy in New Zealand. Royal Commission on Social Policy, Wellington.

Oppenheim, A.N. 1970. *Questionnaire Design and Attitude Measurement*. Heinemann, London.

Park, R.E. 1936. Human Ecology. *American Journal of Sociology, XL11(1)*: 1-15.

Renouf, J. and Taylor C.N. 1984. Economic restructuring: the role and responsibility of social impact assessment. Paper presented at the ASSR/NZSA Social Policy Conference, Wellington, 31 October - 2 November 1984.

Richardson, H.W. 1972. *Input-output and Regional Economics*. Wiley, New York.

Rickson, R.E.; Western, J.S. and Burdge, R.J. 1994. Social impact assessment, knowledge and development, in R.J. Burdge, *A Conceptual Approach to Social Impact Assessment*, Social Ecology Press, Middleton, Wisconsin.

Roberts, Richard 2003. Involving the public. Chapter 16 in Henk Becker and Frank Vanclay (Eds.), *Handbook of Social Impact Assessment, Conceptual and Methodological Advances*, Edward Elgar, Cheltenham.

Rothman, J. 1974. *Planning and Organising for Change: Action Principles from Social Science Research.* Columbia University Press, New York.

Samya, M.; Snow, H. and Bryan, H. 2003. Integrating social impact assessment with research: the case of methyl mercury in fish in the Mobile-Alabama River Basin. *Impact Assessment and Project Appraisal*, 21(2): 133-140.

Sarkissian, Wendy 1997. Community participation: a practical guide. Institute for Science and Technology Policy, Murdoch University, Western Australia.

Schnaiberg, A. 1975. Social synthesis of the societal-environmental dialectic: the role of distributional impacts. *Social Science Quarterly, 56(1)*: 5-20.

Schnaiberg, A. 1980. *The Environment: from Surplus to Scarcity.* Oxford University Press, New York.

Shell International Exploration and Production B.V. 1996. Social Impact Assessment. HSE Manual EP 95-0371, The Hague.

Slootweg, R.; Vanclay, F. and Schooten, M. v 2001. Function evaluation as a framework for the integration of social and environmental impact assessment. *Impact Assessment and Project Appraisal*, 19(1): 19-28.

Statistics New Zealand 1995. A guide to good survey design. Statistics New Zealand, Wellington.

Statistics New Zealand 2003. Regional input-output study. Statistics New Zealand, Wellington.

Sudman, S. and Bradburn, N.M. 1982. *Asking Questions: a Practical Guide to Questionnaire Design.* Jersey Bass, San Francisco.

Taranaki United Council, 1986. Taranaki hill country: a study of attitudes, service provision and economic circumstances. Taranaki United Council, New Plymouth.

Taylor, N. and Dale A. 2001. Conclusions. In A. Dale; N. Taylor and M. Lane (Eds.), *Social Assessment in Natural Resource Management Institutions,* CSIRO Publishing, Collingwood.

Taylor, C.N. and Fitzgerald, G. 1988. New Zealand resource communities: impact assessment and management in response to rapid economic change. *Impact Assessment Bulletin, 6(2)*: 55-70.

Taylor, C.N. and McClintock, W.L. 1984. Major resource development projects in a regional context: a framework for a New Zealand analysis. *Australia and New Zealand Journal of Sociology, 20(3)*: 377-392.

Taylor, C.N. and Sharp, B. 1983. Social impacts of major resource development projects: concerns for research and planning. Discussion Paper. Centre for Resource Management, University of Canterbury and Lincoln College.

Taylor Nick; Fitzgerald, Gerard and McClintock, Wayne 2001. Resource communities in New Zealand: perspectives on community formation and change. Chapter 9 in Geoffrey Lawrence, Vaughan Higgins and Stewart Lockie (Eds.), *Environment, Society and Natural Resource Management, Theoretical Perspectives from Australasia and the Americas*, Edward Elgar, Cheltenham.

Taylor, Nick; McClintock, Wayne and Buckenham, Brigid 2003. Social impacts of out-of-centre shopping centres on town centres: a New Zealand case study. *Impact Assessment and Project Appraisal*, 21(2): 147-154.

Taylor Baines and Associates 2002. Cooperation and Commitment: The Chatham Islands Economic Review, 2002. Christchurch.

Taylor Baines and Lincoln International 1989. Review of the Chatham Islands economy. Report to Department of Internal Affairs, Taylor, Baines and Lincoln International, Christchurch.

Tester, F.J. and Mykes, W. 1981. *Social Impact Assessment: Theory, Method and Practice*. Detselig, Calgary.

Tester, F.J. 1985. The social impacts of environmental protection: a New Zealand case study. Paper presented at the International Association for Impact Assessment Conference, Calgary.

Vanclay, Frank 2003. International principles for social impact assessment. *Impact Assessment and Project Appraisal*, 21(1): 5-12.

Vanclay, Frank. 2002. Social impact assessment. In M. Tolba, (Ed.), *Responding to Environmental Change*, Volume 4 of *Encyclopaedia of Environmental Change*, Wiley and Sons, Chichester: 387-393.

Vanclay, Frank and Bronstein, D. A. (Eds.) 1995. *Environmental and Social Impact Assessment*. Wiley and Sons, Chichester.

Verberg, K. 1975. The carrying capacity of recreational lands: a review. *Occasional Paper No. 1*. Parks Canada Planning Div., Prairie Regional Office.

Verloo, Mieke and Roggeband, Connie 1996. Gender impact assessment: the development of a new instrument in the Netherlands. *Impact Assessment*, 14: 13-20.

Warren, Julie A.; Taylor, C. N.; Davidson, Carl and Goodrich, C. G. 1992. Social assessment and systems theory. Paper prepared for the Annual Meetings of the International Association for Impact Assessment, Washington, DC.

Weber, B.A. and Howell, R.E. (Eds.) 1982. *Coping with Rapid Growth in Rural Communities*. Westview Press, Boulder, Colorado.

Weisberg, H.F. and Bowan, B.D. 1977. *An Introduction to Survey Research and Data Analysis*. W.H. Freeman and Co., San Francisco.

Wildman, P.H. 1985. Social impact analysis in Australia: policy issues for the 1980s. *Australian Journal of Social Issues, 20(2)*: 136-151.

Wildman, P. and Barker, G. 1985. *The social impact assessment handbook: how to assess and evaluate the social impacts of resource development on local communities*. Social Impacts Publications, Armidale, New South Wales.

Wilkinson, K.P. 1985. Implementing a national strategy of rural development. *Rural Sociologist, 4(5)*: 348-353.

Wilkinson, Kenneth P. 1986. In search of community in the changing countryside. *Rural Sociology,* 51(1): 1-17.

Wolf, C.P. 1983. Social impact assessment: a methodological overview. In K. Finsterbusch, L.G. Llewellyn and C.P. Wolf, (Eds.), *Social Impact Assessment Methods*, Sage, Beverly Hills.

World Bank, Environment Department, 1991. Environmental Assessment Sourcebook, Three Volumes. World Bank Technical Paper Numbers, 139-141, Washington, D.C.

World Commission on Environment and Development (Brundtland Commission) 1987. *Our Common Future*. Oxford University Press, Oxford.

# INDEX

# SOCIAL ECOLOGY PRESS
## Social Impact Assessment
## Natural Resource, Rural Sociology Books

SOCIAL ASSESSMENT: THEORY, PROCESS & METHODS, 3RD Edition
by C. Nicholas Taylor, C. Hobson Bryan & Colin G. Goodrich ......$18.95

THE CONCEPTS, PROCESS and METHODS of SOCIAL IMPACT ASSESSMENT
by Rabel J. Burdge, New 2004 ...........................................$19.95

A COMMUNITY GUIDE to SOCIAL IMPACT ASSESSMENT: 3RD Edition
by Rabel J. Burdge ....................................................$18.95

*Classics in Rural Sociology:*

DAYDREAMS and NIGHTMARES
by William R. Burch, Jr .................................................$14.95

DIFFUSION RESEARCH in RURAL SOCIOLOGY
by Frederick C. Fliegel with contributions from Peter Korsching ...$14.95

MAN, MIND and LAND
by Walter Firey ............................................................ $14.95

RURAL SOCIOLOGY and THE ENVIRONMENT
by Donald R. Field & William R. Burch ...............................$14.95

THE COMMUNITY in RURAL AMERICA
by Kenneth Wilkinson ..................................................$14.95

THREE IRON MINING TOWNS
by Paul H. Landis ........................................................$14.95

Send Orders to: Social Ecology Press
P.O. Box 620863
Middleton, WI 53562-0863, USA

Phone and FAX (608) 831-1410
Toll Free in U.S. (888) 364-3277

Shipping costs in United States: $6.95 for first two books; $1.00 each additional book.
Foreign Customers: Payment must be made in U.S. funds drawn on a US bank, with all
monetary conversions paid by the purchaser.

(Shipping based on current postal rates. Prices of books and shipping subject to change.)

Order online using a credit card at: http://www.dog-eared.com/socialecologypress

E-mail: field@chorus.net

Credit Cards Accepted: Visa and MasterCard

Inquire about discounts for bulk orders and alternative and foreign shipping